MARVEL

SPIDER-MAN

CITY AT WAR

Based on a story by **Jon Paquette**, **Bryan Intihar** and the **Insomniac Games Writing Team**; co-written by **Christos Gage** with additional story contributions by **Dan Slott**.

EIGHT YEARS HAVE PASSED SINCE PETER FIRST DONNED THE WEBS, AND WHILE HE HAS GROWN INTO HIS OWN AS A CRIMEFIGHTER, IT DOESN'T MEAN LIFE HAS GOTTEN ANY EASIER...

WRITER
DENNIS "HOPELESS" HALLUM

ARTISTS
MICHELE BANDINI (#1-6) WITH **LUCA MARESCA** (#5)

INKERS
MICHELE BANDINI (#1-6) WITH **ELISABETTA D'AMICO** (#6)

COLORIST
DAVID CURIEL

LETTERER
VC'S TRAVIS LANHAM

COVER ART
CLAYTON CRAIN

ASSISTANT EDITOR
MARTIN BIRO

EDITOR
MARK BASSO

FOR INSOMNIAC GAMES & MARVEL GAMES

STUDIO ART DIRECTOR, INSOMNIAC GAMES
JACINDA CHEW

LEAD WRITER, INSOMNIAC GAMES
JON PAQUETTE

DIRECTOR OF GAME PRODUCTION, MARVEL GAMES
ERIC MONACELLI

VP & CREATIVE DIRECTOR, MARVEL GAMES
BILL ROSEMANN

SPIDER-MAN
CREATED BY
STAN LEE & STEVE DITKO

COLLECTION EDITOR **MARK D. BEAZLEY**
ASSISTANT EDITOR **CAITLIN O'CONNELL**
ASSOCIATE MANAGING EDITOR **KATERI WOODY**
SENIOR EDITOR, SPECIAL PROJECTS **JENNIFER GRÜNWALD**
VP PRODUCTION & SPECIAL PROJECTS **JEFF YOUNGQUIST**
BOOK DESIGNER **ADAM DEL RE** WITH **NICK RUSSELL**

SVP PRINT, SALES & MARKETING **DAVID GABRIEL**
DIRECTOR, LICENSED PUBLISHING **SVEN LARSEN**
EDITOR IN CHIEF **C.B. CEBULSKI**
CHIEF CREATIVE OFFICER **JOE QUESADA**
PRESIDENT **DAN BUCKLEY**
EXECUTIVE PRODUCER **ALAN FINE**

MARVEL'S SPIDER-MAN: CITY AT WAR. Contains material originally published in magazine form as MARVEL'S SPIDER-MAN: CITY AT WAR #1-6. First printing 2019. ISBN 978-1-302-91901-6. Published by MARVEL WORLDWIDE, INC., a subsidiary of MARVEL ENTERTAINMENT, LLC. OFFICE OF PUBLICATION: 135 West 50th Street, New York, NY 10020. © 2019 MARVEL No similarity between any of the names, characters, persons, and/or institutions in this magazine with those of any living or dead person or institution is intended, and any such similarity which may exist is purely coincidental. **Printed in the U.S.A.** DAN BUCKLEY, President, Marvel Entertainment; JOHN NEE, Publisher; JOE QUESADA, Chief Creative Officer; TOM BREVOORT, SVP of Publishing; DAVID BOGART, Associate Publisher & SVP of Talent Affairs; DAVID GABRIEL, SVP of Sales & Marketing, Publishing; JEFF YOUNGQUIST, VP of Production & Special Projects; DAN CARR, Executive Director of Publishing Technology; ALEX MORALES, Director of Publishing Operations; DAN EDINGTON, Managing Editor; SUSAN CRESPI, Production Manager; STAN LEE, Chairman Emeritus. For information regarding advertising in Marvel Comics or on Marvel.com, please contact Vit DeBellis, Custom Solutions & Integrated Advertising Manager, at vdebellis@marvel.com. For Marvel subscription inquiries, please call 888-511-5480. **Manufactured between 8/23/2019 and 9/24/2019 by LSC COMMUNICATIONS INC., KENDALLVILLE, IN, USA.**

10 9 8 7 6 5 4 3 2 1

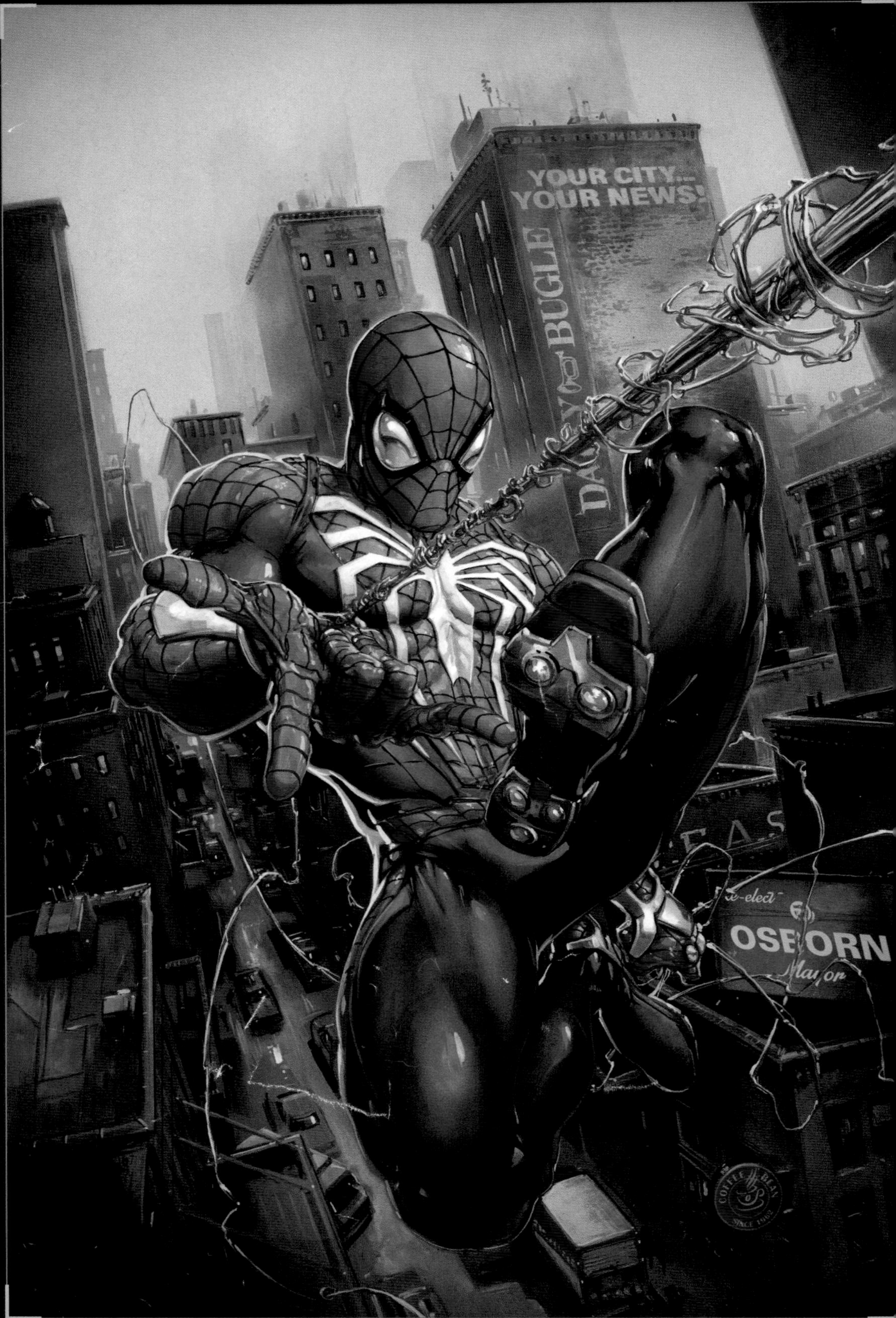
YOUR CITY...
YOUR NEWS!
DAILY BUGLE
Re-elect
OSBORN
Mayor

1

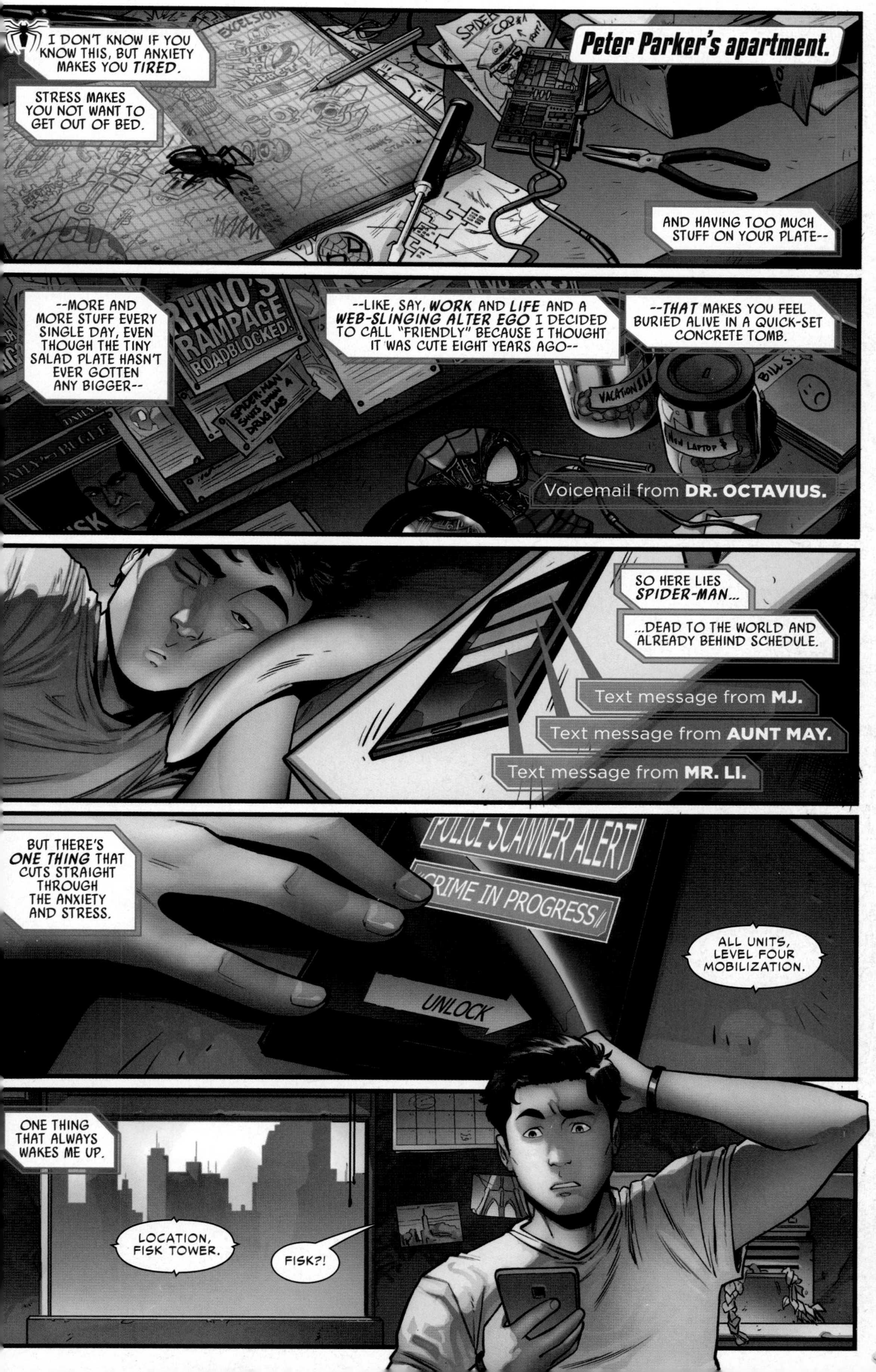
Peter Parker's apartment.
I DON'T KNOW IF YOU KNOW THIS, BUT ANXIETY MAKES YOU TIRED.
STRESS MAKES YOU NOT WANT TO GET OUT OF BED.
AND HAVING TOO MUCH STUFF ON YOUR PLATE--
--MORE AND MORE STUFF EVERY SINGLE DAY, EVEN THOUGH THE TINY SALAD PLATE HASN'T EVER GOTTEN ANY BIGGER--
--LIKE, SAY, WORK AND LIFE AND A WEB-SLINGING ALTER EGO I DECIDED TO CALL "FRIENDLY" BECAUSE I THOUGHT IT WAS CUTE EIGHT YEARS AGO--
--THAT MAKES YOU FEEL BURIED ALIVE IN A QUICK-SET CONCRETE TOMB.
RHINO'S RAMPAGE ROADBLOCKED!
SPIDER-MAN SHUTS DOWN A DRUG LAB
DAILY BUGLE
VACATION
NEW LAPTOP
Voicemail from DR. OCTAVIUS.
SO HERE LIES SPIDER-MAN...
...DEAD TO THE WORLD AND ALREADY BEHIND SCHEDULE.
Text message from MJ.
Text message from AUNT MAY.
Text message from MR. LI.
BUT THERE'S ONE THING THAT CUTS STRAIGHT THROUGH THE ANXIETY AND STRESS.
POLICE SCANNER ALERT
CRIME IN PROGRESS
ALL UNITS, LEVEL FOUR MOBILIZATION.
UNLOCK
ONE THING THAT ALWAYS WAKES ME UP.
LOCATION, FISK TOWER.
FISK?!

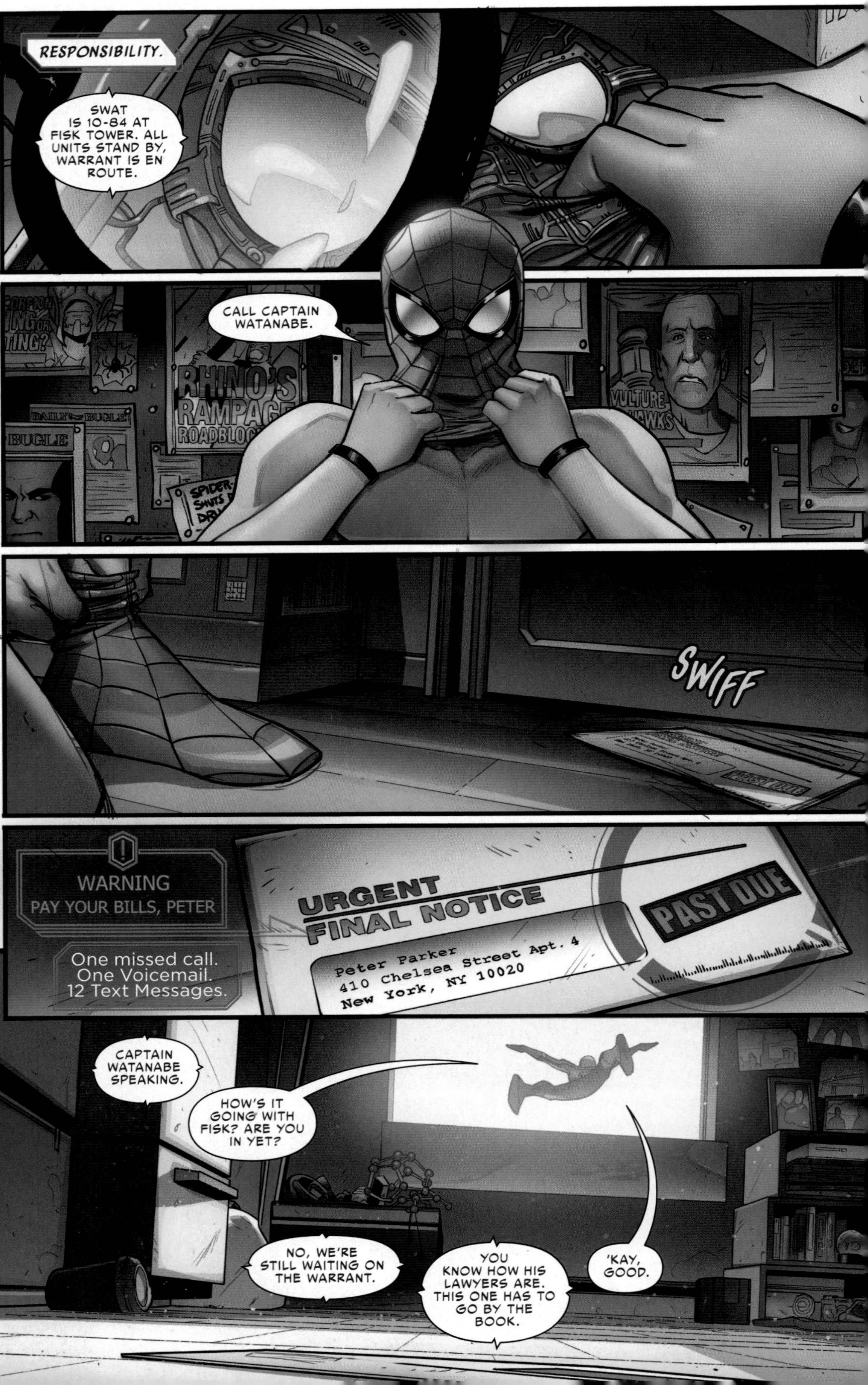
RESPONSIBILITY.
SWAT IS 10-84 AT FISK TOWER. ALL UNITS STAND BY, WARRANT IS EN ROUTE.
CALL CAPTAIN WATANABE.
RHINO'S RAMPAGE ROADBLOCK
VULTURE
SPIDER-
BUGLE
SWIFF
WARNING
PAY YOUR BILLS, PETER
One missed call.
One Voicemail.
12 Text Messages.
URGENT
FINAL NOTICE
PAST DUE
Peter Parker
410 Chelsea Street Apt. 4
New York, NY 10020
CAPTAIN WATANABE SPEAKING.
HOW'S IT GOING WITH FISK? ARE YOU IN YET?
NO, WE'RE STILL WAITING ON THE WARRANT.
YOU KNOW HOW HIS LAWYERS ARE. THIS ONE HAS TO GO BY THE BOOK.
'KAY, GOOD.

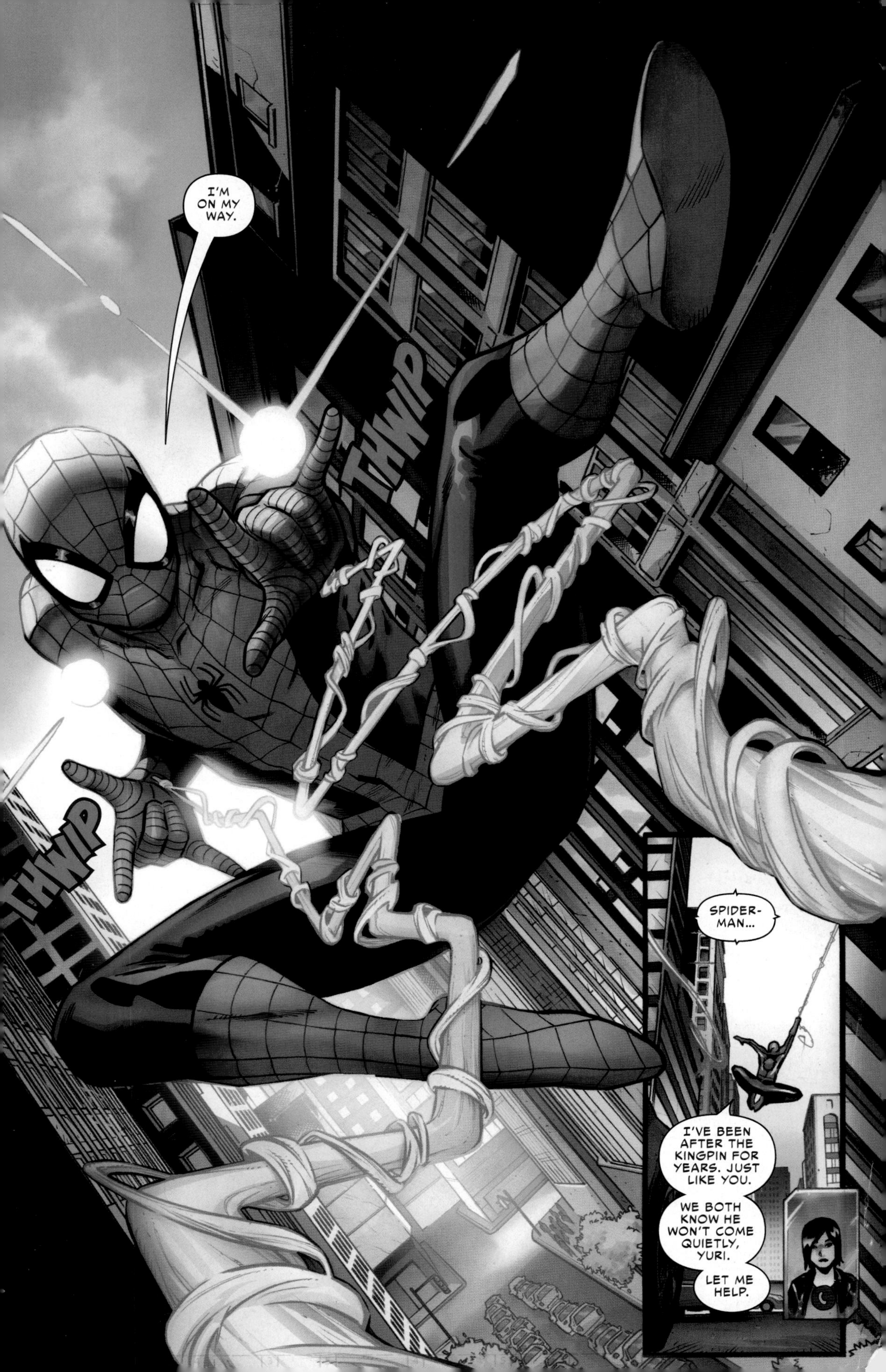
I'M ON MY WAY.
THWIP
THWIP
SPIDER-MAN...
I'VE BEEN AFTER THE KINGPIN FOR YEARS. JUST LIKE YOU.
WE BOTH KNOW HE WON'T COME QUIETLY, YURI.
LET ME HELP.

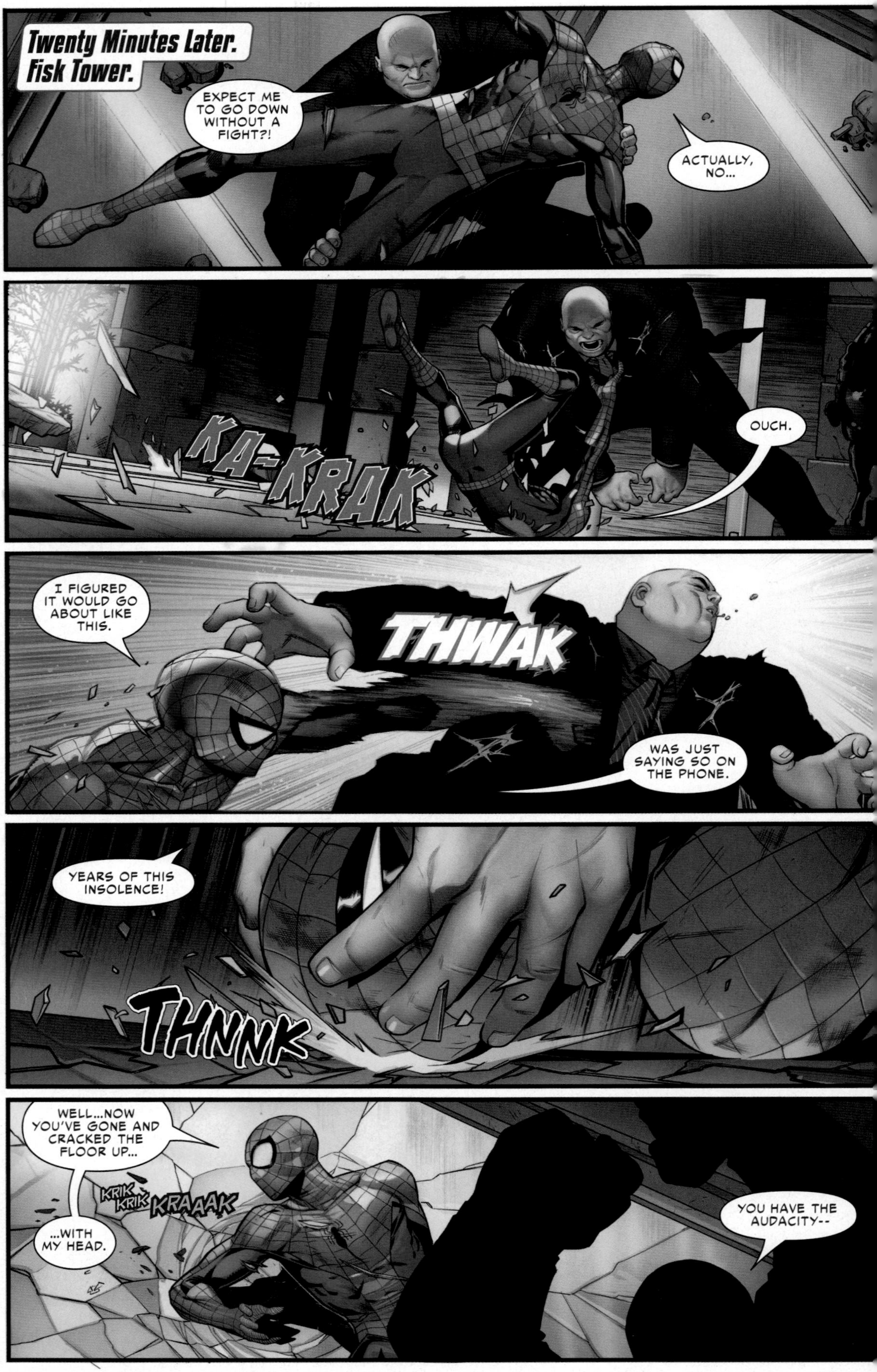
Twenty Minutes Later.
Fisk Tower.
EXPECT ME TO GO DOWN WITHOUT A FIGHT?!
ACTUALLY, NO...
KA-KRAK
OUCH.
I FIGURED IT WOULD GO ABOUT LIKE THIS.
THWAK
WAS JUST SAYING SO ON THE PHONE.
YEARS OF THIS INSOLENCE!
THNNK
WELL...NOW YOU'VE GONE AND CRACKED THE FLOOR UP...
KRIK KRIK KRAAAK
...WITH MY HEAD.
YOU HAVE THE AUDACITY--

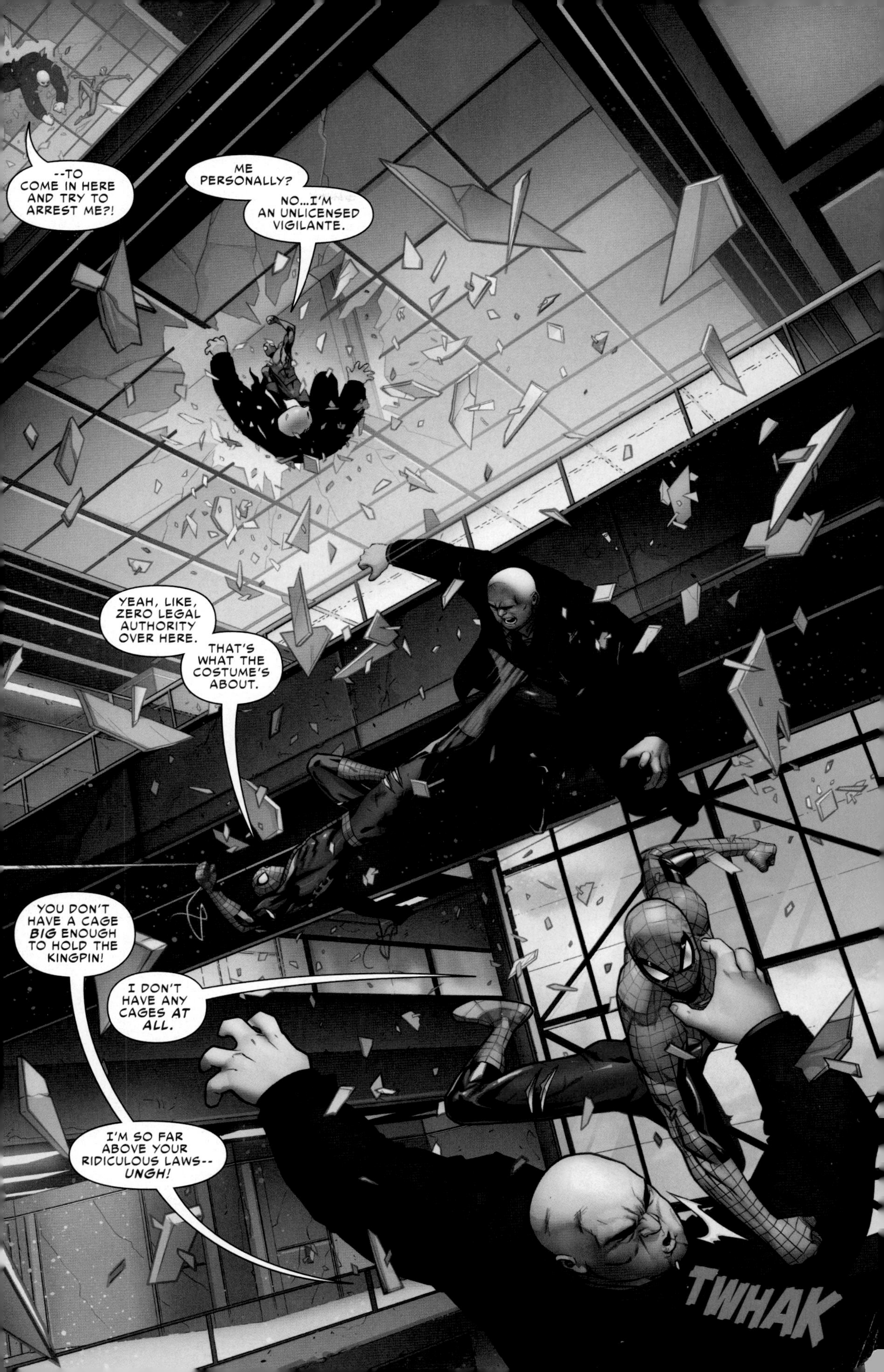
--TO COME IN HERE AND TRY TO ARREST ME?!
ME PERSONALLY?
NO...I'M AN UNLICENSED VIGILANTE.
YEAH, LIKE, ZERO LEGAL AUTHORITY OVER HERE.
THAT'S WHAT THE COSTUME'S ABOUT.
YOU DON'T HAVE A CAGE BIG ENOUGH TO HOLD THE KINGPIN!
I DON'T HAVE ANY CAGES AT ALL.
I'M SO FAR ABOVE YOUR RIDICULOUS LAWS-- UNGH!
TWHAK

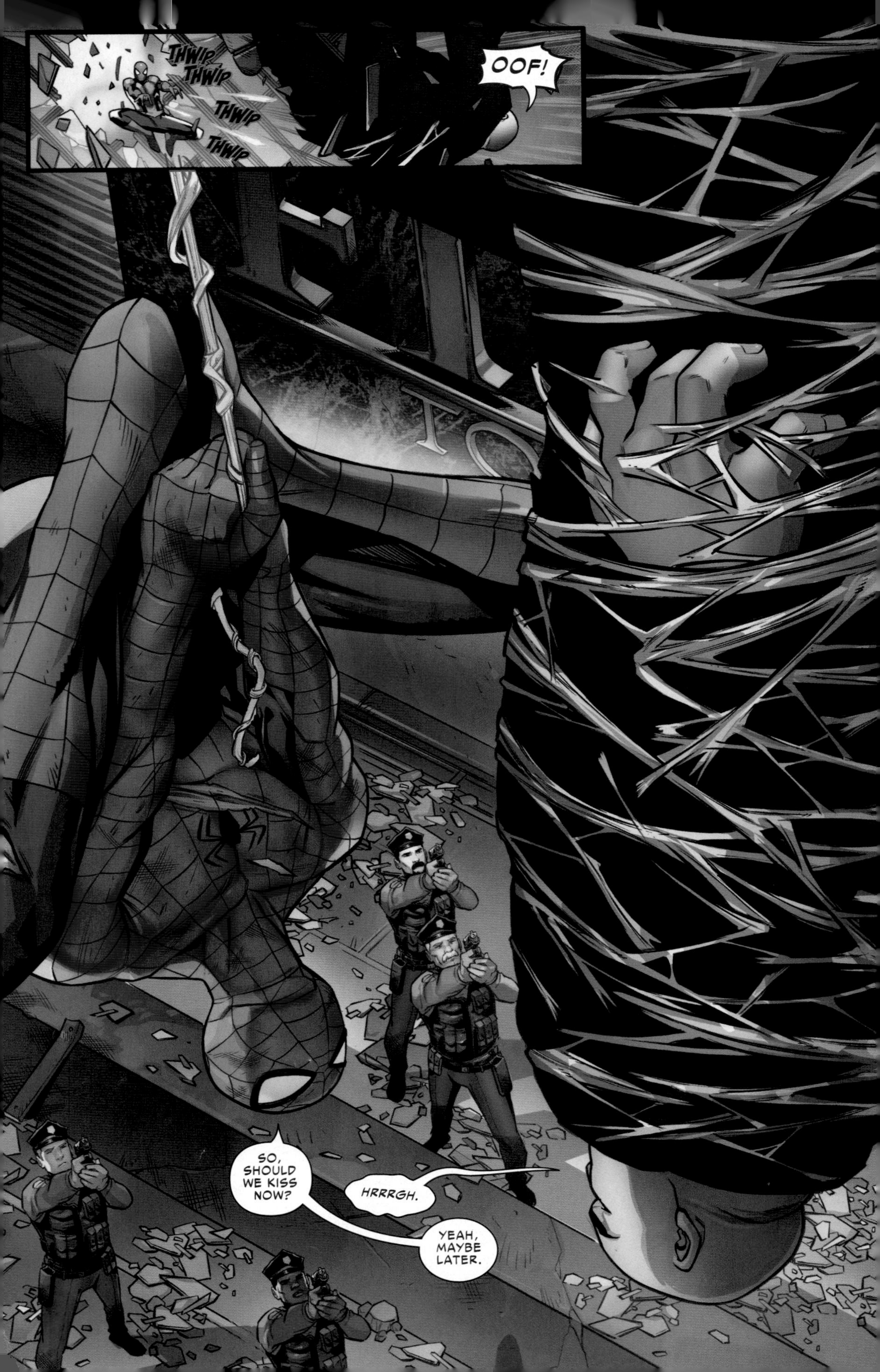
THWIP
THWIP
THWIP
THWIP
OOF!
SO, SHOULD WE KISS NOW?
HRRRGH.
YEAH, MAYBE LATER.

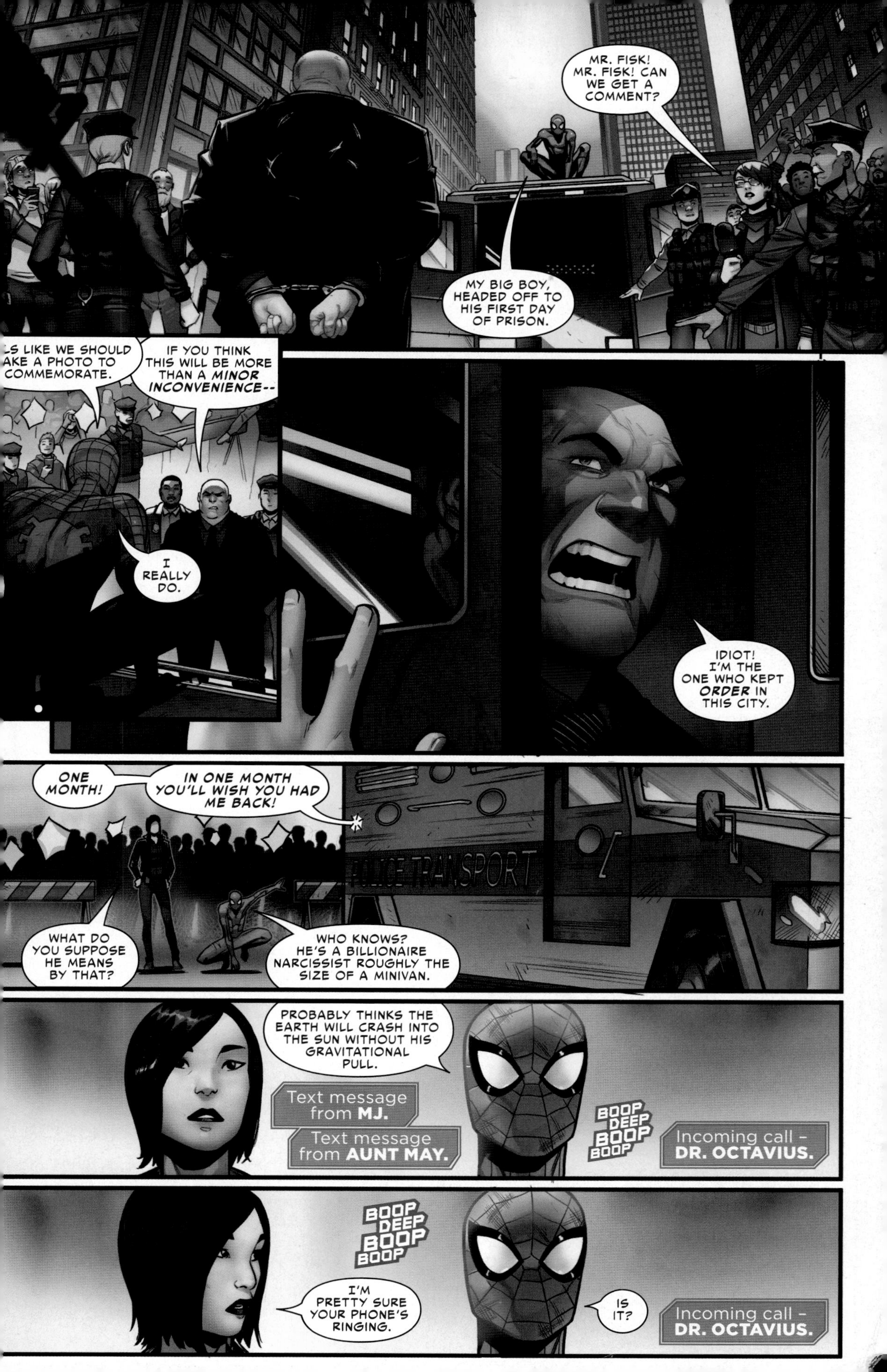
MR. FISK! MR. FISK! CAN WE GET A COMMENT?
MY BIG BOY, HEADED OFF TO HIS FIRST DAY OF PRISON.
...LS LIKE WE SHOULD ...AKE A PHOTO TO COMMEMORATE.
IF YOU THINK THIS WILL BE MORE THAN A MINOR INCONVENIENCE--
I REALLY DO.
IDIOT! I'M THE ONE WHO KEPT ORDER IN THIS CITY.
ONE MONTH!
IN ONE MONTH YOU'LL WISH YOU HAD ME BACK!
POLICE TRANSPORT
WHAT DO YOU SUPPOSE HE MEANS BY THAT?
WHO KNOWS? HE'S A BILLIONAIRE NARCISSIST ROUGHLY THE SIZE OF A MINIVAN.
PROBABLY THINKS THE EARTH WILL CRASH INTO THE SUN WITHOUT HIS GRAVITATIONAL PULL.
Text message from MJ.
Text message from AUNT MAY.
BOOP DEEP BOOP BOOP
Incoming call – DR. OCTAVIUS.
BOOP DEEP BOOP BOOP
I'M PRETTY SURE YOUR PHONE'S RINGING.
IS IT?
Incoming call – DR. OCTAVIUS.

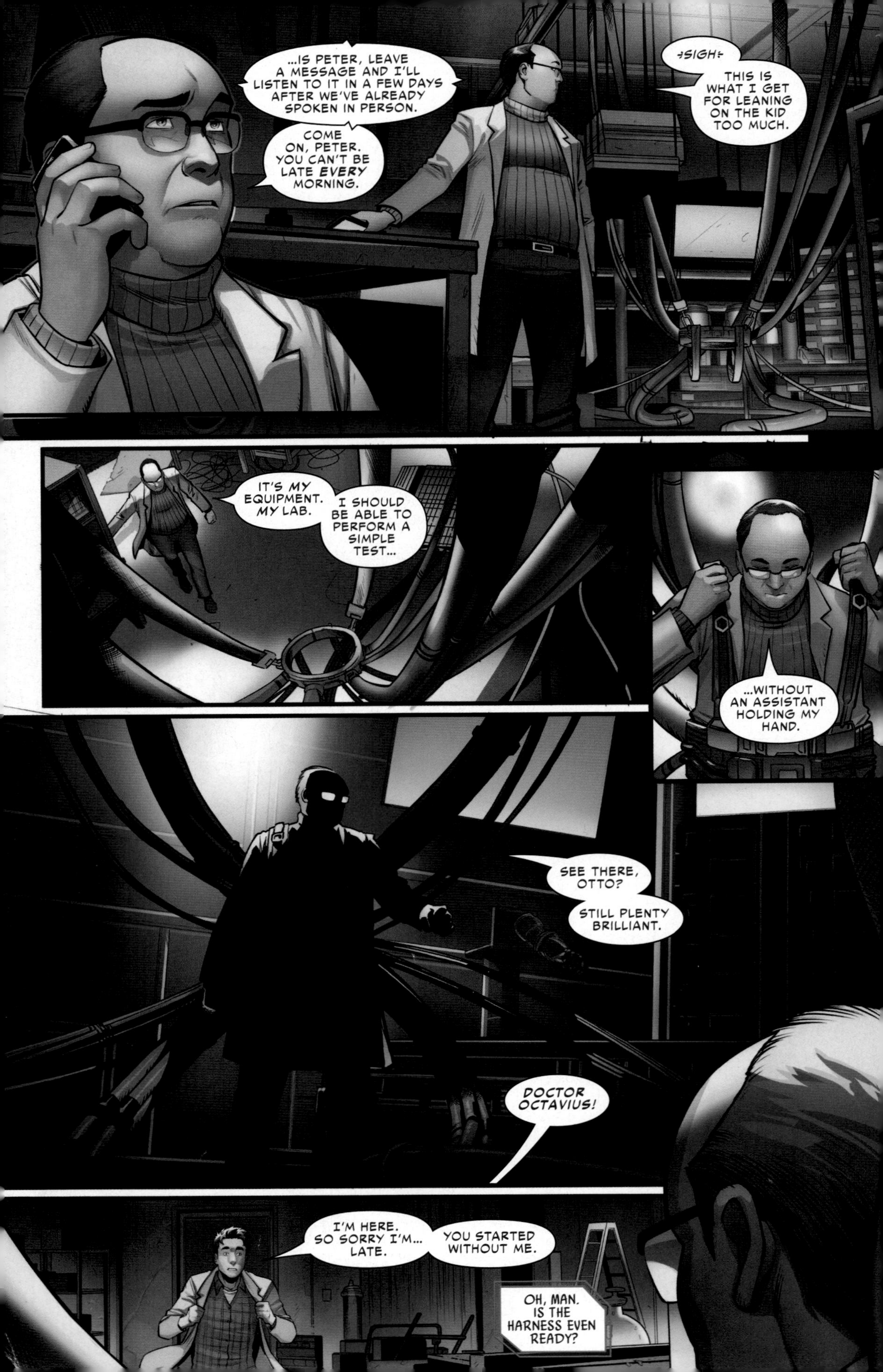
...IS PETER, LEAVE A MESSAGE AND I'LL LISTEN TO IT IN A FEW DAYS AFTER WE'VE ALREADY SPOKEN IN PERSON.
COME ON, PETER. YOU CAN'T BE LATE EVERY MORNING.
SIGH
THIS IS WHAT I GET FOR LEANING ON THE KID TOO MUCH.
IT'S MY EQUIPMENT. MY LAB.
I SHOULD BE ABLE TO PERFORM A SIMPLE TEST...
...WITHOUT AN ASSISTANT HOLDING MY HAND.
SEE THERE, OTTO?
STILL PLENTY BRILLIANT.
DOCTOR OCTAVIUS!
I'M HERE. SO SORRY I'M... LATE.
YOU STARTED WITHOUT ME.
OH, MAN. IS THE HARNESS EVEN READY?

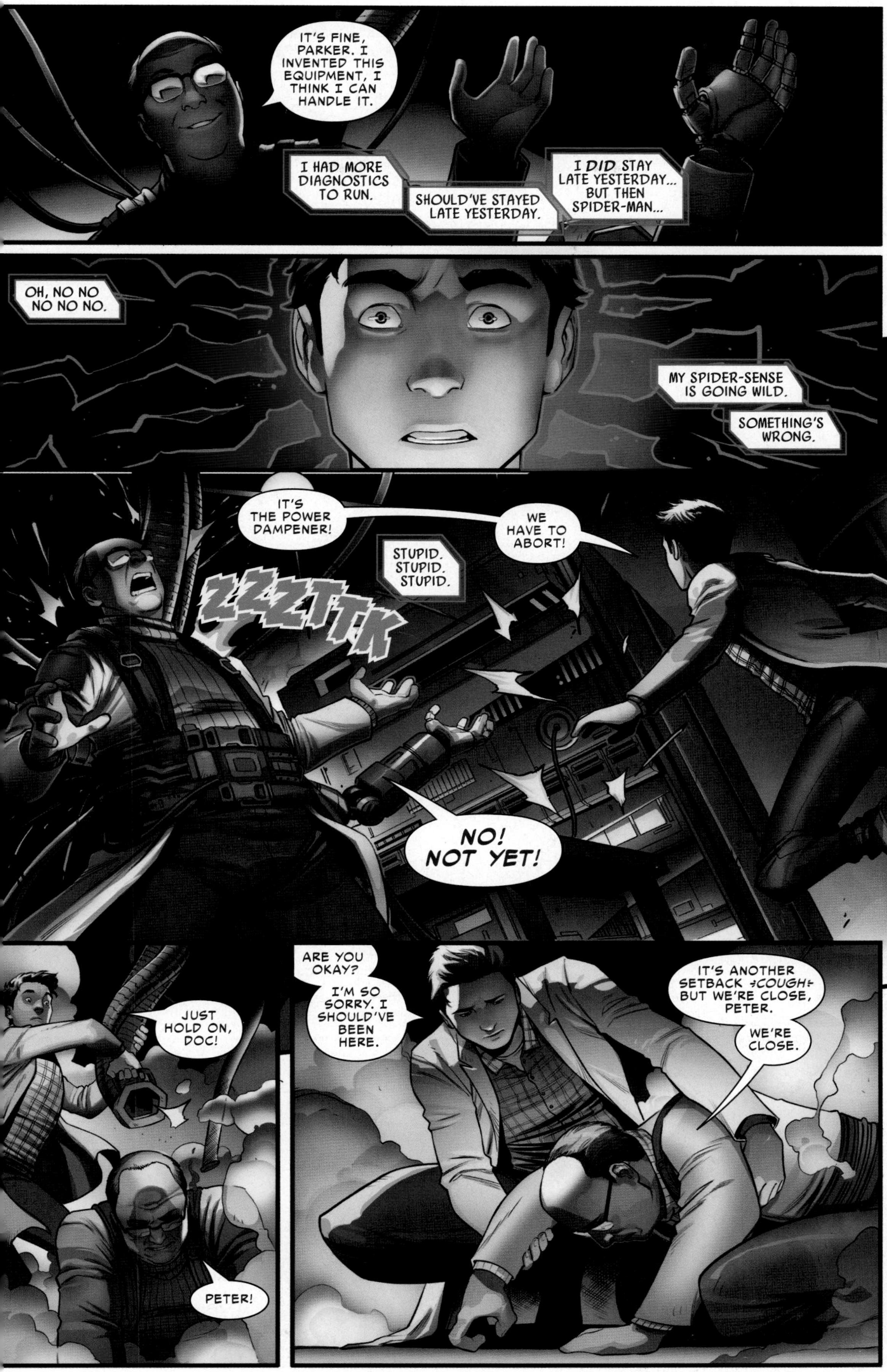
IT'S FINE, PARKER. I INVENTED THIS EQUIPMENT, I THINK I CAN HANDLE IT.
I HAD MORE DIAGNOSTICS TO RUN.
SHOULD'VE STAYED LATE YESTERDAY.
I *DID* STAY LATE YESTERDAY... BUT THEN SPIDER-MAN...
OH, NO NO NO NO NO.
MY SPIDER-SENSE IS GOING WILD.
SOMETHING'S WRONG.
IT'S THE POWER DAMPENER!
WE HAVE TO ABORT!
STUPID. STUPID. STUPID.
ZZZTTK
NO! NOT YET!
JUST HOLD ON, DOC!
PETER!
ARE YOU OKAY?
I'M SO SORRY. I SHOULD'VE BEEN HERE.
IT'S ANOTHER SETBACK *COUGH* BUT WE'RE CLOSE, PETER.
WE'RE CLOSE.

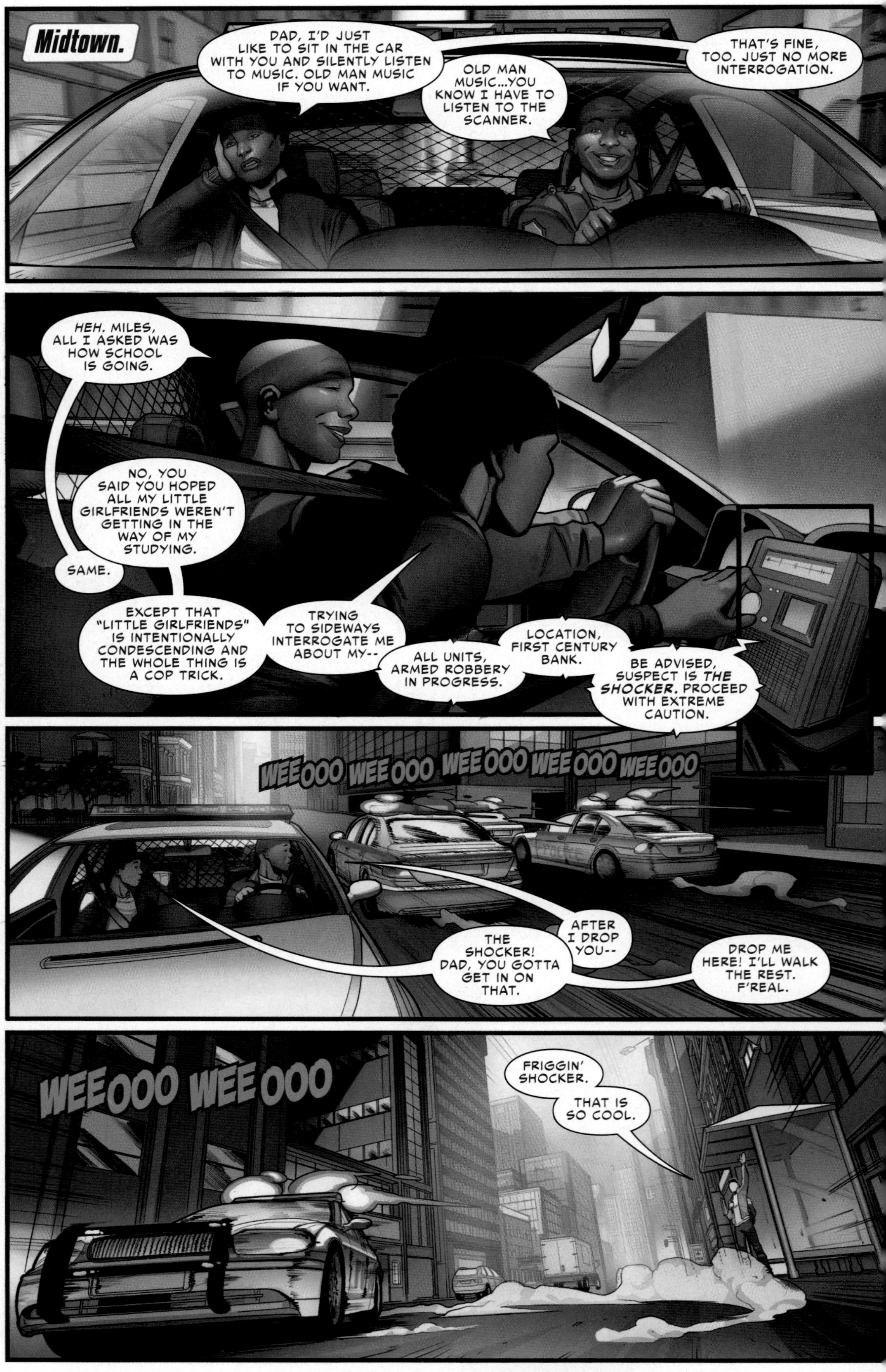
Midtown.
DAD, I'D JUST LIKE TO SIT IN THE CAR WITH YOU AND SILENTLY LISTEN TO MUSIC. OLD MAN MUSIC IF YOU WANT.
OLD MAN MUSIC...YOU KNOW I HAVE TO LISTEN TO THE SCANNER.
THAT'S FINE, TOO. JUST NO MORE INTERROGATION.
HEH. MILES, ALL I ASKED WAS HOW SCHOOL IS GOING.
NO, YOU SAID YOU HOPED ALL MY LITTLE GIRLFRIENDS WEREN'T GETTING IN THE WAY OF MY STUDYING.
SAME.
EXCEPT THAT "LITTLE GIRLFRIENDS" IS INTENTIONALLY CONDESCENDING AND THE WHOLE THING IS A COP TRICK.
TRYING TO SIDEWAYS INTERROGATE ME ABOUT MY--
ALL UNITS, ARMED ROBBERY IN PROGRESS.
LOCATION, FIRST CENTURY BANK.
BE ADVISED, SUSPECT IS THE SHOCKER. PROCEED WITH EXTREME CAUTION.
WEEOOO WEEOOO WEEOOO WEEOOO WEEOOO
THE SHOCKER! DAD, YOU GOTTA GET IN ON THAT.
AFTER I DROP YOU--
DROP ME HERE! I'LL WALK THE REST. F'REAL.
WEEOOO WEEOOO
FRIGGIN' SHOCKER.
THAT IS SO COOL.

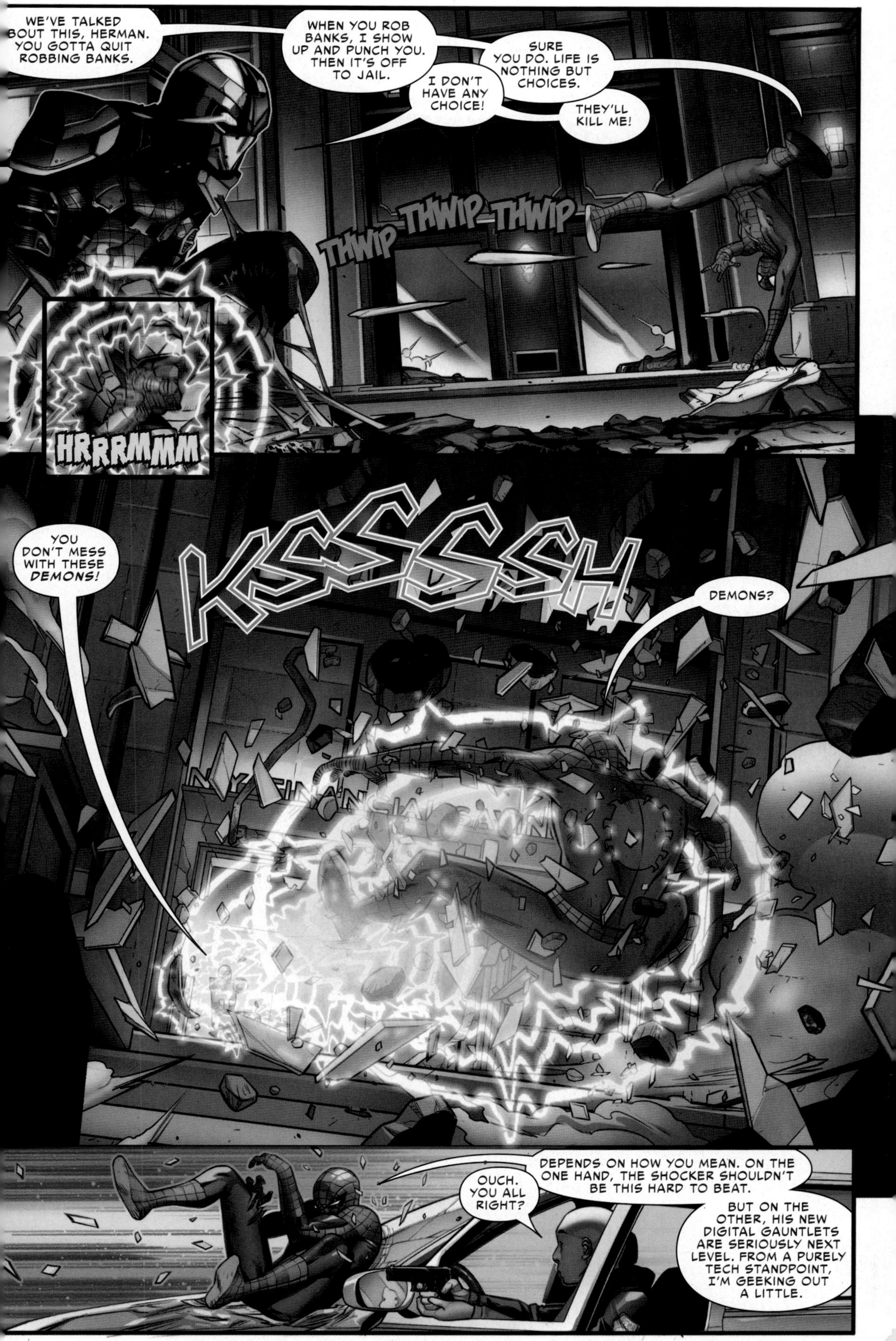
WE'VE TALKED BOUT THIS, HERMAN. YOU GOTTA QUIT ROBBING BANKS.
WHEN YOU ROB BANKS, I SHOW UP AND PUNCH YOU. THEN IT'S OFF TO JAIL.
SURE YOU DO. LIFE IS NOTHING BUT CHOICES.
I DON'T HAVE ANY CHOICE!
THEY'LL KILL ME!
THWIP THWIP THWIP
HRRRMMMM
KSSSSH
YOU DON'T MESS WITH THESE DEMONS!
DEMONS?
OUCH. YOU ALL RIGHT?
DEPENDS ON HOW YOU MEAN. ON THE ONE HAND, THE SHOCKER SHOULDN'T BE THIS HARD TO BEAT.
BUT ON THE OTHER, HIS NEW DIGITAL GAUNTLETS ARE SERIOUSLY NEXT LEVEL. FROM A PURELY TECH STANDPOINT, I'M GEEKING OUT A LITTLE.

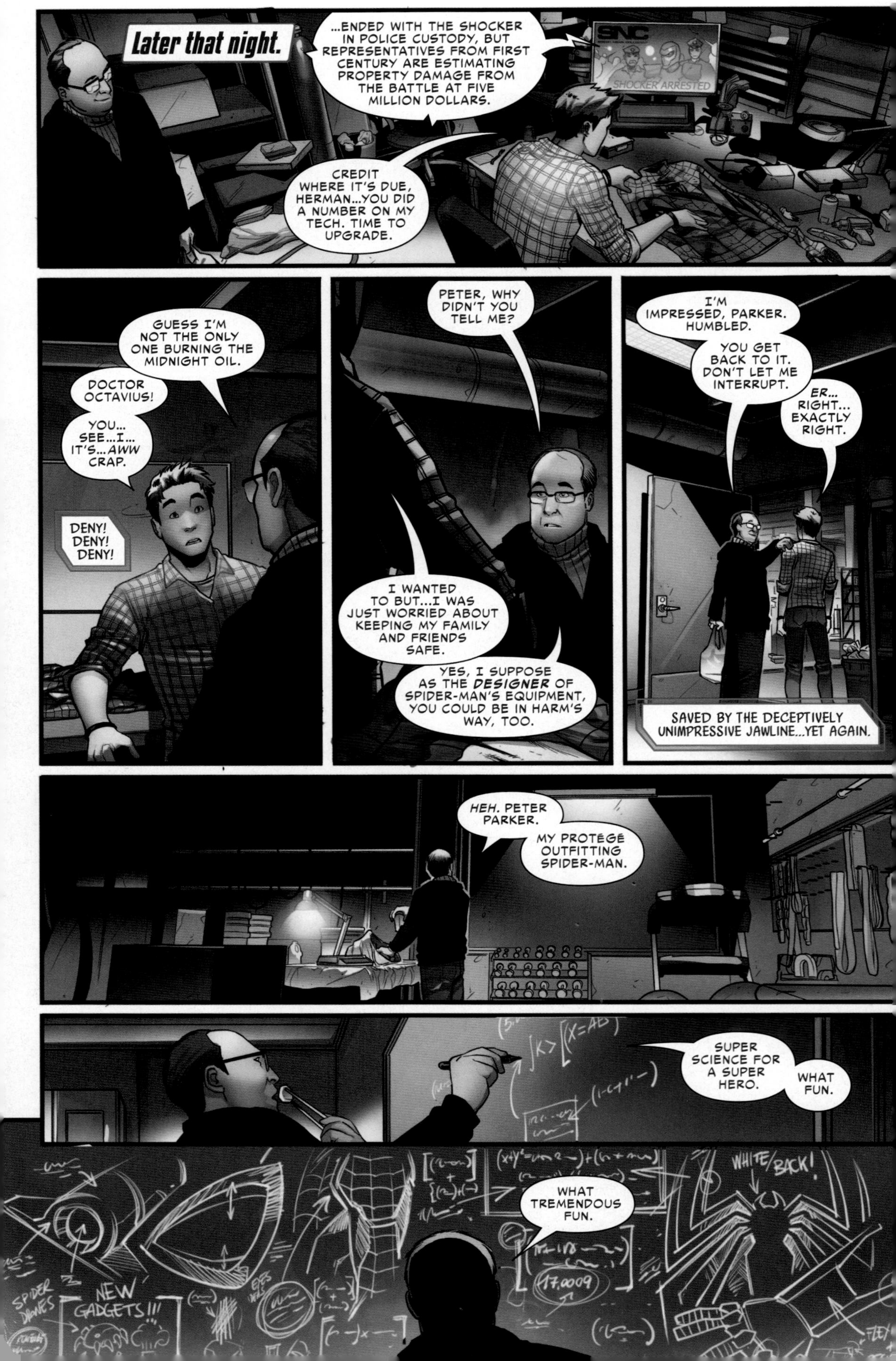
Later that night.
...ENDED WITH THE SHOCKER IN POLICE CUSTODY, BUT REPRESENTATIVES FROM FIRST CENTURY ARE ESTIMATING PROPERTY DAMAGE FROM THE BATTLE AT FIVE MILLION DOLLARS.
SNC
SHOCKER ARRESTED
CREDIT WHERE IT'S DUE, HERMAN...YOU DID A NUMBER ON MY TECH. TIME TO UPGRADE.
GUESS I'M NOT THE ONLY ONE BURNING THE MIDNIGHT OIL.
DOCTOR OCTAVIUS!
YOU... SEE...I... IT'S...AWW CRAP.
DENY! DENY! DENY!
PETER, WHY DIDN'T YOU TELL ME?
I WANTED TO BUT...I WAS JUST WORRIED ABOUT KEEPING MY FAMILY AND FRIENDS SAFE.
YES, I SUPPOSE AS THE *DESIGNER* OF SPIDER-MAN'S EQUIPMENT, YOU COULD BE IN HARM'S WAY, TOO.
I'M IMPRESSED, PARKER. HUMBLED.
YOU GET BACK TO IT. DON'T LET ME INTERRUPT.
ER... RIGHT... EXACTLY RIGHT.
SAVED BY THE DECEPTIVELY UNIMPRESSIVE JAWLINE...YET AGAIN.
HEH. PETER PARKER.
MY PROTÉGÉ OUTFITTING SPIDER-MAN.
SUPER SCIENCE FOR A SUPER HERO.
WHAT FUN.
WHAT TREMENDOUS FUN.
WHITE/BACK!
NEW GADGETS!!!
SPIDER DRONES
EYES
17,0009

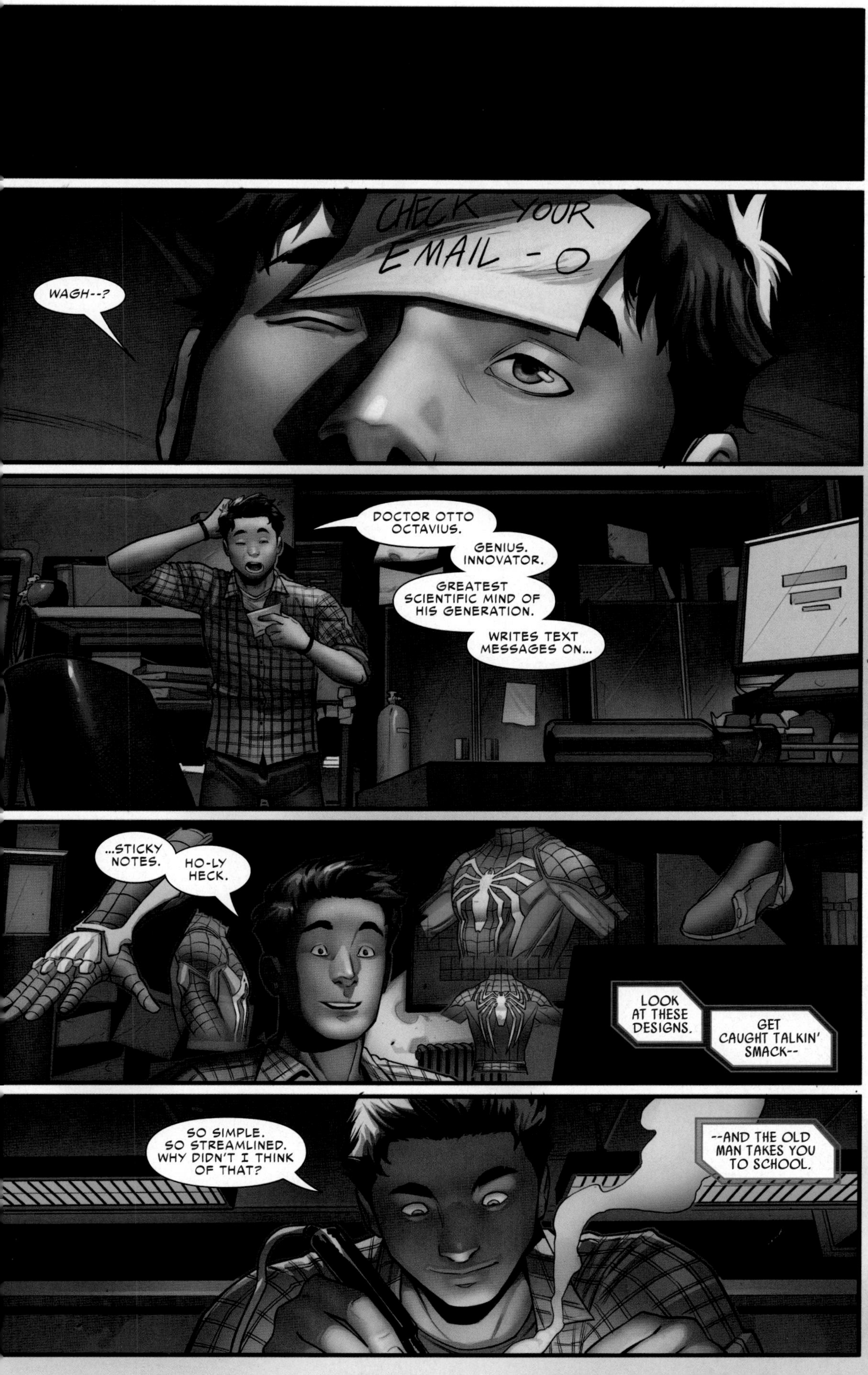
CHECK YOUR EMAIL -O
WAGH--?
DOCTOR OTTO OCTAVIUS.
GENIUS. INNOVATOR.
GREATEST SCIENTIFIC MIND OF HIS GENERATION.
WRITES TEXT MESSAGES ON...
...STICKY NOTES.
HO-LY HECK.
LOOK AT THESE DESIGNS.
GET CAUGHT TALKIN' SMACK--
SO SIMPLE. SO STREAMLINED. WHY DIDN'T I THINK OF THAT?
--AND THE OLD MAN TAKES YOU TO SCHOOL.

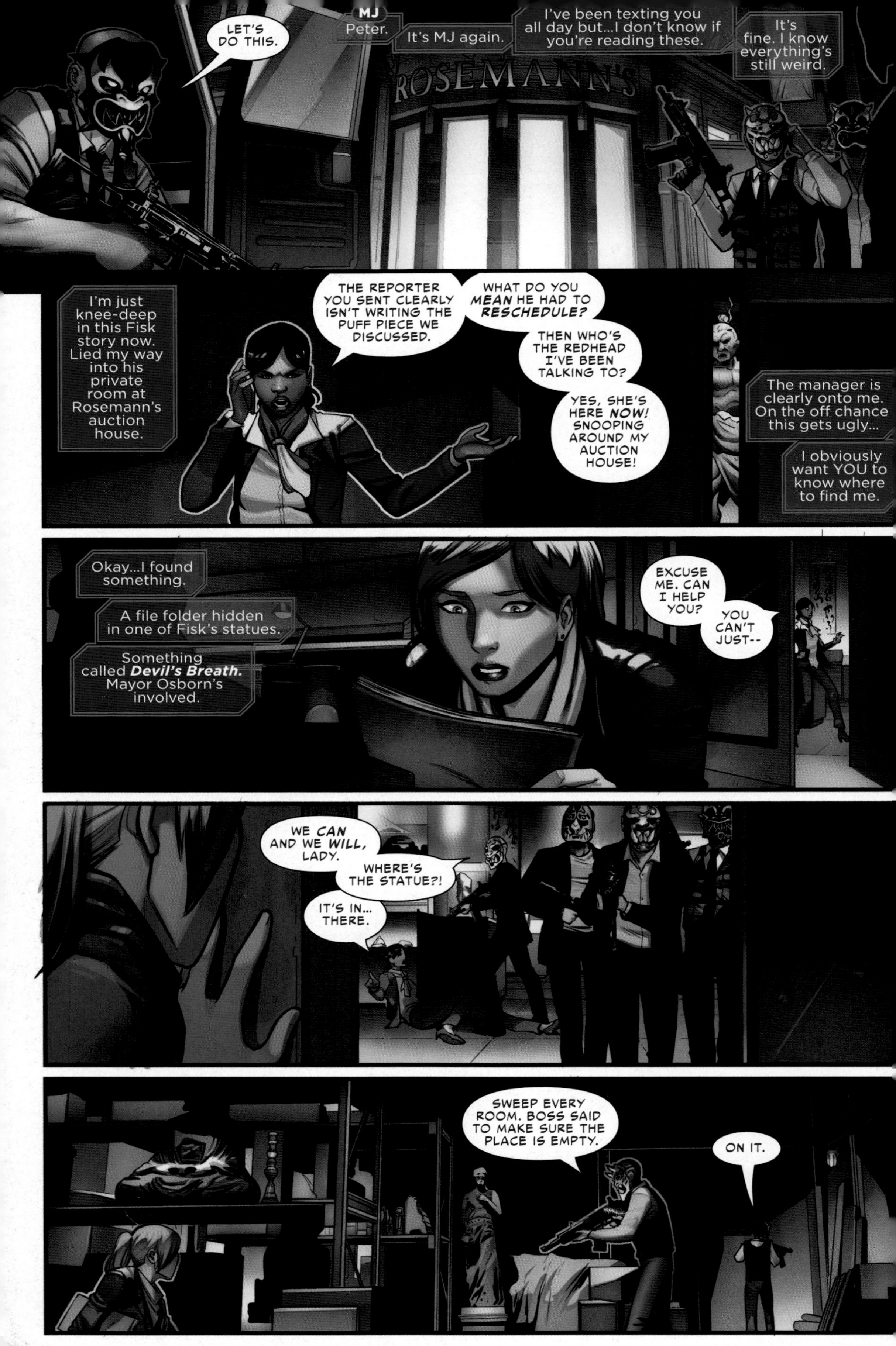
LET'S DO THIS.
MJ
Peter.
It's MJ again.
I've been texting you all day but...I don't know if you're reading these.
It's fine. I know everything's still weird.
ROSEMANN'S
I'm just knee-deep in this Fisk story now. Lied my way into his private room at Rosemann's auction house.
THE REPORTER YOU SENT CLEARLY ISN'T WRITING THE PUFF PIECE WE DISCUSSED.
WHAT DO YOU MEAN HE HAD TO RESCHEDULE?
THEN WHO'S THE REDHEAD I'VE BEEN TALKING TO?
YES, SHE'S HERE NOW! SNOOPING AROUND MY AUCTION HOUSE!
The manager is clearly onto me. On the off chance this gets ugly...
I obviously want YOU to know where to find me.
Okay...I found something.
A file folder hidden in one of Fisk's statues.
Something called Devil's Breath. Mayor Osborn's involved.
EXCUSE ME. CAN I HELP YOU?
YOU CAN'T JUST--
WE CAN AND WE WILL, LADY.
WHERE'S THE STATUE?!
IT'S IN... THERE.
SWEEP EVERY ROOM. BOSS SAID TO MAKE SURE THE PLACE IS EMPTY.
ON IT.

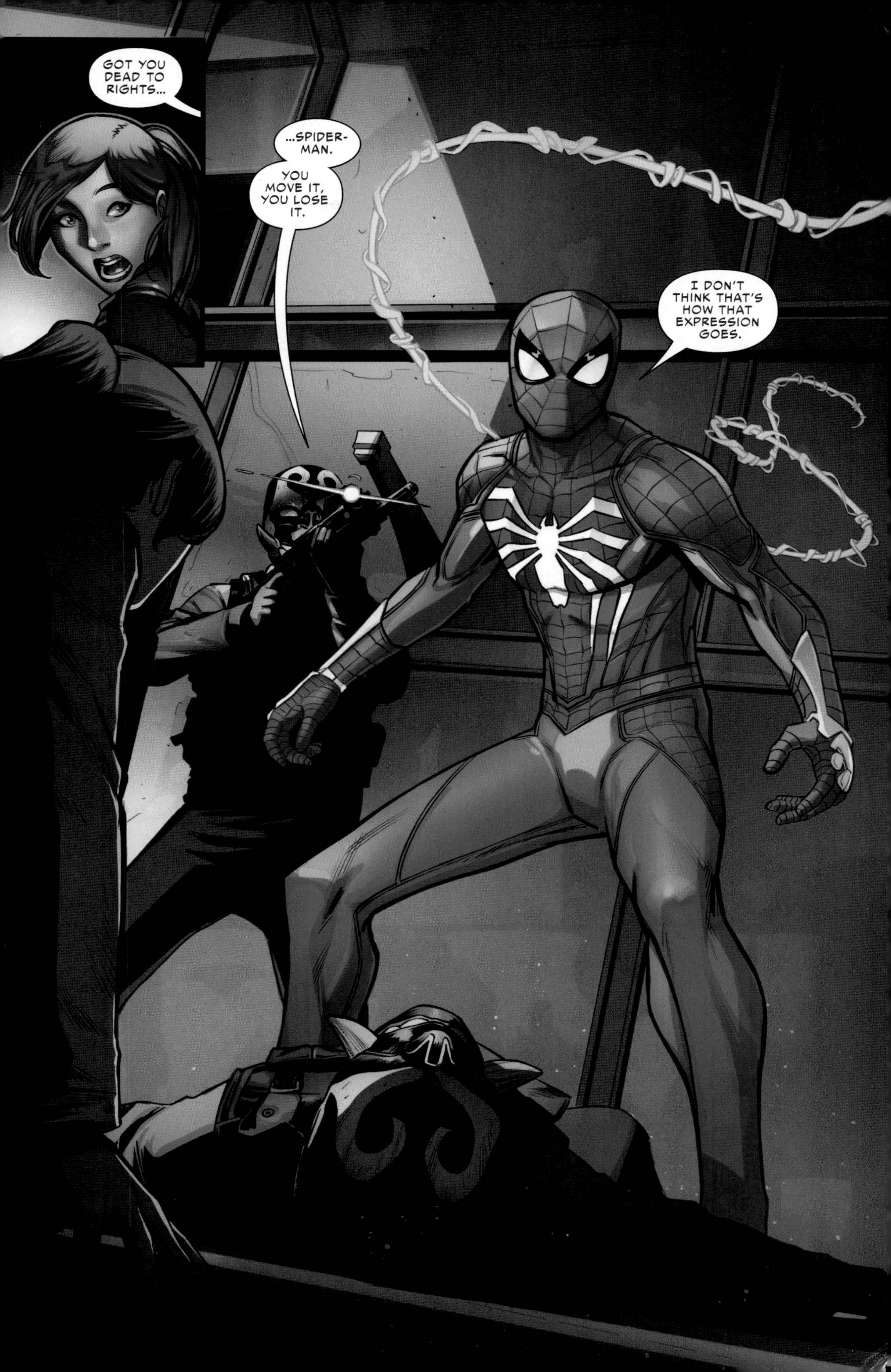
GOT YOU DEAD TO RIGHTS...
...SPIDER-MAN.
YOU MOVE IT, YOU LOSE IT.
I DON'T THINK THAT'S HOW THAT EXPRESSION GOES.

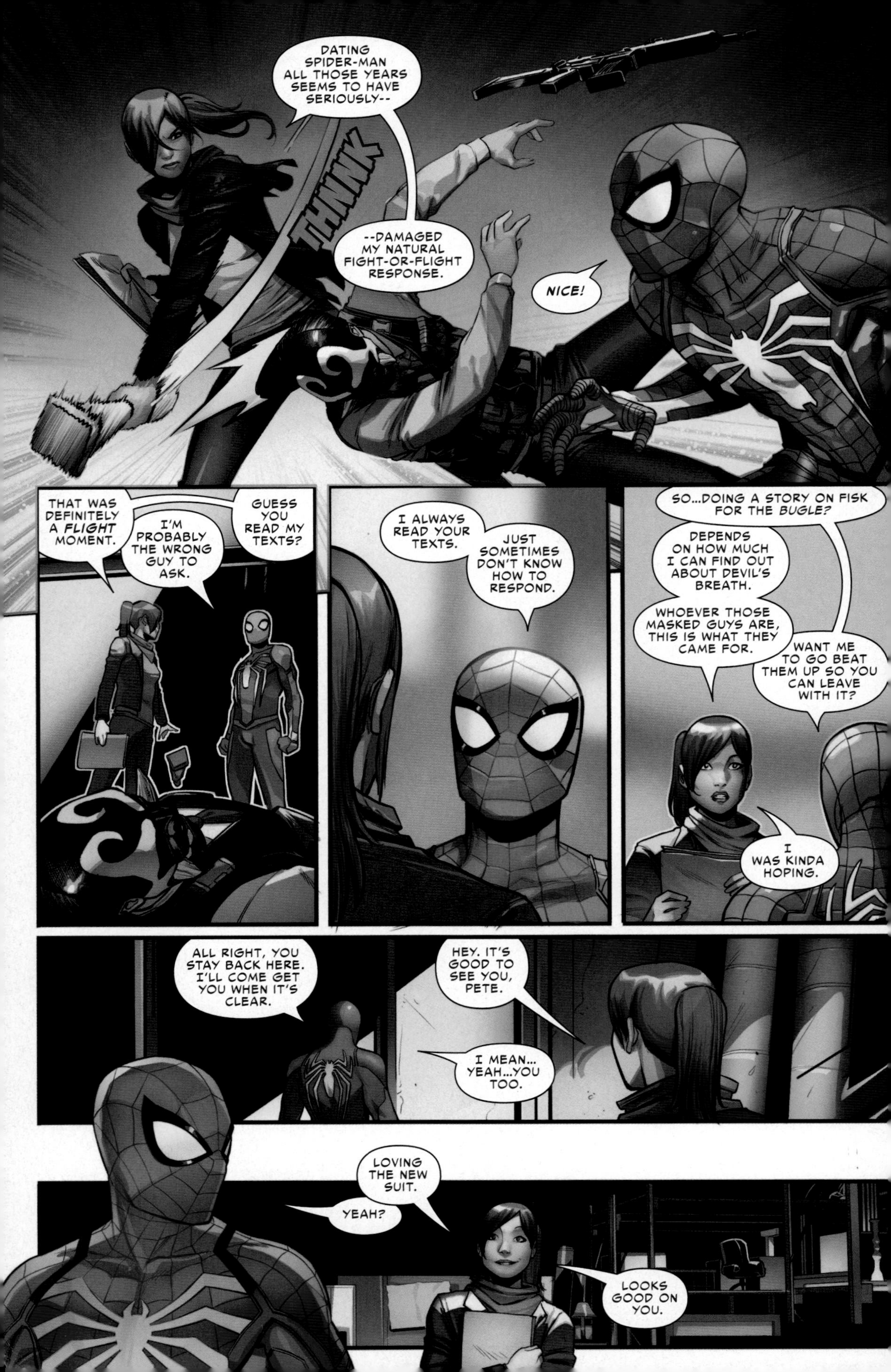
DATING SPIDER-MAN ALL THOSE YEARS SEEMS TO HAVE SERIOUSLY--
THWK
--DAMAGED MY NATURAL FIGHT-OR-FLIGHT RESPONSE.
NICE!
THAT WAS DEFINITELY A *FLIGHT* MOMENT.
I'M PROBABLY THE WRONG GUY TO ASK.
GUESS YOU READ MY TEXTS?
I ALWAYS READ YOUR TEXTS.
JUST SOMETIMES DON'T KNOW HOW TO RESPOND.
SO...DOING A STORY ON FISK FOR THE *BUGLE?*
DEPENDS ON HOW MUCH I CAN FIND OUT ABOUT DEVIL'S BREATH.
WHOEVER THOSE MASKED GUYS ARE, THIS IS WHAT THEY CAME FOR.
WANT ME TO GO BEAT THEM UP SO YOU CAN LEAVE WITH IT?
I WAS KINDA HOPING.
ALL RIGHT, YOU STAY BACK HERE. I'LL COME GET YOU WHEN IT'S CLEAR.
HEY. IT'S GOOD TO SEE YOU, PETE.
I MEAN... YEAH...YOU TOO.
LOVING THE NEW SUIT.
YEAH?
LOOKS GOOD ON YOU.

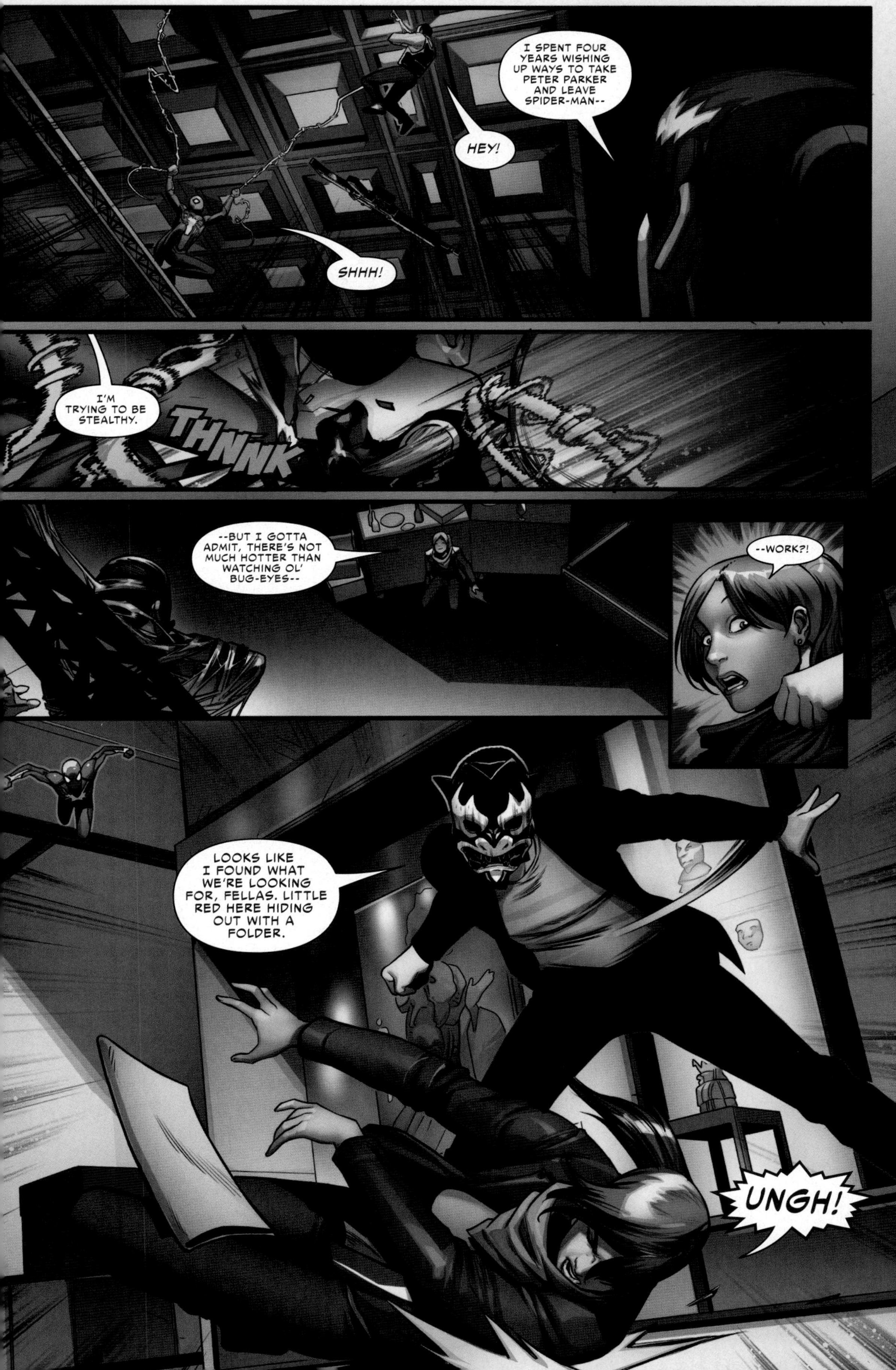
I SPENT FOUR YEARS WISHING UP WAYS TO TAKE PETER PARKER AND LEAVE SPIDER-MAN--
HEY!
SHHH!
I'M TRYING TO BE STEALTHY.
THNNK
--BUT I GOTTA ADMIT, THERE'S NOT MUCH HOTTER THAN WATCHING OL' BUG-EYES--
--WORK?!
LOOKS LIKE I FOUND WHAT WE'RE LOOKING FOR, FELLAS. LITTLE RED HERE HIDING OUT WITH A FOLDER.
UNGH!

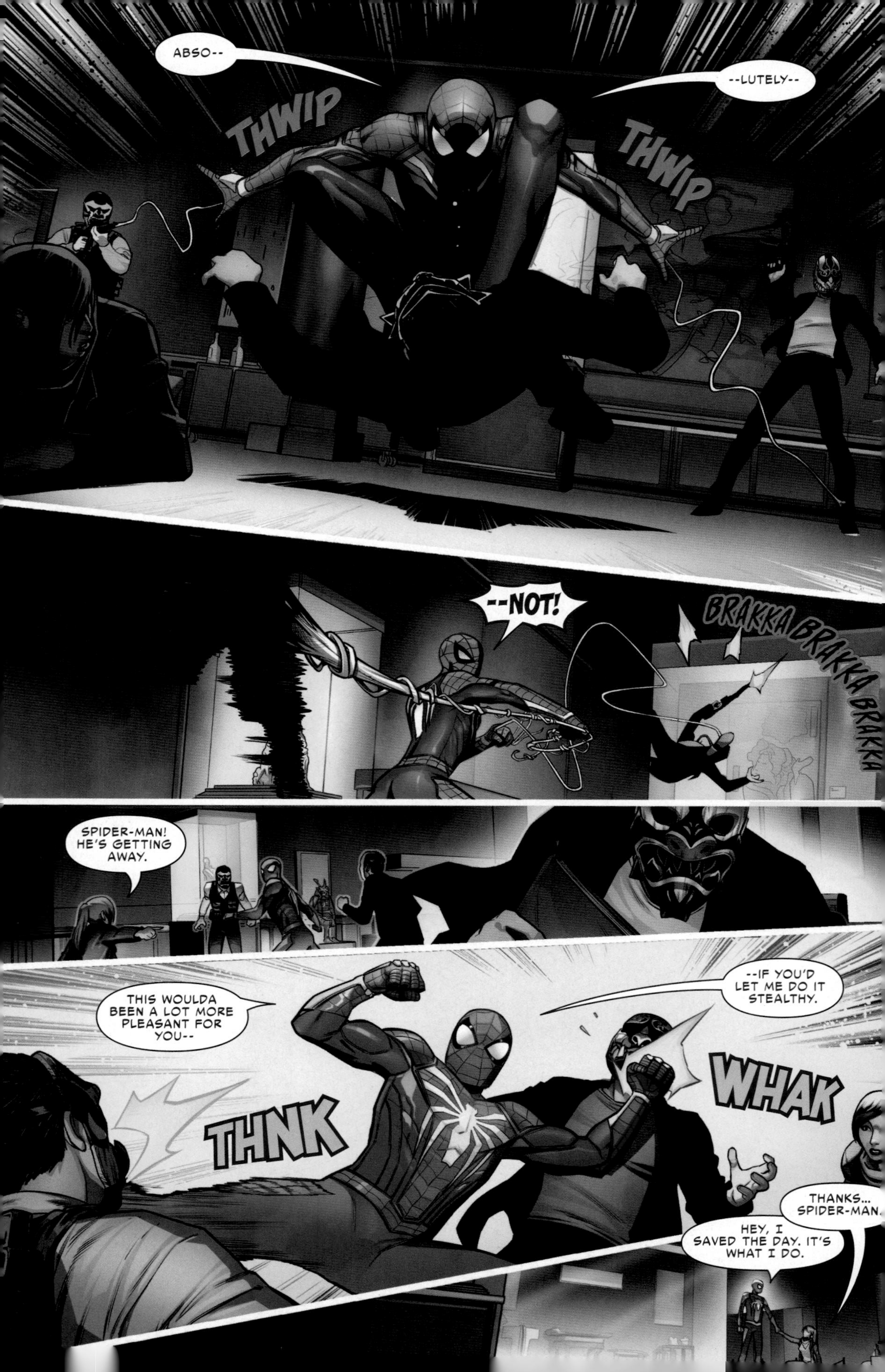
ABSO--
--LUTELY--
THWIP
THWIP
--NOT!
BRAKKA BRAKKA BRAKKA
SPIDER-MAN! HE'S GETTING AWAY.
THIS WOULDA BEEN A LOT MORE PLEASANT FOR YOU--
--IF YOU'D LET ME DO IT STEALTHY.
THNK
WHAK
THANKS... SPIDER-MAN.
HEY, I SAVED THE DAY. IT'S WHAT I DO.

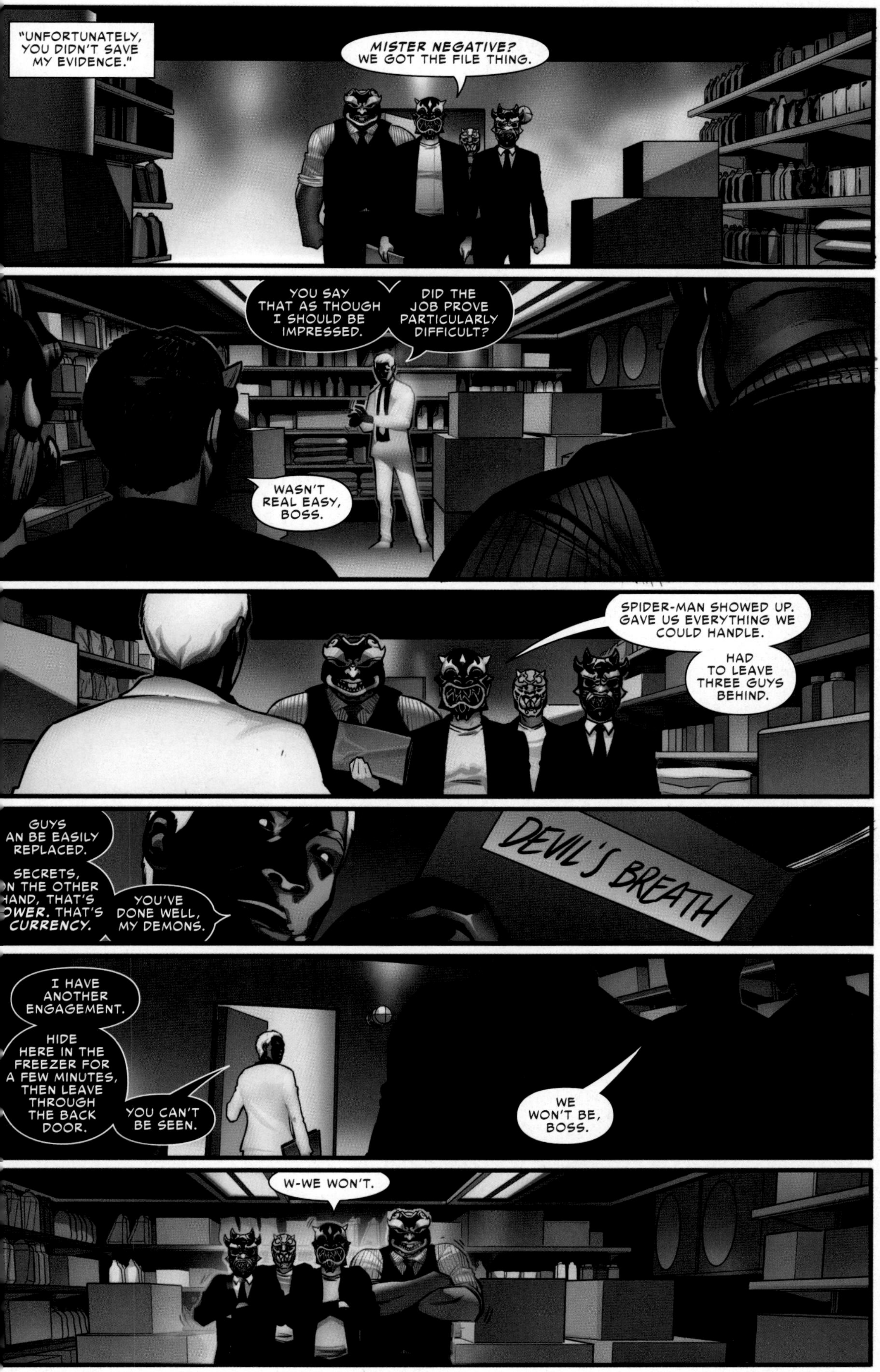
"UNFORTUNATELY, YOU DIDN'T SAVE MY EVIDENCE."
MISTER NEGATIVE? WE GOT THE FILE THING.
YOU SAY THAT AS THOUGH I SHOULD BE IMPRESSED.
DID THE JOB PROVE PARTICULARLY DIFFICULT?
WASN'T REAL EASY, BOSS.
SPIDER-MAN SHOWED UP. GAVE US EVERYTHING WE COULD HANDLE.
HAD TO LEAVE THREE GUYS BEHIND.
GUYS AN BE EASILY REPLACED.
SECRETS, N THE OTHER HAND, THAT'S OWER. THAT'S CURRENCY.
YOU'VE DONE WELL, MY DEMONS.
DEVIL'S BREATH
I HAVE ANOTHER ENGAGEMENT.
HIDE HERE IN THE FREEZER FOR A FEW MINUTES, THEN LEAVE THROUGH THE BACK DOOR.
YOU CAN'T BE SEEN.
WE WON'T BE, BOSS.
W-WE WON'T.

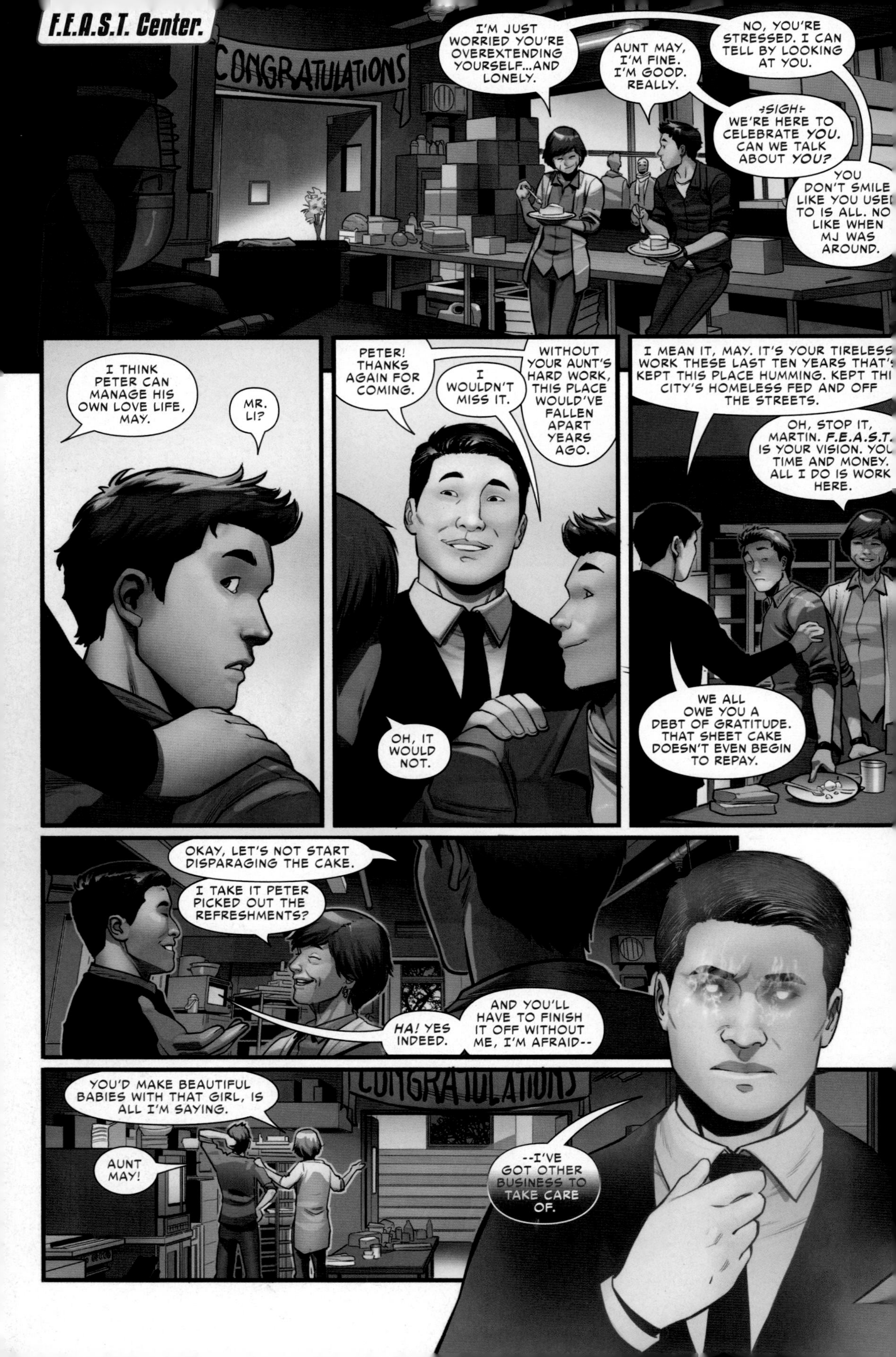
F.E.A.S.T. Center.
CONGRATULATIONS
I'M JUST WORRIED YOU'RE OVEREXTENDING YOURSELF...AND LONELY.
AUNT MAY, I'M FINE. I'M GOOD. REALLY.
NO, YOU'RE STRESSED. I CAN TELL BY LOOKING AT YOU.
-SIGH- WE'RE HERE TO CELEBRATE YOU. CAN WE TALK ABOUT YOU?
YOU DON'T SMILE LIKE YOU USED TO IS ALL. NOT LIKE WHEN MJ WAS AROUND.
I THINK PETER CAN MANAGE HIS OWN LOVE LIFE, MAY.
MR. LI?
PETER! THANKS AGAIN FOR COMING.
I WOULDN'T MISS IT.
WITHOUT YOUR AUNT'S HARD WORK, THIS PLACE WOULD'VE FALLEN APART YEARS AGO.
OH, IT WOULD NOT.
I MEAN IT, MAY. IT'S YOUR TIRELESS WORK THESE LAST TEN YEARS THAT'S KEPT THIS PLACE HUMMING. KEPT THIS CITY'S HOMELESS FED AND OFF THE STREETS.
OH, STOP IT, MARTIN. F.E.A.S.T. IS YOUR VISION. YOUR TIME AND MONEY. ALL I DO IS WORK HERE.
WE ALL OWE YOU A DEBT OF GRATITUDE. THAT SHEET CAKE DOESN'T EVEN BEGIN TO REPAY.
OKAY, LET'S NOT START DISPARAGING THE CAKE.
I TAKE IT PETER PICKED OUT THE REFRESHMENTS?
HA! YES INDEED.
AND YOU'LL HAVE TO FINISH IT OFF WITHOUT ME, I'M AFRAID--
YOU'D MAKE BEAUTIFUL BABIES WITH THAT GIRL, IS ALL I'M SAYING.
AUNT MAY!
CONGRATULATIONS
--I'VE GOT OTHER BUSINESS TO TAKE CARE OF.

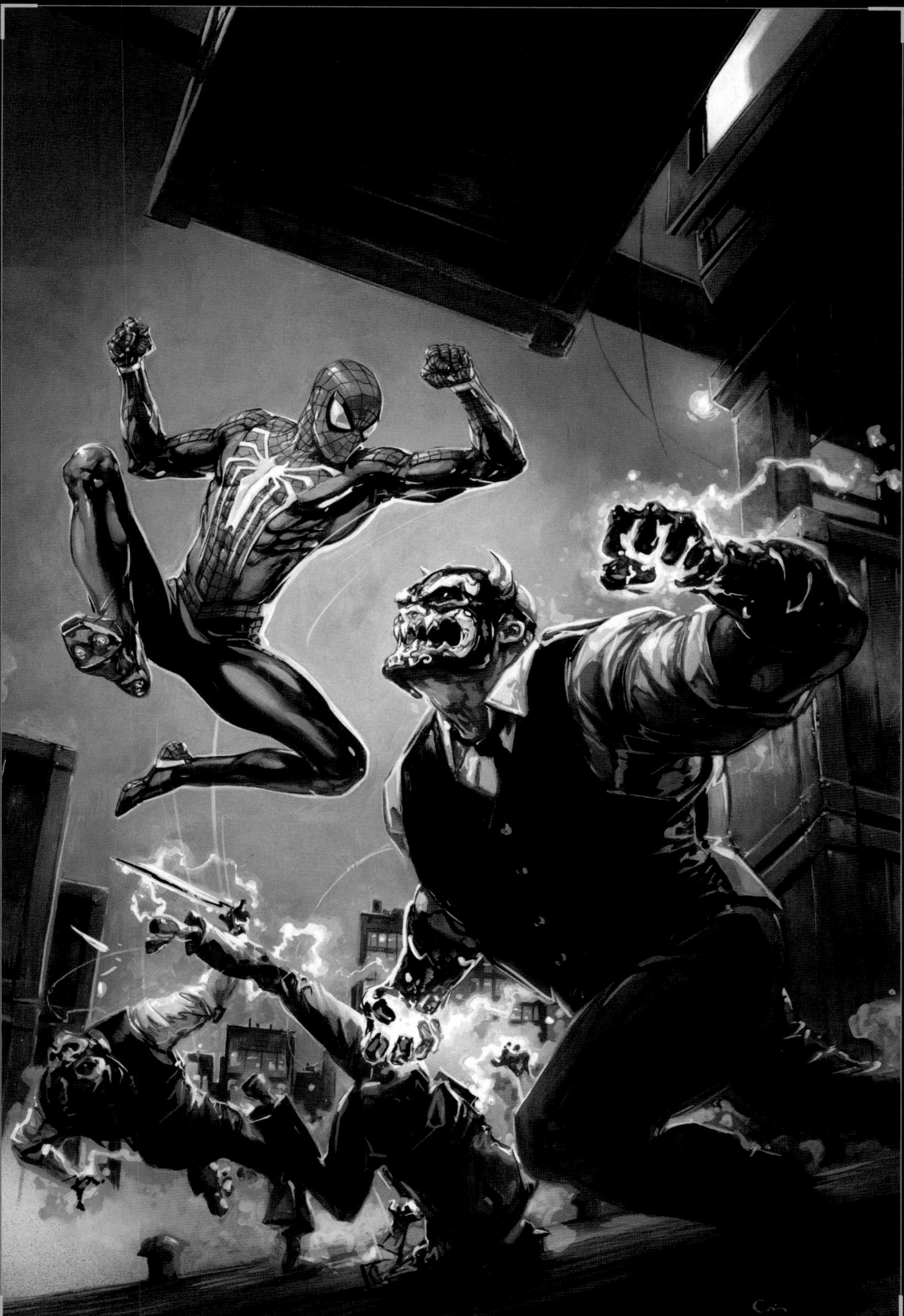

2

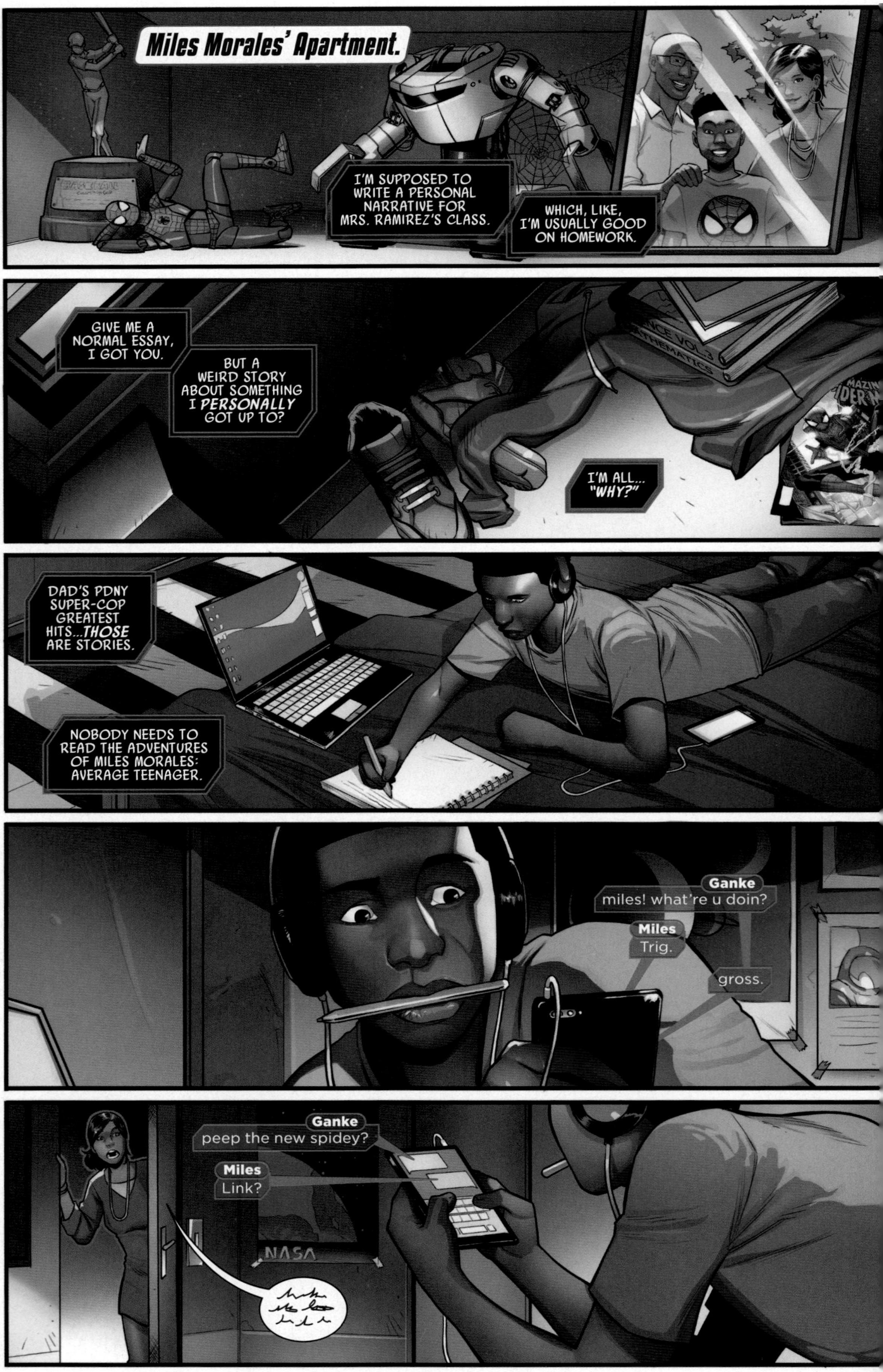
Miles Morales' Apartment.
I'M SUPPOSED TO WRITE A PERSONAL NARRATIVE FOR MRS. RAMIREZ'S CLASS.
WHICH, LIKE, I'M USUALLY GOOD ON HOMEWORK.
GIVE ME A NORMAL ESSAY, I GOT YOU.
BUT A WEIRD STORY ABOUT SOMETHING I *PERSONALLY* GOT UP TO?
I'M ALL... *"WHY?"*
DAD'S PDNY SUPER-COP GREATEST HITS...*THOSE* ARE STORIES.
NOBODY NEEDS TO READ THE ADVENTURES OF MILES MORALES: AVERAGE TEENAGER.
Ganke
miles! what're u doin?
Miles
Trig.
gross.
Ganke
peep the new spidey?
Miles
Link?
NASA

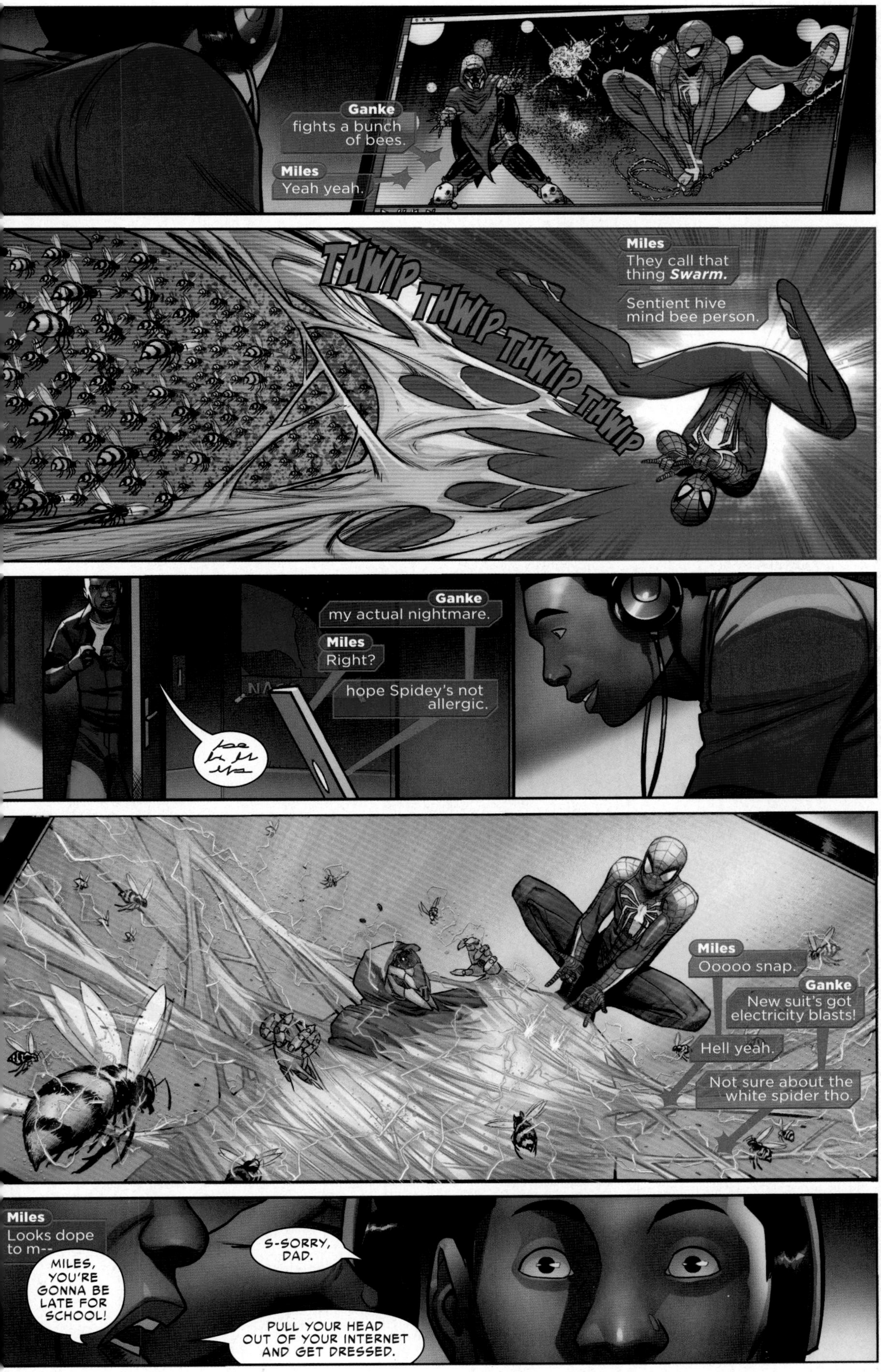
Ganke
fights a bunch of bees.
Miles
Yeah yeah.
THWIP THWIP THWIP THWIP
Miles
They call that thing *Swarm.*
Sentient hive mind bee person.
Ganke
my actual nightmare.
Miles
Right?
hope Spidey's not allergic.
Miles
Ooooo snap.
Ganke
New suit's got electricity blasts!
Hell yeah.
Not sure about the white spider tho.
Miles
Looks dope to m--
MILES, YOU'RE GONNA BE LATE FOR SCHOOL!
S-SORRY, DAD.
PULL YOUR HEAD OUT OF YOUR INTERNET AND GET DRESSED.

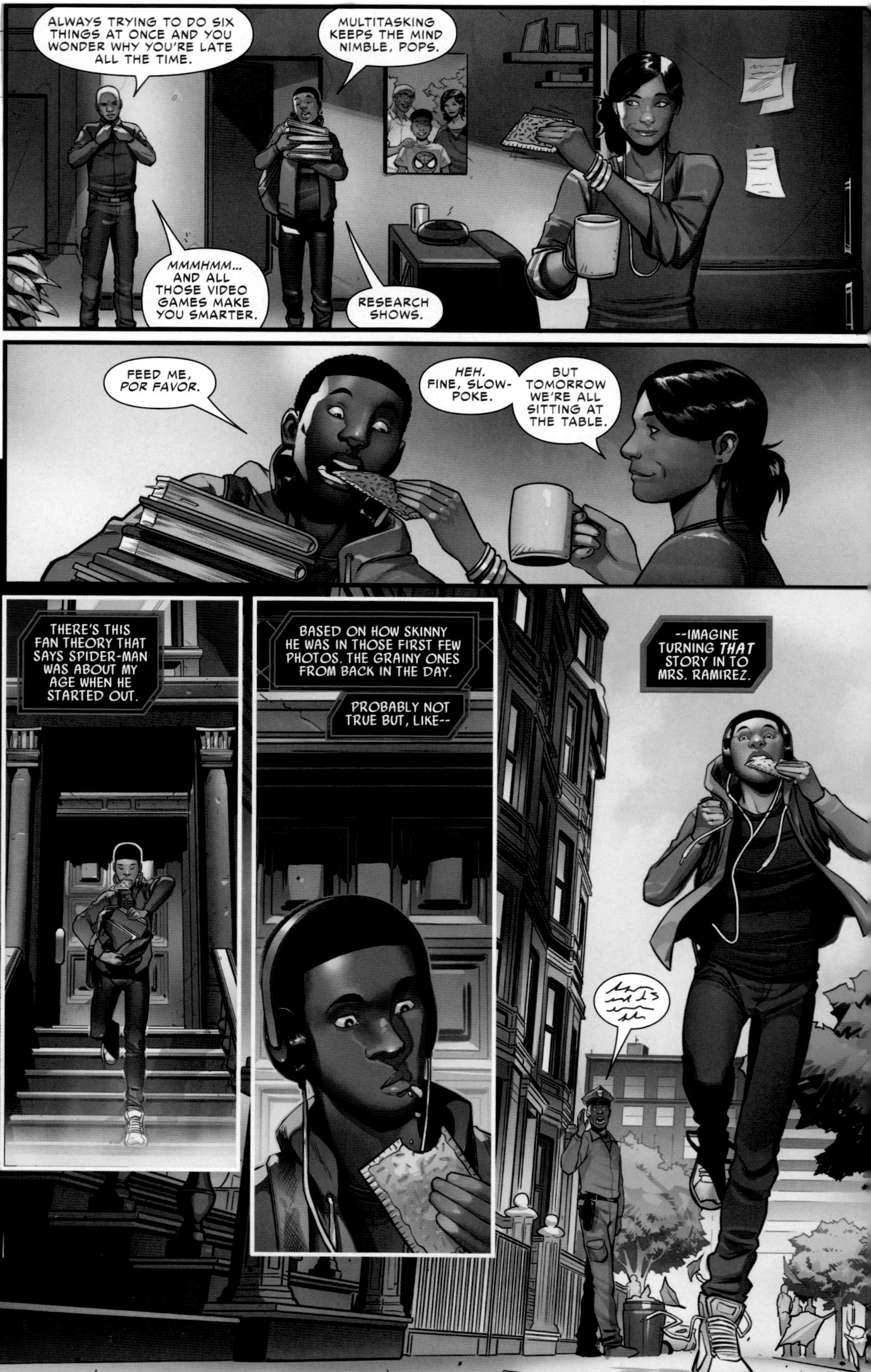
ALWAYS TRYING TO DO SIX THINGS AT ONCE AND YOU WONDER WHY YOU'RE LATE ALL THE TIME.
MULTITASKING KEEPS THE MIND NIMBLE, POPS.
MMMHMM... AND ALL THOSE VIDEO GAMES MAKE YOU SMARTER.
RESEARCH SHOWS.
FEED ME, POR FAVOR.
HEH. FINE, SLOW-POKE.
BUT TOMORROW WE'RE ALL SITTING AT THE TABLE.
THERE'S THIS FAN THEORY THAT SAYS SPIDER-MAN WAS ABOUT MY AGE WHEN HE STARTED OUT.
BASED ON HOW SKINNY HE WAS IN THOSE FIRST FEW PHOTOS. THE GRAINY ONES FROM BACK IN THE DAY.
PROBABLY NOT TRUE BUT, LIKE--
--IMAGINE TURNING THAT STORY IN TO MRS. RAMIREZ.

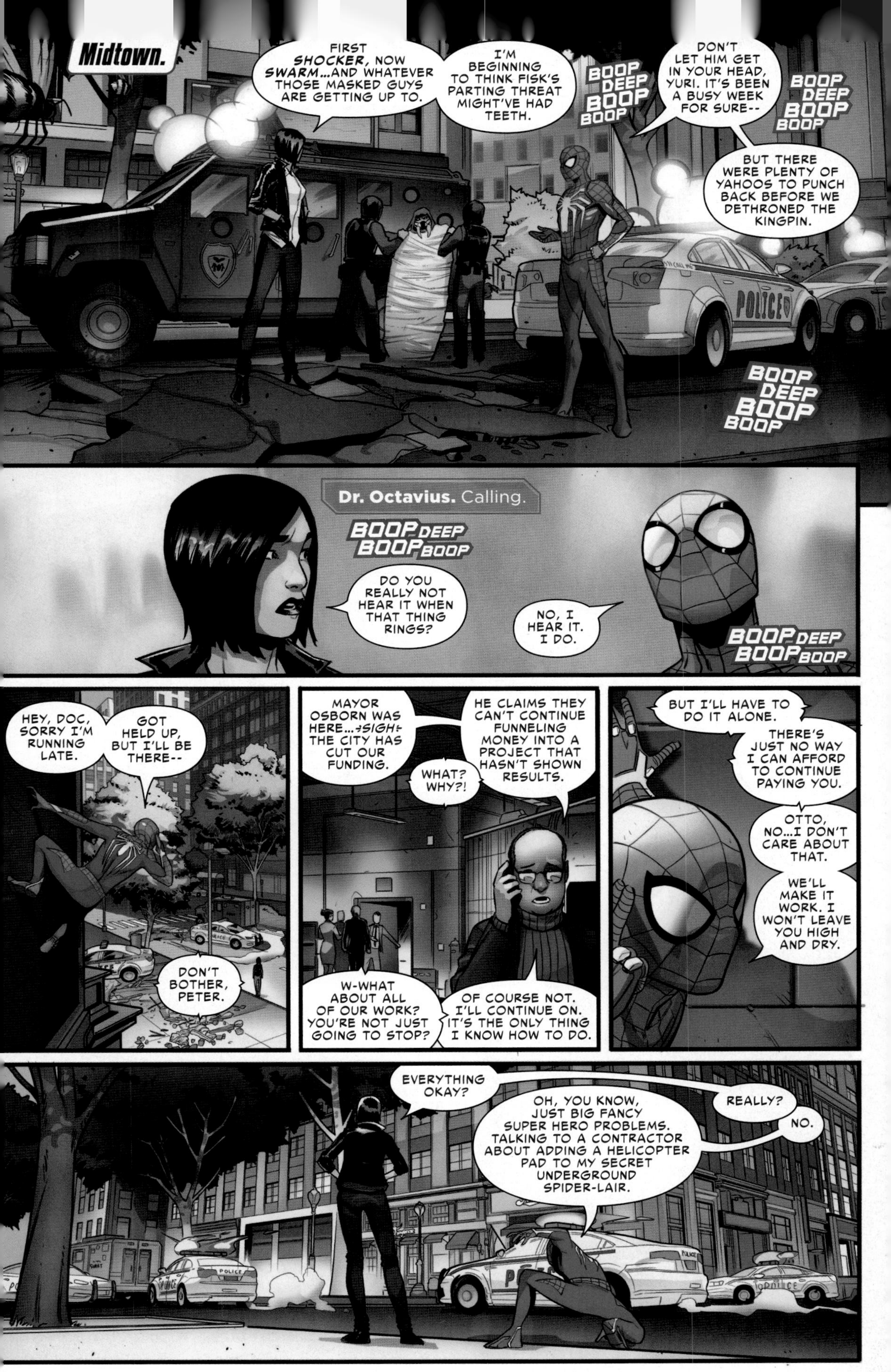

Midtown.
FIRST SHOCKER, NOW SWARM...AND WHATEVER THOSE MASKED GUYS ARE GETTING UP TO.
I'M BEGINNING TO THINK FISK'S PARTING THREAT MIGHT'VE HAD TEETH.
BOOP DEEP BOOP BOOP
DON'T LET HIM GET IN YOUR HEAD, YURI. IT'S BEEN A BUSY WEEK FOR SURE--
BOOP DEEP BOOP BOOP
BUT THERE WERE PLENTY OF YAHOOS TO PUNCH BACK BEFORE WE DETHRONED THE KINGPIN.
BOOP DEEP BOOP BOOP
Dr. Octavius. Calling.
BOOP DEEP BOOP BOOP
DO YOU REALLY NOT HEAR IT WHEN THAT THING RINGS?
NO, I HEAR IT. I DO.
BOOP DEEP BOOP BOOP
HEY, DOC, SORRY I'M RUNNING LATE.
GOT HELD UP, BUT I'LL BE THERE--
DON'T BOTHER, PETER.
MAYOR OSBORN WAS HERE... *SIGH* THE CITY HAS CUT OUR FUNDING.
WHAT? WHY?!
HE CLAIMS THEY CAN'T CONTINUE FUNNELING MONEY INTO A PROJECT THAT HASN'T SHOWN RESULTS.
W-WHAT ABOUT ALL OF OUR WORK? YOU'RE NOT JUST GOING TO STOP?
OF COURSE NOT. I'LL CONTINUE ON. IT'S THE ONLY THING I KNOW HOW TO DO.
BUT I'LL HAVE TO DO IT ALONE.
THERE'S JUST NO WAY I CAN AFFORD TO CONTINUE PAYING YOU.
OTTO, NO...I DON'T CARE ABOUT THAT.
WE'LL MAKE IT WORK. I WON'T LEAVE YOU HIGH AND DRY.
EVERYTHING OKAY?
OH, YOU KNOW, JUST BIG FANCY SUPER HERO PROBLEMS. TALKING TO A CONTRACTOR ABOUT ADDING A HELICOPTER PAD TO MY SECRET UNDERGROUND SPIDER-LAIR.
REALLY?
NO.

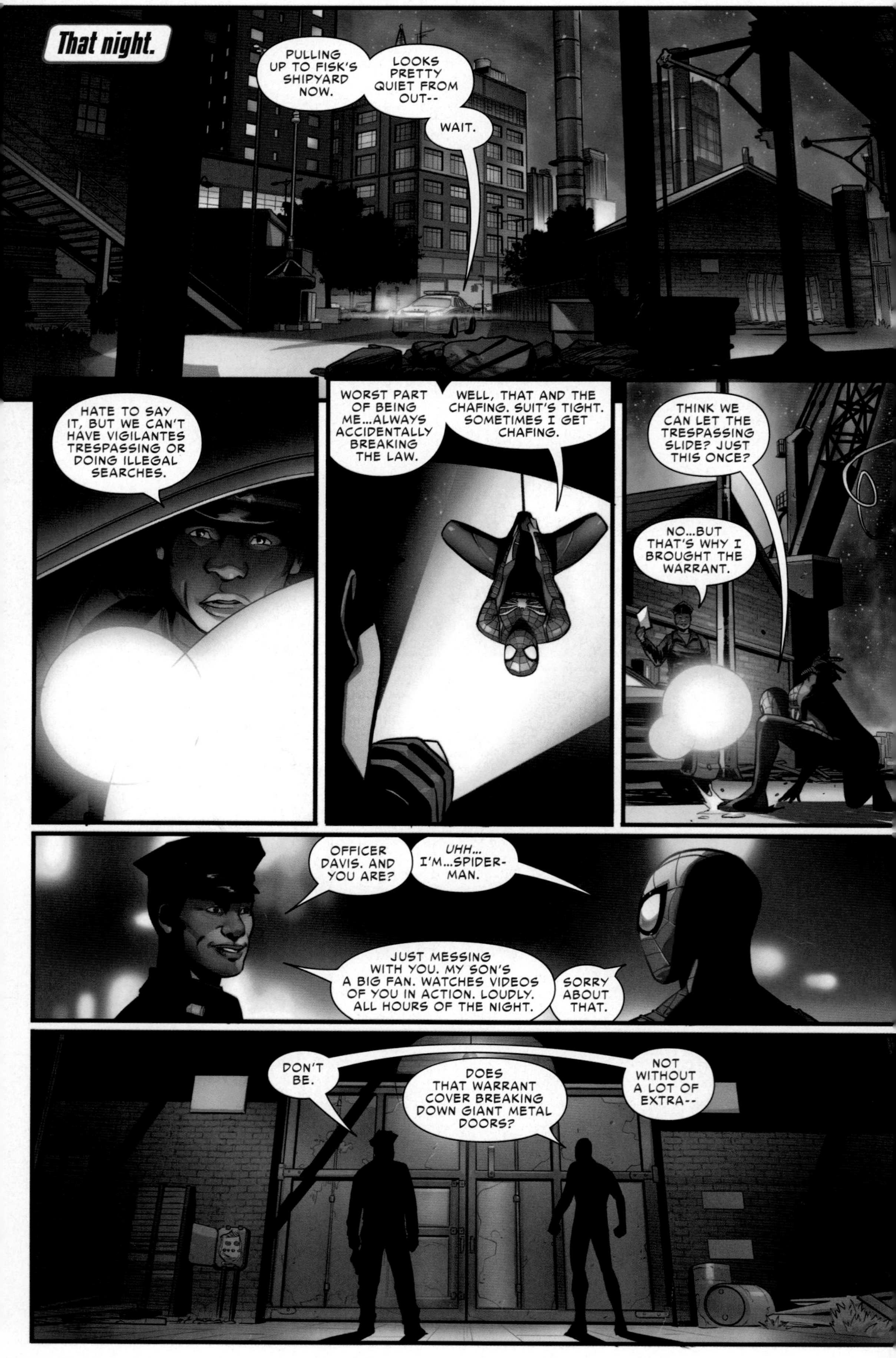
That night.
PULLING UP TO FISK'S SHIPYARD NOW.
LOOKS PRETTY QUIET FROM OUT--
WAIT.
HATE TO SAY IT, BUT WE CAN'T HAVE VIGILANTES TRESPASSING OR DOING ILLEGAL SEARCHES.
WORST PART OF BEING ME...ALWAYS ACCIDENTALLY BREAKING THE LAW.
WELL, THAT AND THE CHAFING. SUIT'S TIGHT. SOMETIMES I GET CHAFING.
THINK WE CAN LET THE TRESPASSING SLIDE? JUST THIS ONCE?
NO...BUT THAT'S WHY I BROUGHT THE WARRANT.
OFFICER DAVIS. AND YOU ARE?
UHH... I'M...SPIDER-MAN.
JUST MESSING WITH YOU. MY SON'S A BIG FAN. WATCHES VIDEOS OF YOU IN ACTION. LOUDLY. ALL HOURS OF THE NIGHT.
SORRY ABOUT THAT.
DON'T BE.
DOES THAT WARRANT COVER BREAKING DOWN GIANT METAL DOORS?
NOT WITHOUT A LOT OF EXTRA--

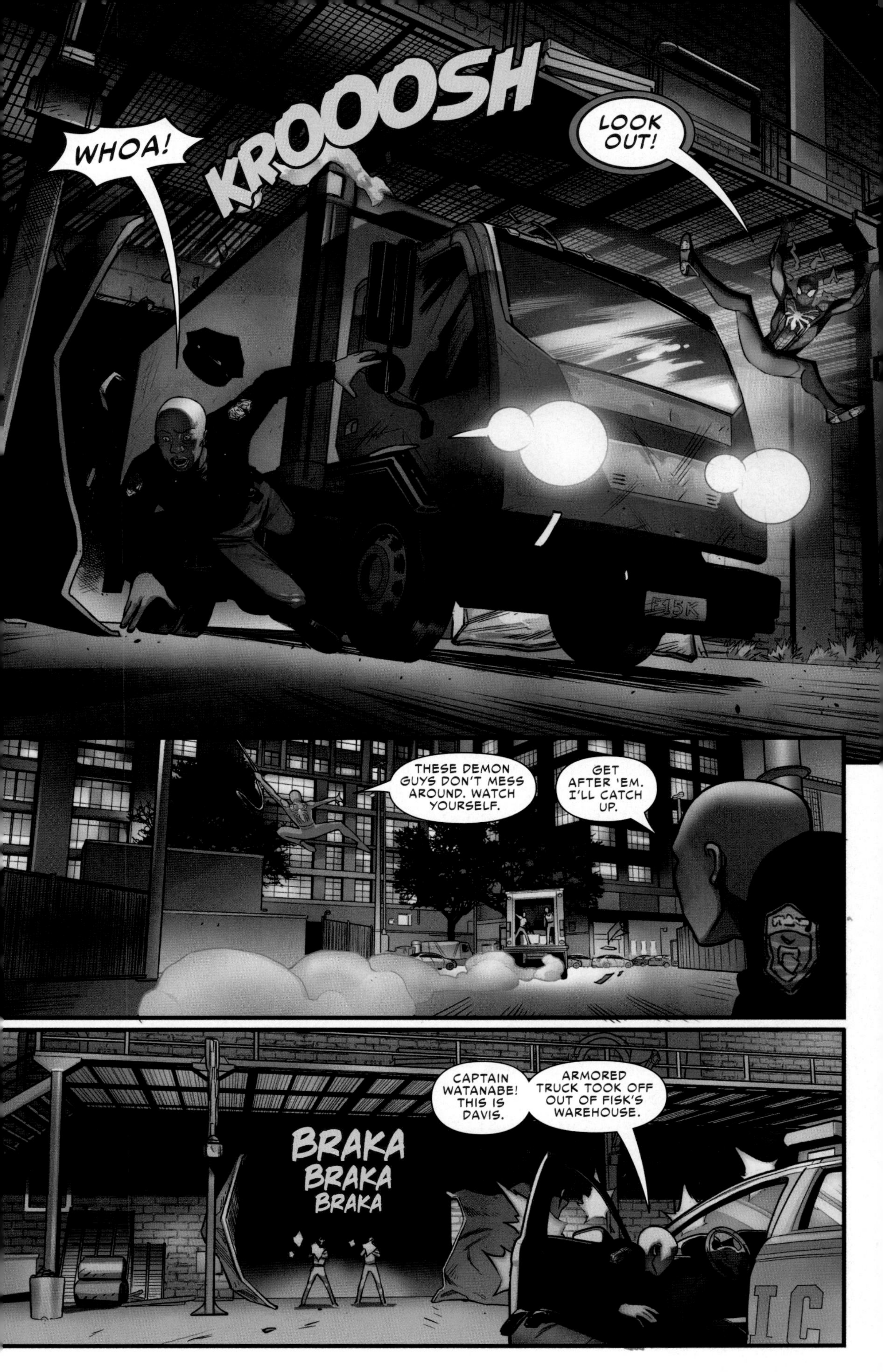
WHOA!
KROOOSH
LOOK OUT!
THESE DEMON GUYS DON'T MESS AROUND. WATCH YOURSELF.
GET AFTER 'EM. I'LL CATCH UP.
BRAKA BRAKA BRAKA
CAPTAIN WATANABE! THIS IS DAVIS.
ARMORED TRUCK TOOK OFF OUT OF FISK'S WAREHOUSE.

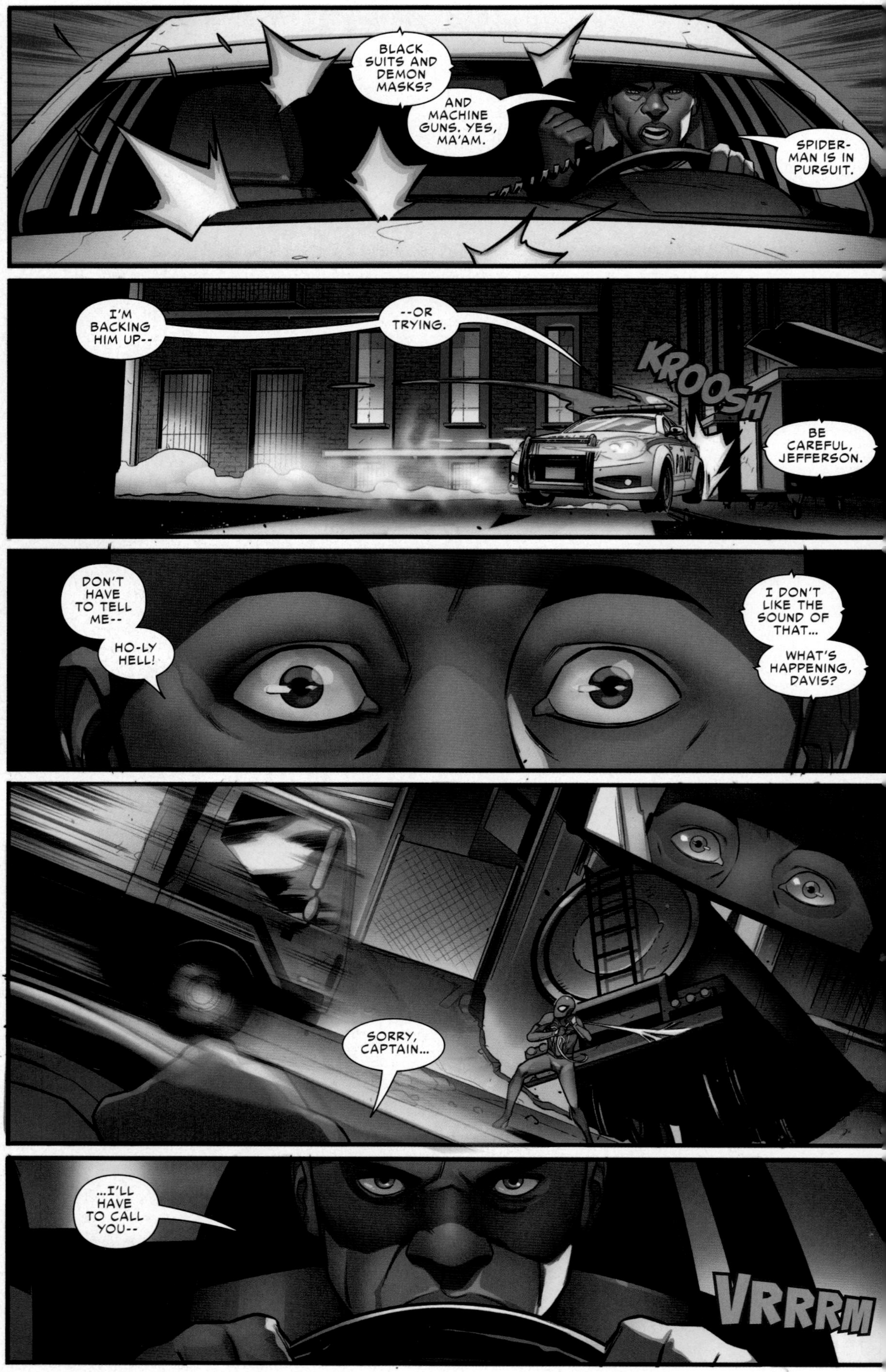
BLACK SUITS AND DEMON MASKS?
AND MACHINE GUNS. YES, MA'AM.
SPIDER-MAN IS IN PURSUIT.
I'M BACKING HIM UP--
--OR TRYING.
KROOSH
BE CAREFUL, JEFFERSON.
DON'T HAVE TO TELL ME--
HO-LY HELL!
I DON'T LIKE THE SOUND OF THAT...
WHAT'S HAPPENING, DAVIS?
SORRY, CAPTAIN...
...I'LL HAVE TO CALL YOU--
VRRRM

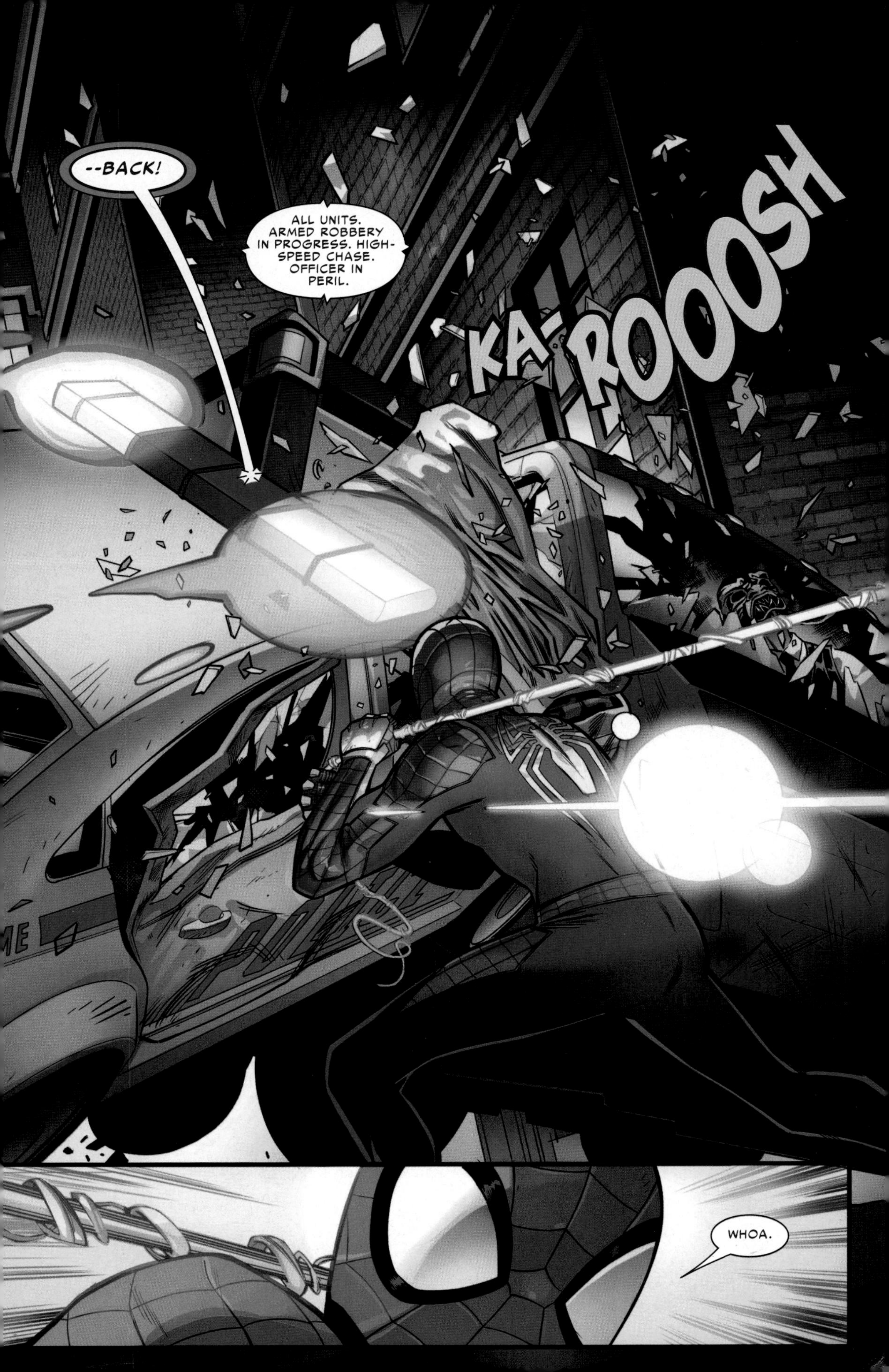
--BACK!
ALL UNITS. ARMED ROBBERY IN PROGRESS. HIGH-SPEED CHASE. OFFICER IN PERIL.
KA-ROOOSH
WHOA.

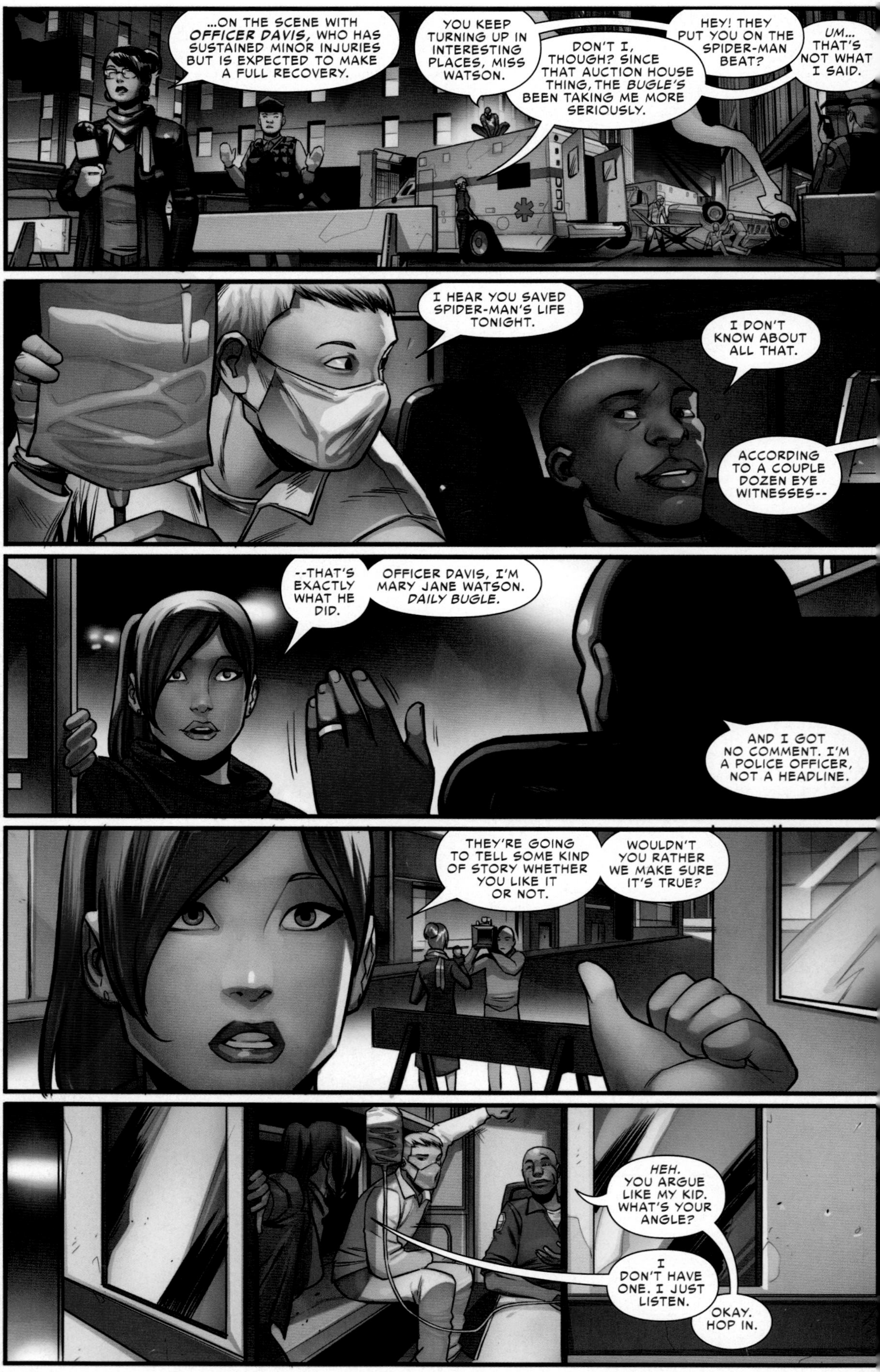
...ON THE SCENE WITH *OFFICER DAVIS,* WHO HAS SUSTAINED MINOR INJURIES BUT IS EXPECTED TO MAKE A FULL RECOVERY.
YOU KEEP TURNING UP IN INTERESTING PLACES, MISS WATSON.
DON'T I, THOUGH? SINCE THAT AUCTION HOUSE THING, THE *BUGLE'S* BEEN TAKING ME MORE SERIOUSLY.
HEY! THEY PUT YOU ON THE SPIDER-MAN BEAT?
UM... THAT'S NOT WHAT I SAID.
I HEAR YOU SAVED SPIDER-MAN'S LIFE TONIGHT.
I DON'T KNOW ABOUT ALL THAT.
ACCORDING TO A COUPLE DOZEN EYE WITNESSES--
--THAT'S EXACTLY WHAT HE DID.
OFFICER DAVIS, I'M MARY JANE WATSON. *DAILY BUGLE.*
AND I GOT NO COMMENT. I'M A POLICE OFFICER, NOT A HEADLINE.
THEY'RE GOING TO TELL SOME KIND OF STORY WHETHER YOU LIKE IT OR NOT.
WOULDN'T YOU RATHER WE MAKE SURE IT'S TRUE?
HEH. YOU ARGUE LIKE MY KID. WHAT'S YOUR ANGLE?
I DON'T HAVE ONE. I JUST LISTEN.
OKAY. HOP IN.

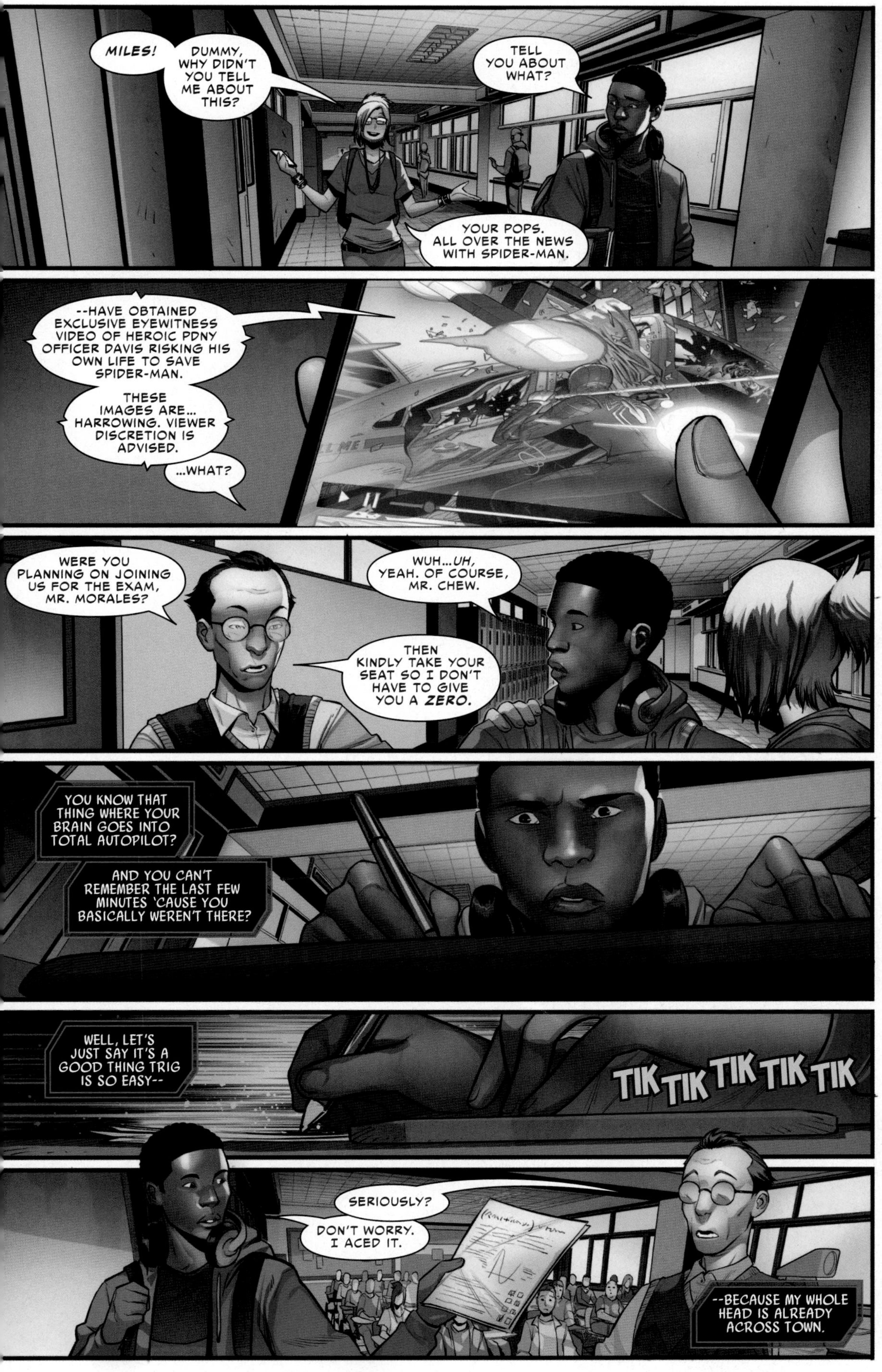
MILES!
DUMMY, WHY DIDN'T YOU TELL ME ABOUT THIS?
TELL YOU ABOUT WHAT?
YOUR POPS. ALL OVER THE NEWS WITH SPIDER-MAN.
--HAVE OBTAINED EXCLUSIVE EYEWITNESS VIDEO OF HEROIC PDNY OFFICER DAVIS RISKING HIS OWN LIFE TO SAVE SPIDER-MAN.
THESE IMAGES ARE... HARROWING. VIEWER DISCRETION IS ADVISED.
...WHAT?
WERE YOU PLANNING ON JOINING US FOR THE EXAM, MR. MORALES?
WUH...UH, YEAH. OF COURSE, MR. CHEW.
THEN KINDLY TAKE YOUR SEAT SO I DON'T HAVE TO GIVE YOU A ZERO.
YOU KNOW THAT THING WHERE YOUR BRAIN GOES INTO TOTAL AUTOPILOT?
AND YOU CAN'T REMEMBER THE LAST FEW MINUTES 'CAUSE YOU BASICALLY WEREN'T THERE?
WELL, LET'S JUST SAY IT'S A GOOD THING TRIG IS SO EASY--
TIK TIK TIK TIK TIK
SERIOUSLY?
DON'T WORRY. I ACED IT.
--BECAUSE MY WHOLE HEAD IS ALREADY ACROSS TOWN.

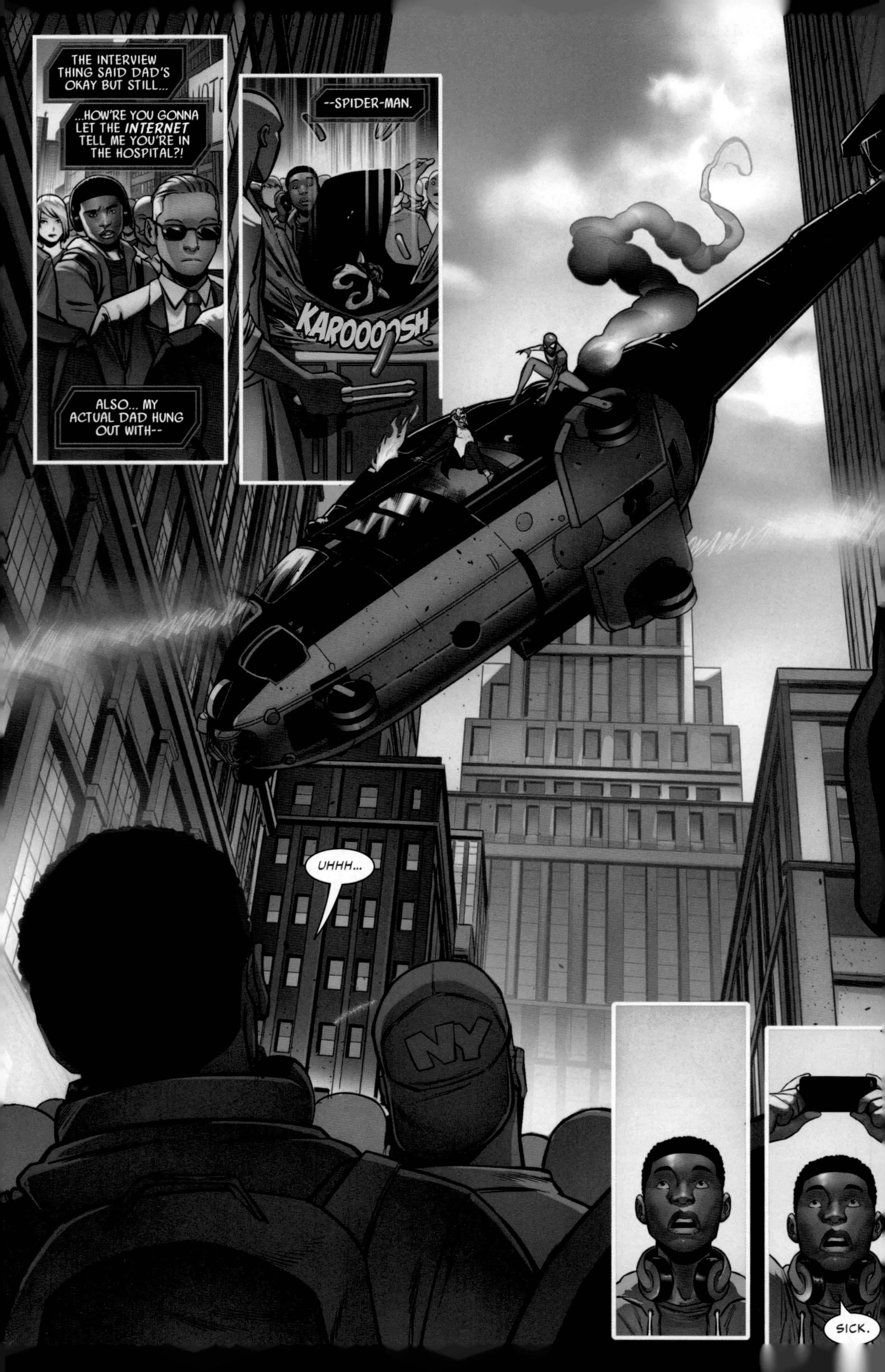
THE INTERVIEW THING SAID DAD'S OKAY BUT STILL...
...HOW'RE YOU GONNA LET THE *INTERNET* TELL ME YOU'RE IN THE HOSPITAL?!
ALSO... MY ACTUAL DAD HUNG OUT WITH--
--SPIDER-MAN.
KAROOOOSH
NY
UHHH...
SICK.

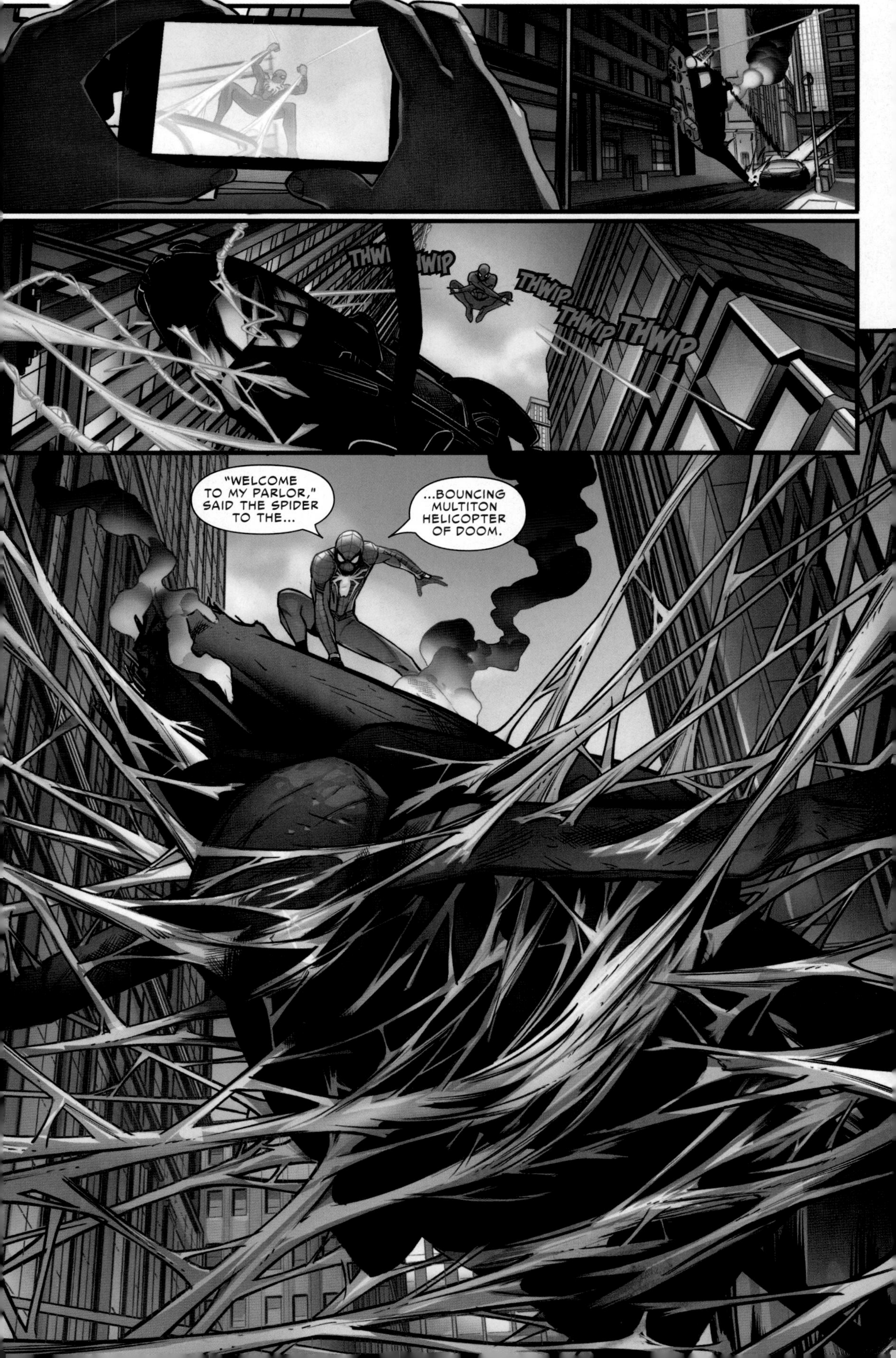
THWIP THWIP
THWIP
THWIP THWIP
"WELCOME TO MY PARLOR," SAID THE SPIDER TO THE...
...BOUNCING MULTITON HELICOPTER OF DOOM.

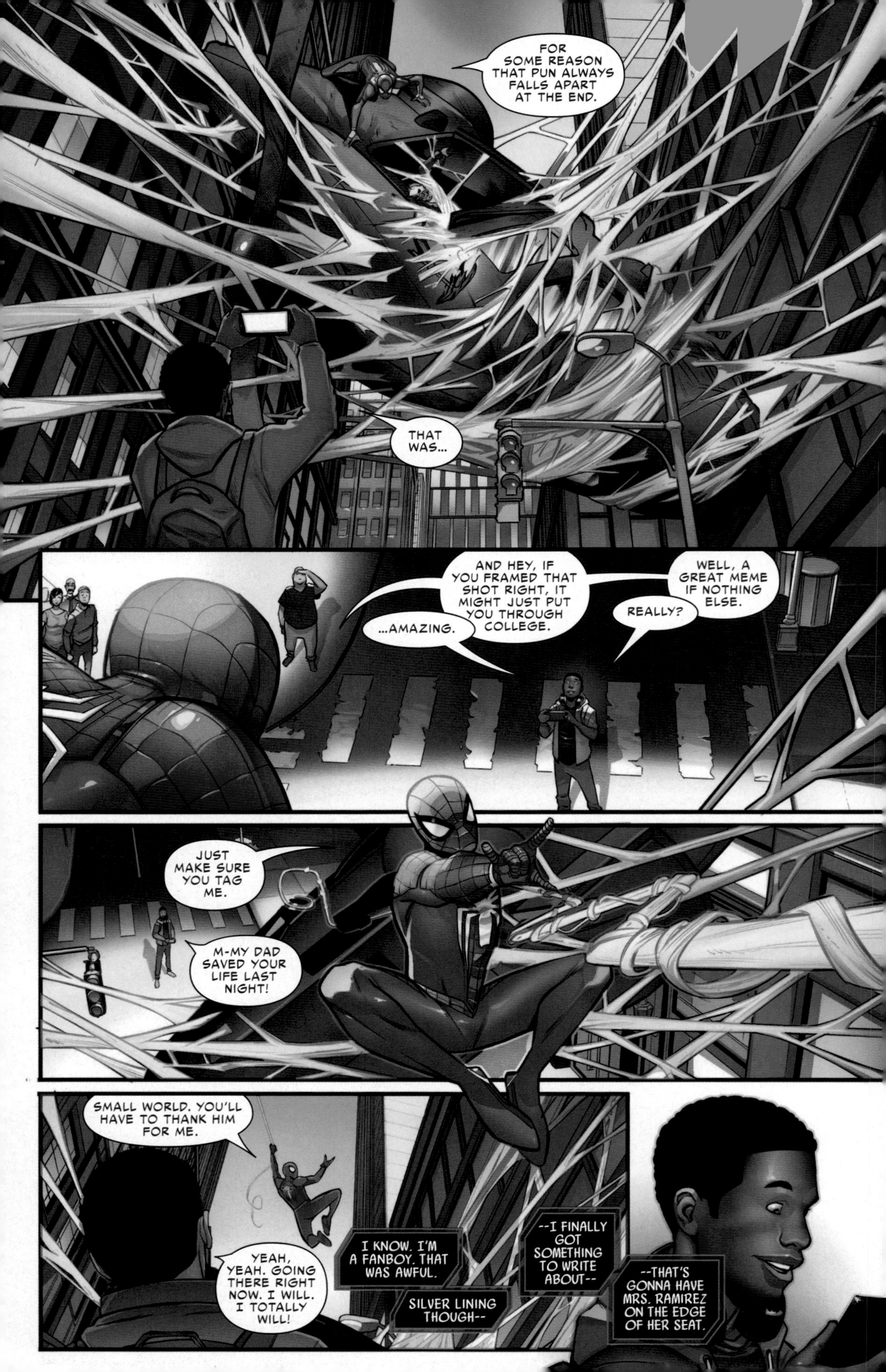
FOR SOME REASON THAT PUN ALWAYS FALLS APART AT THE END.
THAT WAS...
...AMAZING.
AND HEY, IF YOU FRAMED THAT SHOT RIGHT, IT MIGHT JUST PUT YOU THROUGH COLLEGE.
REALLY?
WELL, A GREAT MEME IF NOTHING ELSE.
JUST MAKE SURE YOU TAG ME.
M-MY DAD SAVED YOUR LIFE LAST NIGHT!
SMALL WORLD. YOU'LL HAVE TO THANK HIM FOR ME.
YEAH, YEAH. GOING THERE RIGHT NOW. I WILL. I TOTALLY WILL!
I KNOW. I'M A FANBOY. THAT WAS AWFUL.
SILVER LINING THOUGH--
--I FINALLY GOT SOMETHING TO WRITE ABOUT--
--THAT'S GONNA HAVE MRS. RAMIREZ ON THE EDGE OF HER SEAT.

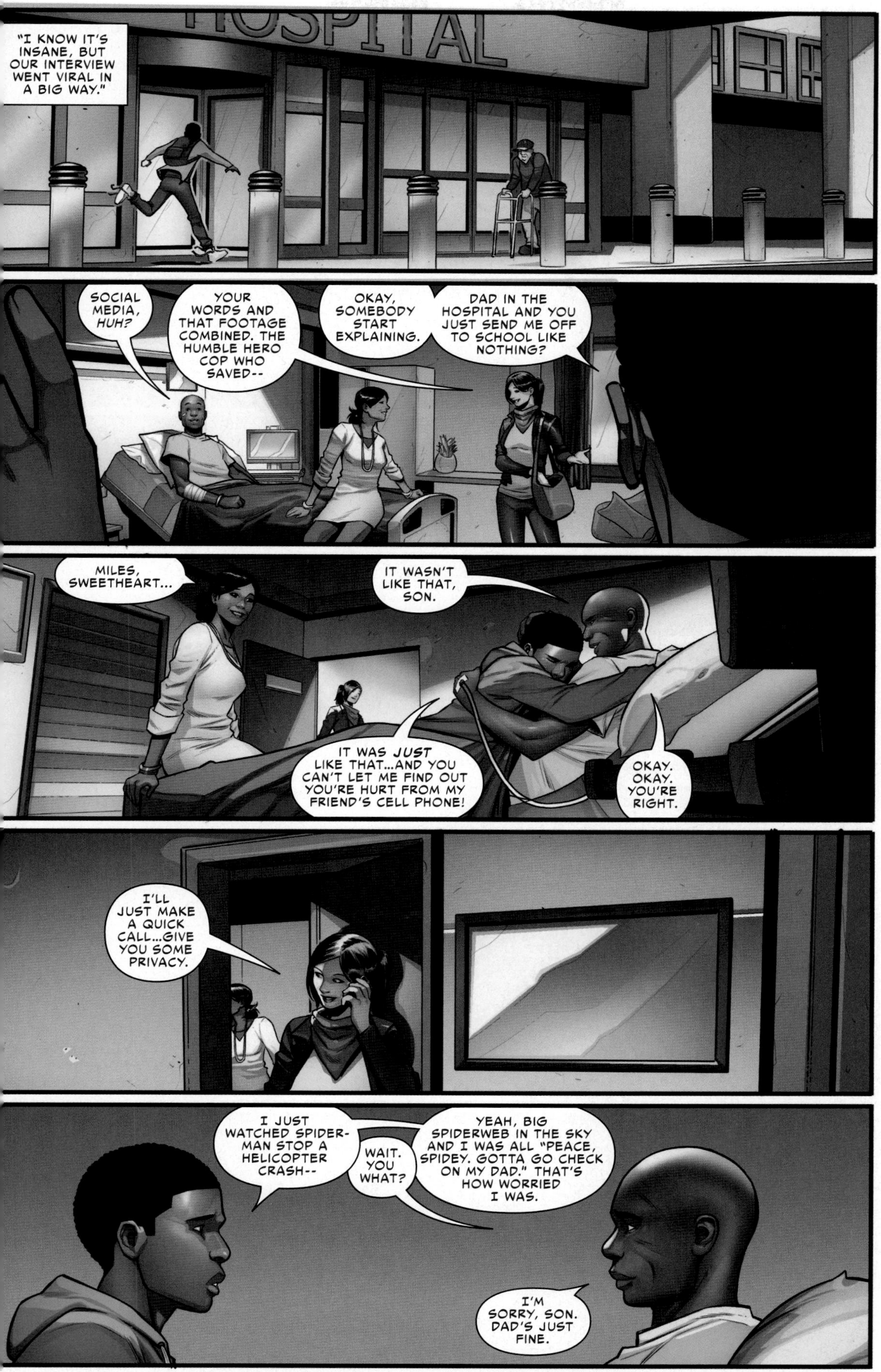
HOSPITAL
"I KNOW IT'S INSANE, BUT OUR INTERVIEW WENT VIRAL IN A BIG WAY."
SOCIAL MEDIA, *HUH?*
YOUR WORDS AND THAT FOOTAGE COMBINED. THE HUMBLE HERO COP WHO SAVED--
OKAY, SOMEBODY START EXPLAINING.
DAD IN THE HOSPITAL AND YOU JUST SEND ME OFF TO SCHOOL LIKE NOTHING?
MILES, SWEETHEART...
IT WASN'T LIKE THAT, SON.
IT WAS *JUST* LIKE THAT...AND YOU CAN'T LET ME FIND OUT YOU'RE HURT FROM MY FRIEND'S CELL PHONE!
OKAY. OKAY. YOU'RE RIGHT.
I'LL JUST MAKE A QUICK CALL...GIVE YOU SOME PRIVACY.
I JUST WATCHED SPIDER-MAN STOP A HELICOPTER CRASH--
WAIT. YOU WHAT?
YEAH, BIG SPIDERWEB IN THE SKY AND I WAS ALL "PEACE, SPIDEY. GOTTA GO CHECK ON MY DAD." THAT'S HOW WORRIED I WAS.
I'M SORRY, SON. DAD'S JUST FINE.

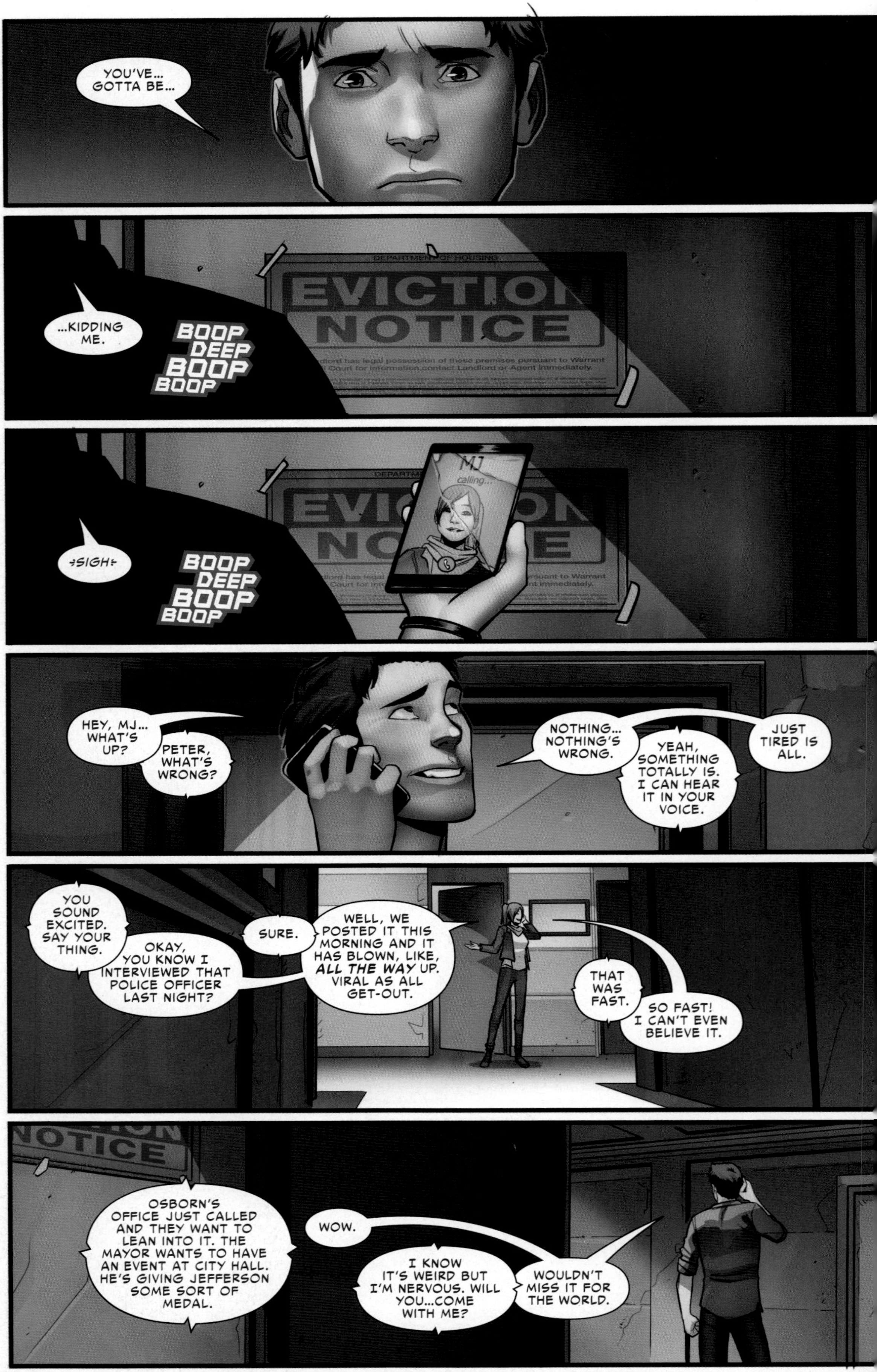
YOU'VE... GOTTA BE...
...KIDDING ME.
BOOP DEEP BOOP BOOP
DEPARTMENT OF HOUSING
EVICTION NOTICE
Landlord has legal possession of these premises pursuant to Warrant
Court for information,contact Landlord or Agent Immediately.
MJ
calling...
¬SIGH¬
BOOP DEEP BOOP BOOP
HEY, MJ... WHAT'S UP?
PETER, WHAT'S WRONG?
NOTHING... NOTHING'S WRONG.
YEAH, SOMETHING TOTALLY IS. I CAN HEAR IT IN YOUR VOICE.
JUST TIRED IS ALL.
YOU SOUND EXCITED. SAY YOUR THING.
OKAY, YOU KNOW I INTERVIEWED THAT POLICE OFFICER LAST NIGHT?
SURE.
WELL, WE POSTED IT THIS MORNING AND IT HAS BLOWN, LIKE, ALL THE WAY UP. VIRAL AS ALL GET-OUT.
THAT WAS FAST.
SO FAST! I CAN'T EVEN BELIEVE IT.
NOTICE
OSBORN'S OFFICE JUST CALLED AND THEY WANT TO LEAN INTO IT. THE MAYOR WANTS TO HAVE AN EVENT AT CITY HALL. HE'S GIVING JEFFERSON SOME SORT OF MEDAL.
WOW.
I KNOW IT'S WEIRD BUT I'M NERVOUS. WILL YOU...COME WITH ME?
WOULDN'T MISS IT FOR THE WORLD.

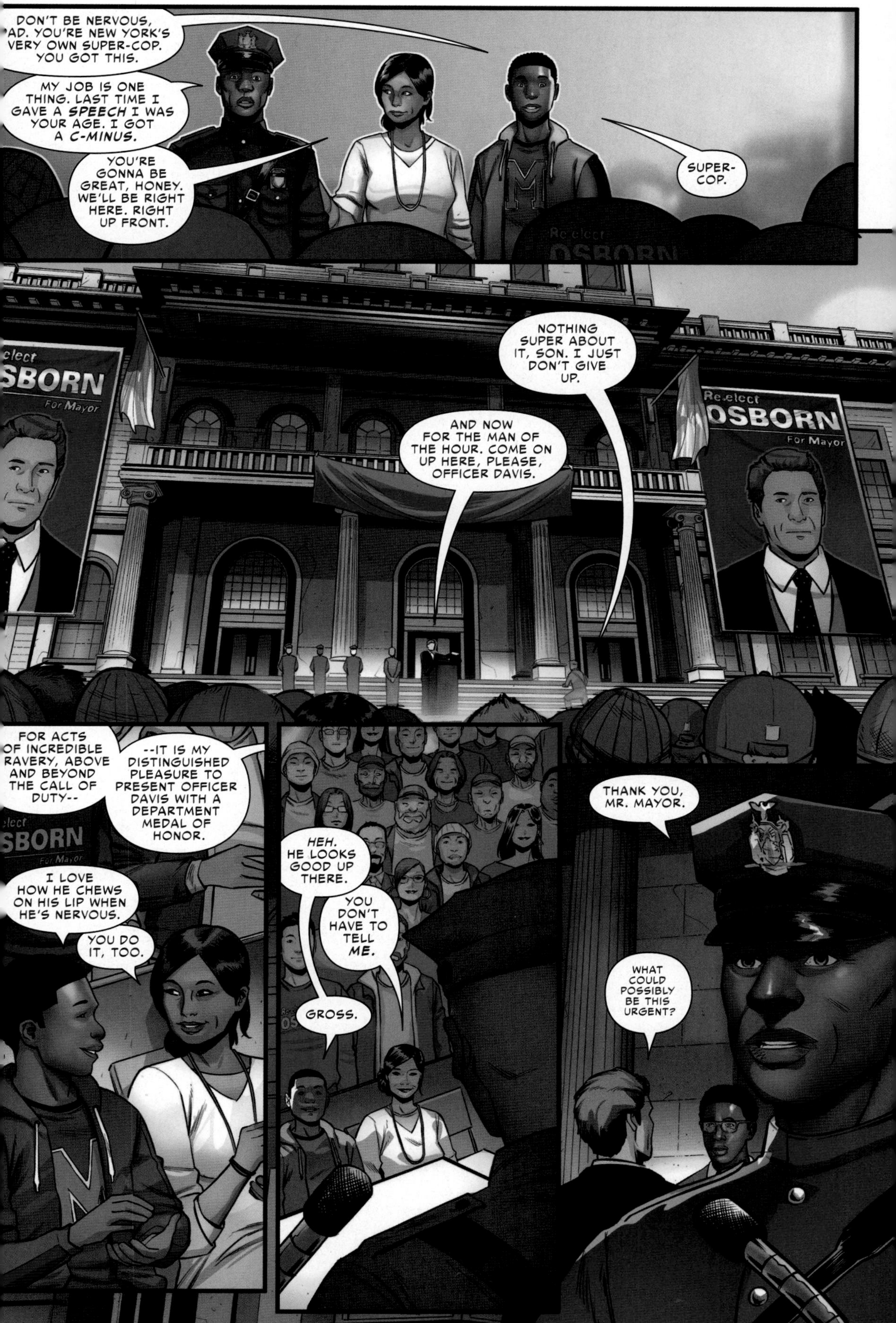
DON'T BE NERVOUS, DAD. YOU'RE NEW YORK'S VERY OWN SUPER-COP. YOU GOT THIS.
MY JOB IS ONE THING. LAST TIME I GAVE A SPEECH I WAS YOUR AGE. I GOT A C-MINUS.
YOU'RE GONNA BE GREAT, HONEY. WE'LL BE RIGHT HERE. RIGHT UP FRONT.
SUPER-COP.
Re-elect OSBORN
NOTHING SUPER ABOUT IT, SON. I JUST DON'T GIVE UP.
AND NOW FOR THE MAN OF THE HOUR. COME ON UP HERE, PLEASE, OFFICER DAVIS.
Re-elect OSBORN For Mayor
Re-elect OSBORN For Mayor
FOR ACTS OF INCREDIBLE BRAVERY, ABOVE AND BEYOND THE CALL OF DUTY--
--IT IS MY DISTINGUISHED PLEASURE TO PRESENT OFFICER DAVIS WITH A DEPARTMENT MEDAL OF HONOR.
I LOVE HOW HE CHEWS ON HIS LIP WHEN HE'S NERVOUS.
YOU DO IT, TOO.
HEH. HE LOOKS GOOD UP THERE.
YOU DON'T HAVE TO TELL ME.
GROSS.
THANK YOU, MR. MAYOR.
WHAT COULD POSSIBLY BE THIS URGENT?

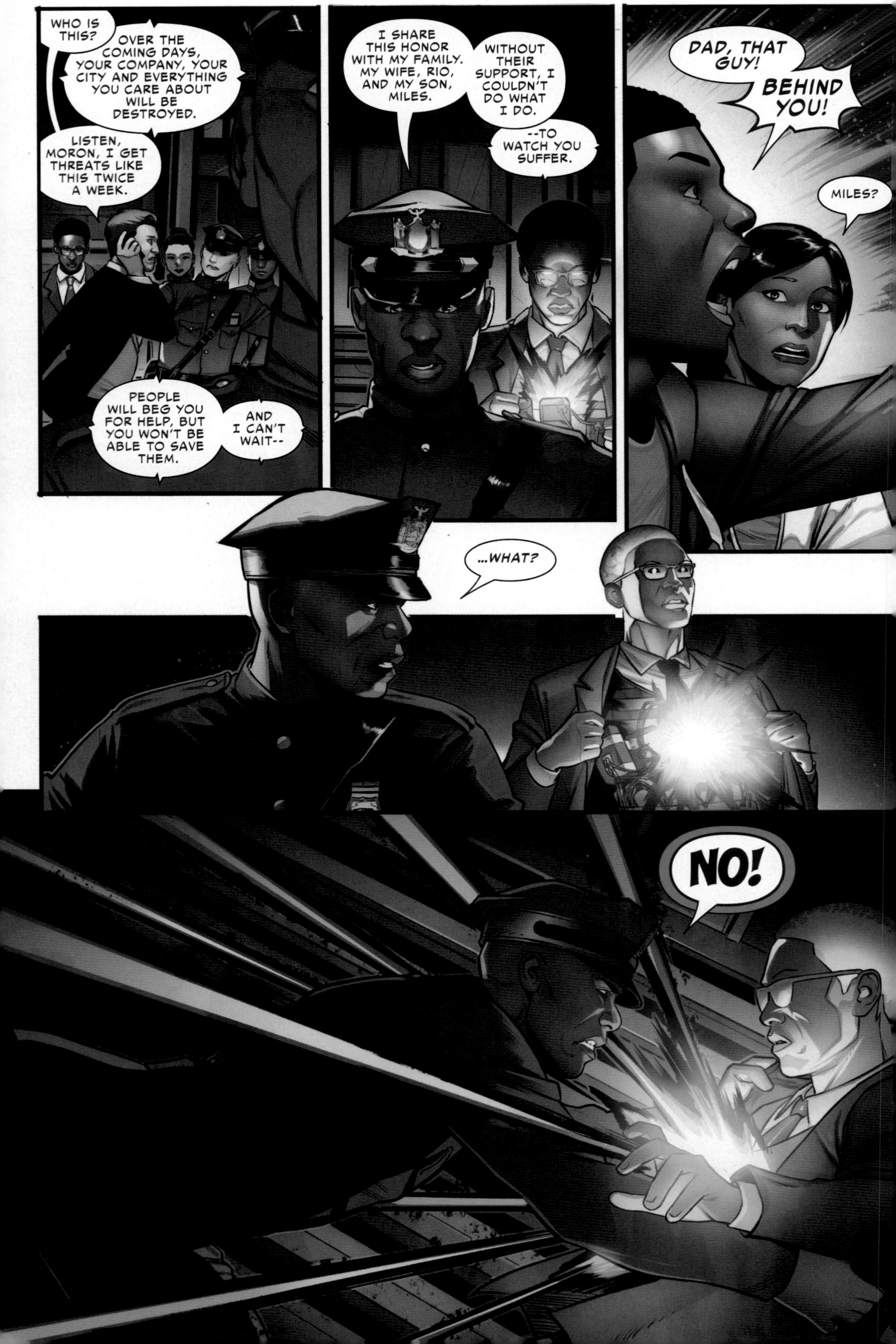
WHO IS THIS?
OVER THE COMING DAYS, YOUR COMPANY, YOUR CITY AND EVERYTHING YOU CARE ABOUT WILL BE DESTROYED.
LISTEN, MORON, I GET THREATS LIKE THIS TWICE A WEEK.
PEOPLE WILL BEG YOU FOR HELP, BUT YOU WON'T BE ABLE TO SAVE THEM.
AND I CAN'T WAIT--
I SHARE THIS HONOR WITH MY FAMILY. MY WIFE, RIO, AND MY SON, MILES.
WITHOUT THEIR SUPPORT, I COULDN'T DO WHAT I DO.
--TO WATCH YOU SUFFER.
DAD, THAT GUY!
BEHIND YOU!
MILES?
...WHAT?
NO!

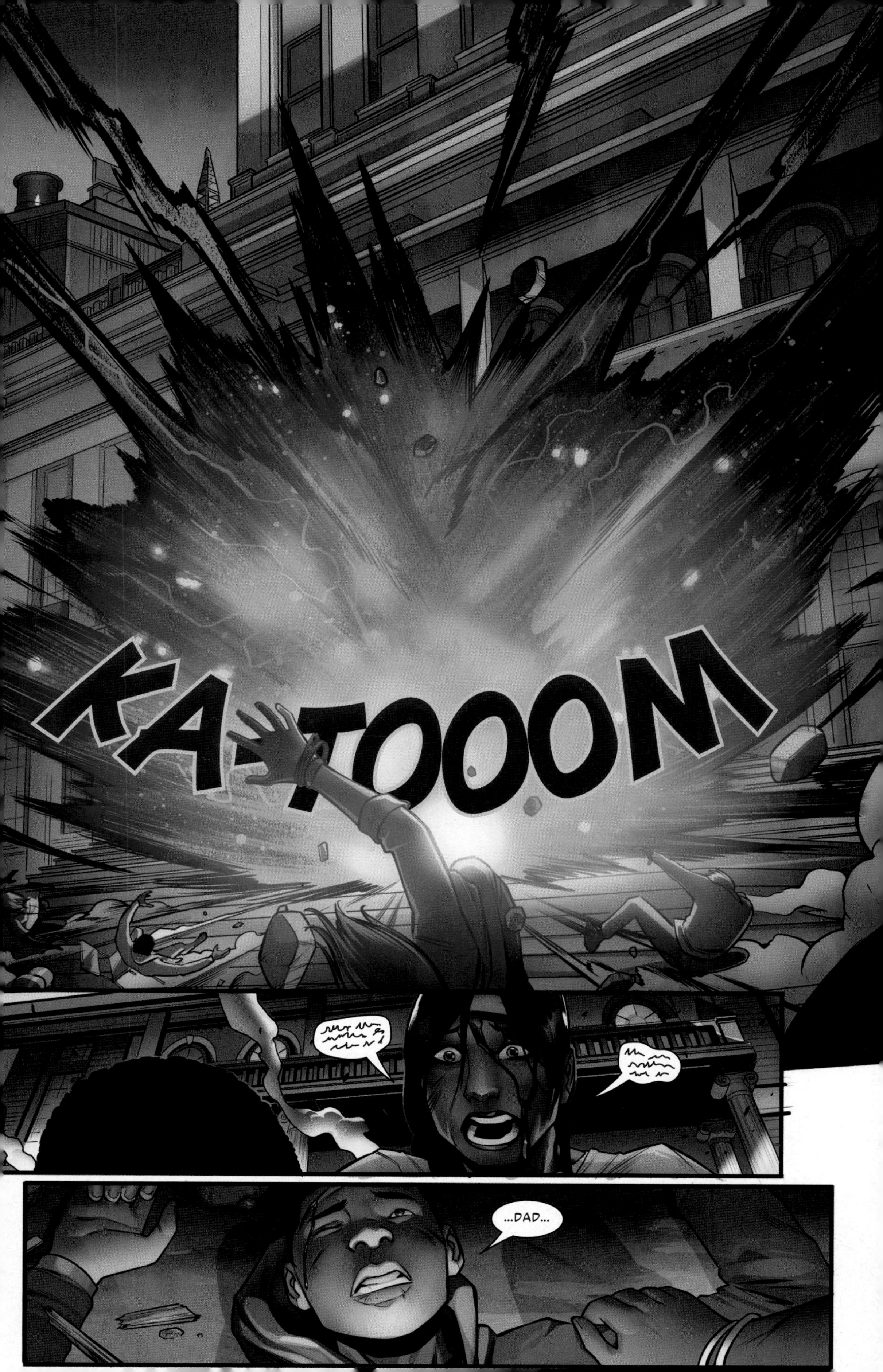
KA-TOOOM
...DAD...

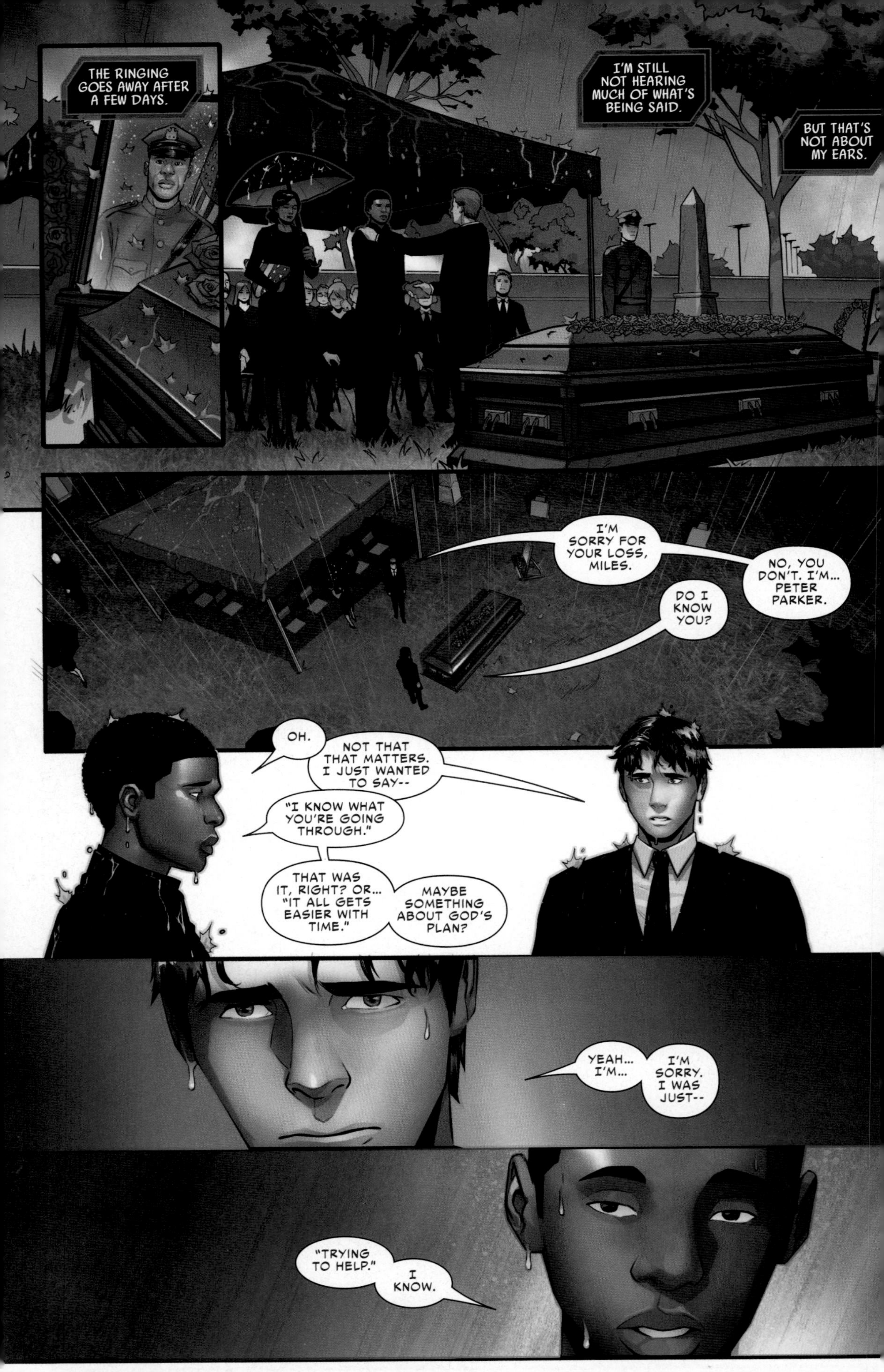
THE RINGING GOES AWAY AFTER A FEW DAYS.
I'M STILL NOT HEARING MUCH OF WHAT'S BEING SAID.
BUT THAT'S NOT ABOUT MY EARS.
I'M SORRY FOR YOUR LOSS, MILES.
DO I KNOW YOU?
NO, YOU DON'T. I'M... PETER PARKER.
OH.
NOT THAT THAT MATTERS. I JUST WANTED TO SAY--
"I KNOW WHAT YOU'RE GOING THROUGH."
THAT WAS IT, RIGHT? OR... "IT ALL GETS EASIER WITH TIME."
MAYBE SOMETHING ABOUT GOD'S PLAN?
YEAH... I'M...
I'M SORRY. I WAS JUST--
"TRYING TO HELP."
I KNOW.

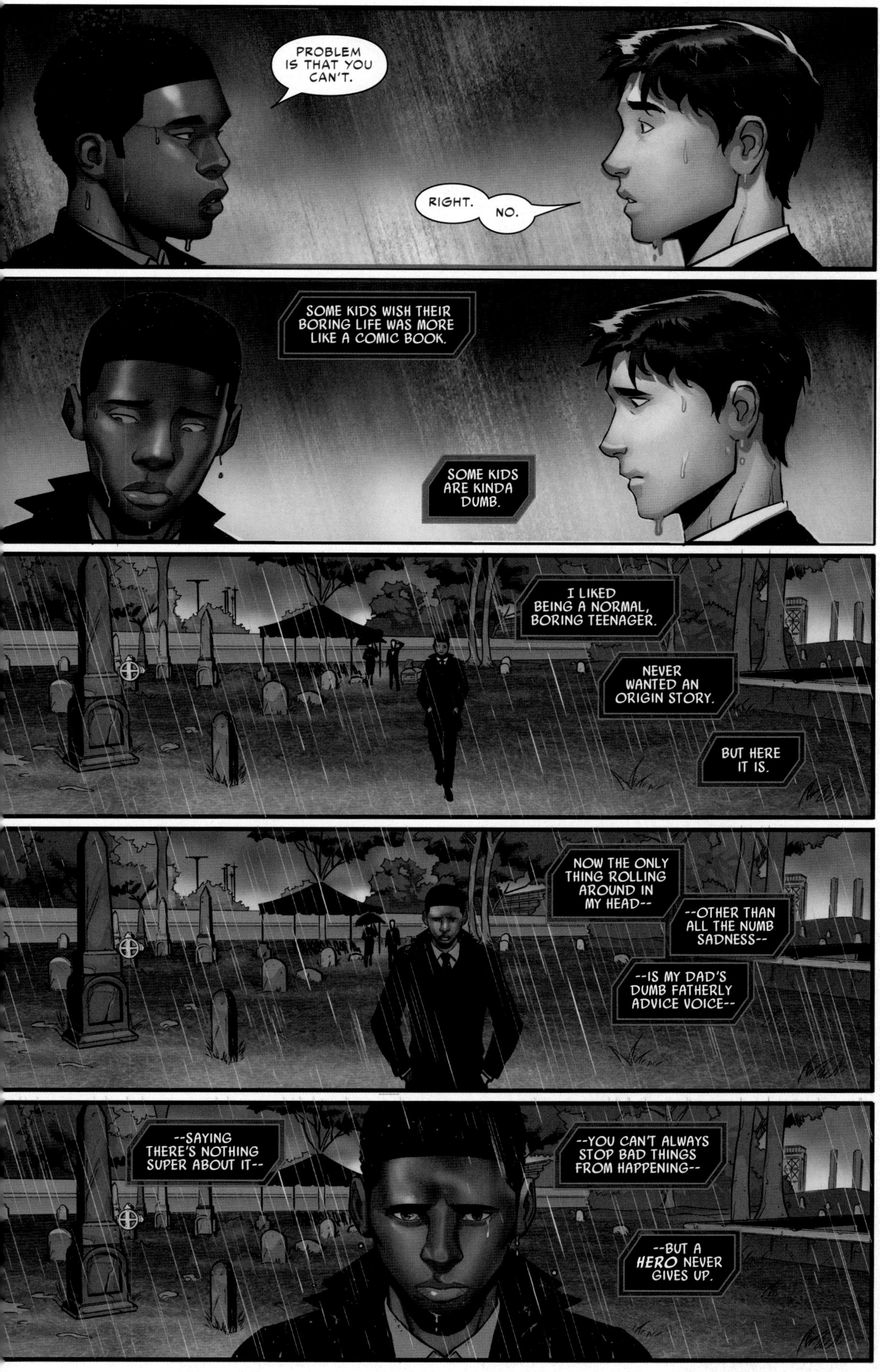
PROBLEM IS THAT YOU CAN'T.
RIGHT.
NO.
SOME KIDS WISH THEIR BORING LIFE WAS MORE LIKE A COMIC BOOK.
SOME KIDS ARE KINDA DUMB.
I LIKED BEING A NORMAL, BORING TEENAGER.
NEVER WANTED AN ORIGIN STORY.
BUT HERE IT IS.
NOW THE ONLY THING ROLLING AROUND IN MY HEAD--
--OTHER THAN ALL THE NUMB SADNESS--
--IS MY DAD'S DUMB FATHERLY ADVICE VOICE--
--SAYING THERE'S NOTHING SUPER ABOUT IT--
--YOU CAN'T ALWAYS STOP BAD THINGS FROM HAPPENING--
--BUT A *HERO* NEVER GIVES UP.

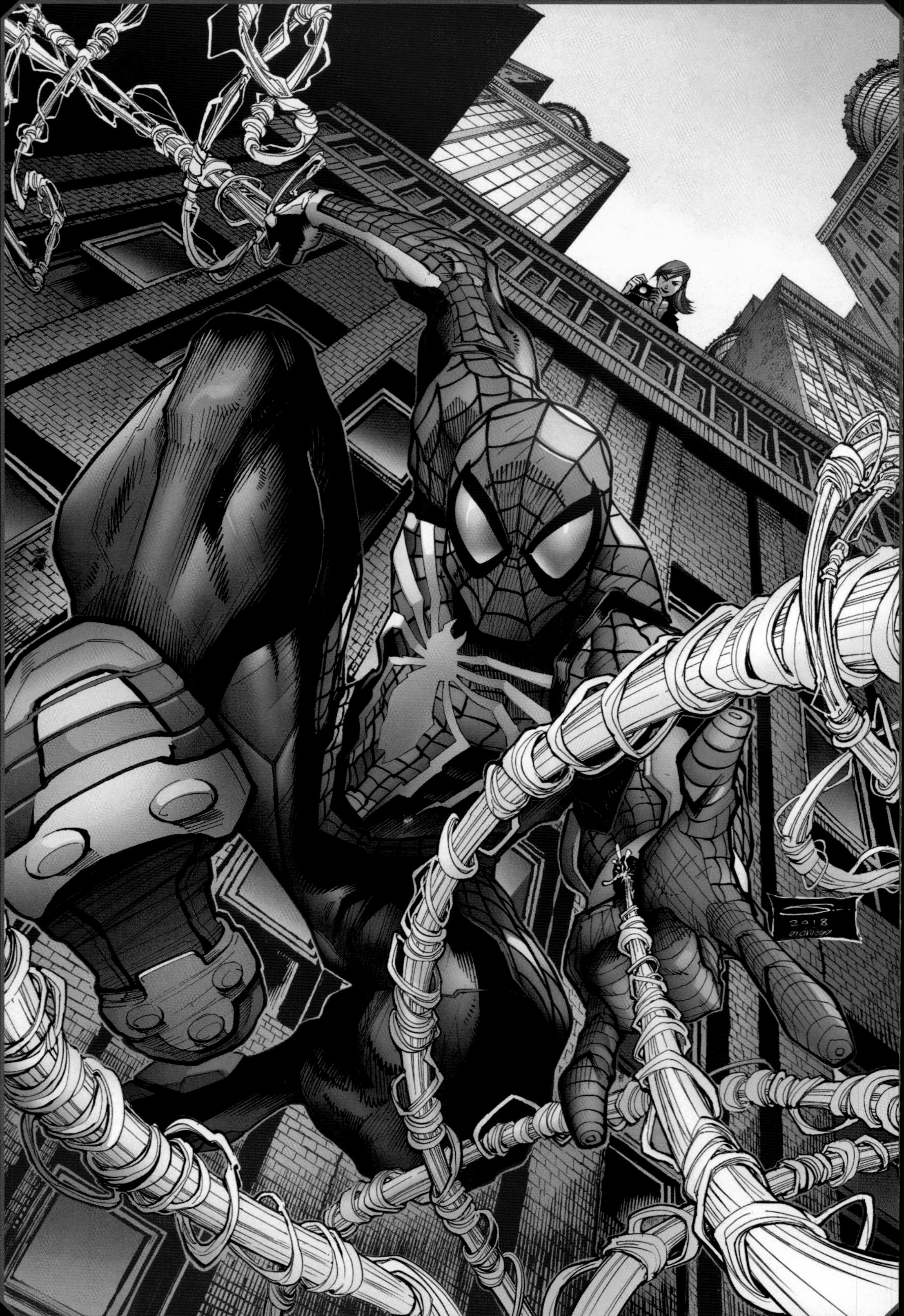
2018
arciniega

GERARDO SANDOVAL & ERICK ARCINIEGA

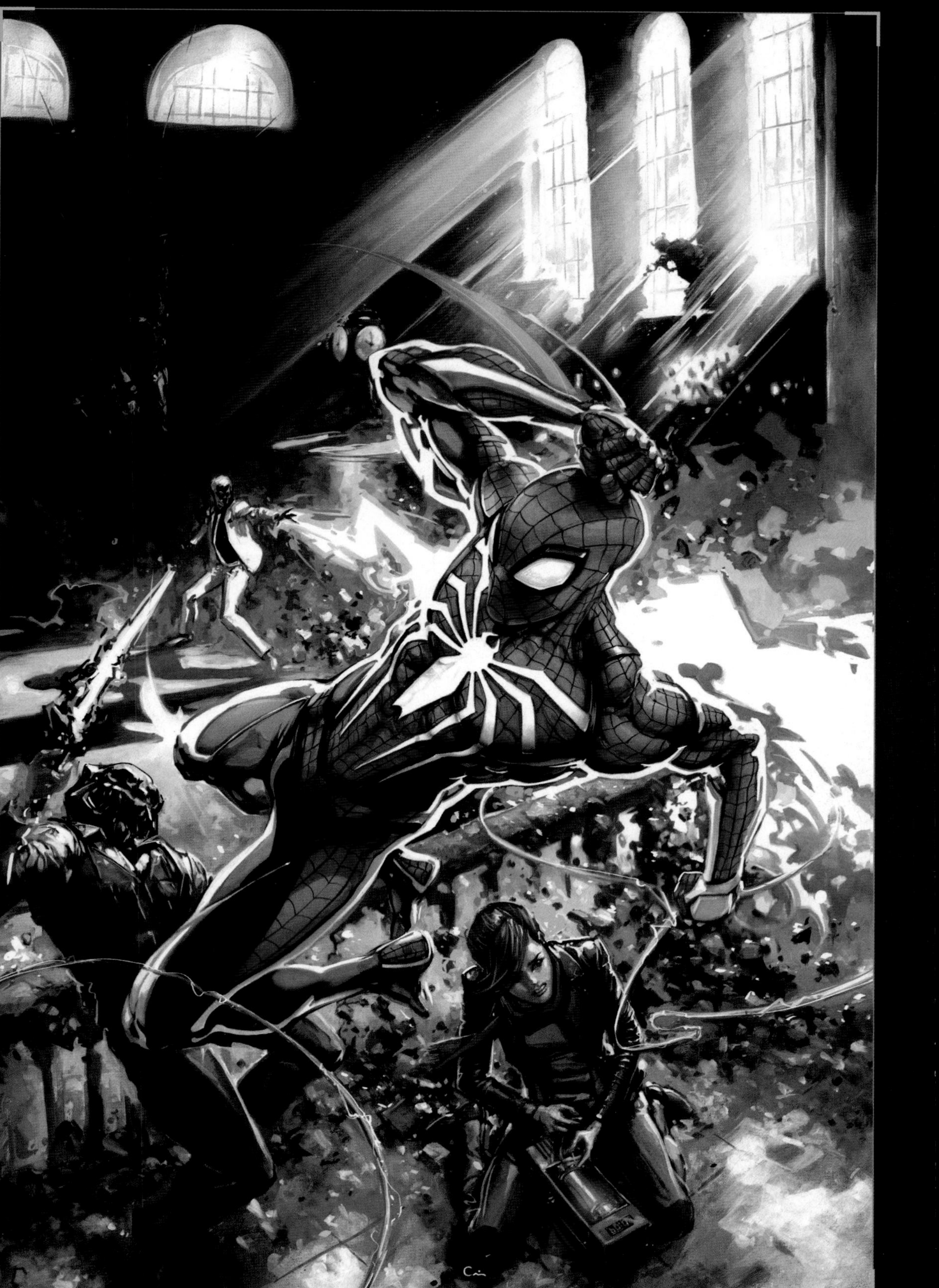

3

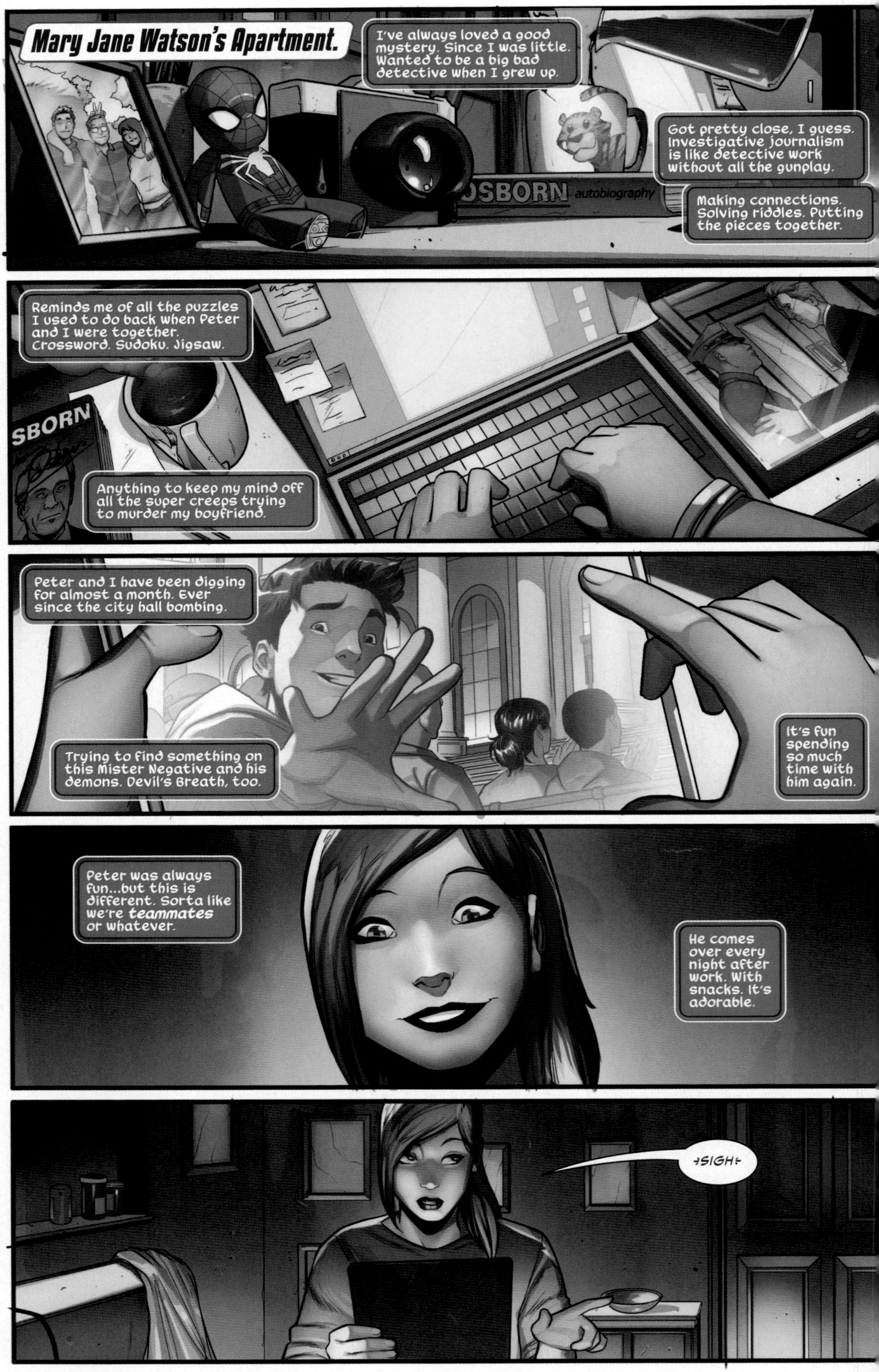
Mary Jane Watson's Apartment.
I've always loved a good mystery. Since I was little. Wanted to be a big bad detective when I grew up.
OSBORN autobiography
Got pretty close, I guess. Investigative journalism is like detective work without all the gunplay.
Making connections. Solving riddles. Putting the pieces together.
Reminds me of all the puzzles I used to do back when Peter and I were together. Crossword. Sudoku. Jigsaw.
SBORN
Anything to keep my mind off all the super creeps trying to murder my boyfriend.
Peter and I have been digging for almost a month. Ever since the city hall bombing.
Trying to find something on this Mister Negative and his demons. Devil's Breath, too.
It's fun spending so much time with him again.
Peter was always fun...but this is different. Sorta like we're *teammates* or whatever.
He comes over every night after work. With snacks. It's adorable.
SIGH

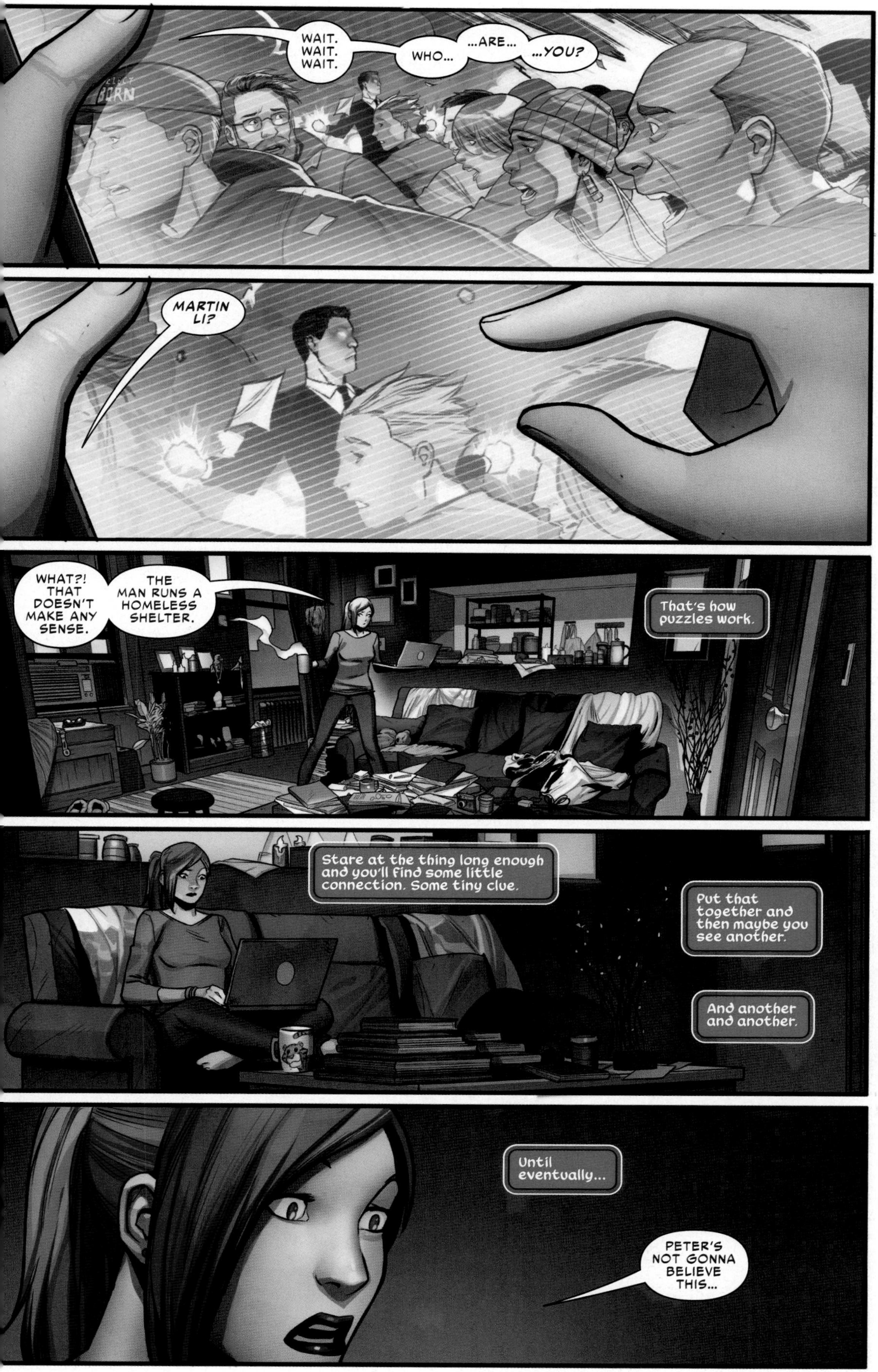
WAIT. WAIT. WAIT.
WHO...
...ARE...
...YOU?
MARTIN LI?
WHAT?! THAT DOESN'T MAKE ANY SENSE.
THE MAN RUNS A HOMELESS SHELTER.
That's how puzzles work.
Stare at the thing long enough and you'll find some little connection. Some tiny clue.
Put that together and then maybe you see another.
And another and another.
Until eventually...
PETER'S NOT GONNA BELIEVE THIS...

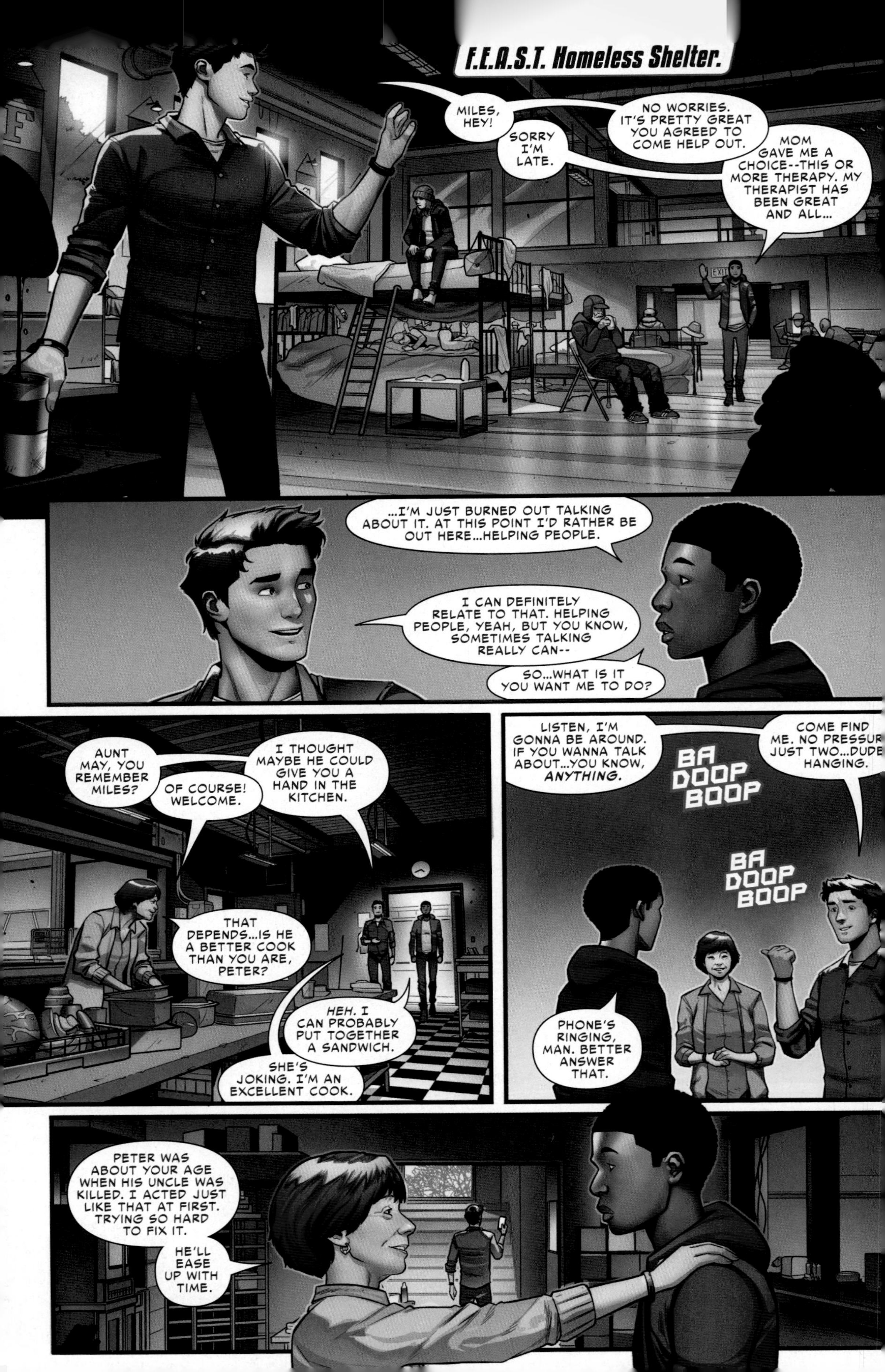
F.E.A.S.T. Homeless Shelter.
MILES, HEY!
SORRY I'M LATE.
NO WORRIES. IT'S PRETTY GREAT YOU AGREED TO COME HELP OUT.
MOM GAVE ME A CHOICE--THIS OR MORE THERAPY. MY THERAPIST HAS BEEN GREAT AND ALL...
...I'M JUST BURNED OUT TALKING ABOUT IT. AT THIS POINT I'D RATHER BE OUT HERE...HELPING PEOPLE.
I CAN DEFINITELY RELATE TO THAT. HELPING PEOPLE, YEAH, BUT YOU KNOW, SOMETIMES TALKING REALLY CAN--
SO...WHAT IS IT YOU WANT ME TO DO?
AUNT MAY, YOU REMEMBER MILES?
I THOUGHT MAYBE HE COULD GIVE YOU A HAND IN THE KITCHEN.
OF COURSE! WELCOME.
THAT DEPENDS...IS HE A BETTER COOK THAN YOU ARE, PETER?
HEH. I CAN PROBABLY PUT TOGETHER A SANDWICH.
SHE'S JOKING. I'M AN EXCELLENT COOK.
LISTEN, I'M GONNA BE AROUND. IF YOU WANNA TALK ABOUT...YOU KNOW, ANYTHING.
BA DOOP BOOP
COME FIND ME. NO PRESSUR JUST TWO...DUDE HANGING.
BA DOOP BOOP
PHONE'S RINGING, MAN. BETTER ANSWER THAT.
PETER WAS ABOUT YOUR AGE WHEN HIS UNCLE WAS KILLED. I ACTED JUST LIKE THAT AT FIRST. TRYING SO HARD TO FIX IT.
HE'LL EASE UP WITH TIME.

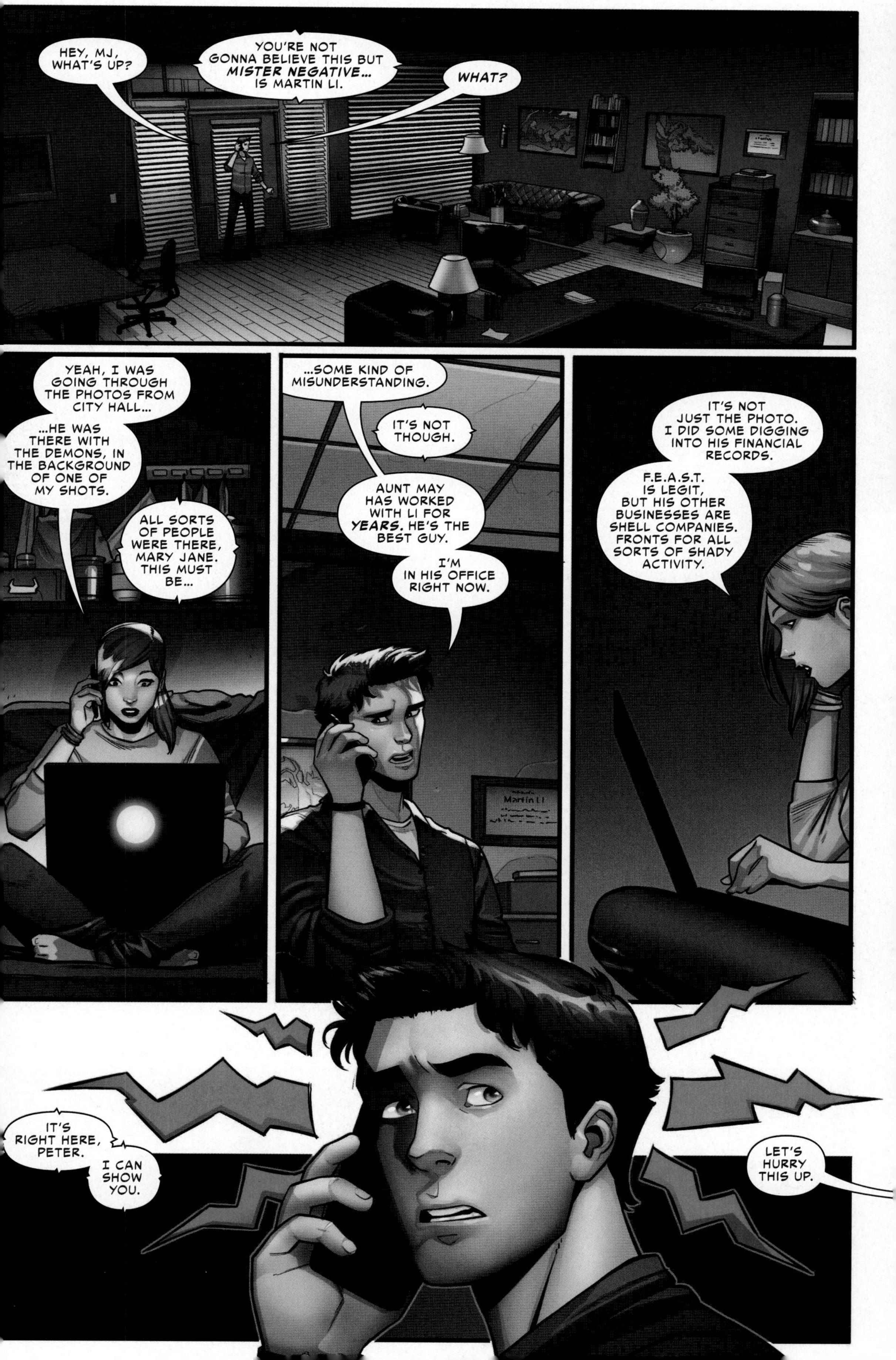
HEY, MJ, WHAT'S UP?
YOU'RE NOT GONNA BELIEVE THIS BUT MISTER NEGATIVE... IS MARTIN LI.
WHAT?
YEAH, I WAS GOING THROUGH THE PHOTOS FROM CITY HALL...
...HE WAS THERE WITH THE DEMONS, IN THE BACKGROUND OF ONE OF MY SHOTS.
ALL SORTS OF PEOPLE WERE THERE, MARY JANE. THIS MUST BE...
...SOME KIND OF MISUNDERSTANDING.
IT'S NOT THOUGH.
AUNT MAY HAS WORKED WITH LI FOR YEARS. HE'S THE BEST GUY.
I'M IN HIS OFFICE RIGHT NOW.
Martin Li
IT'S NOT JUST THE PHOTO. I DID SOME DIGGING INTO HIS FINANCIAL RECORDS.
F.E.A.S.T. IS LEGIT, BUT HIS OTHER BUSINESSES ARE SHELL COMPANIES. FRONTS FOR ALL SORTS OF SHADY ACTIVITY.
IT'S RIGHT HERE, PETER.
I CAN SHOW YOU.
LET'S HURRY THIS UP.

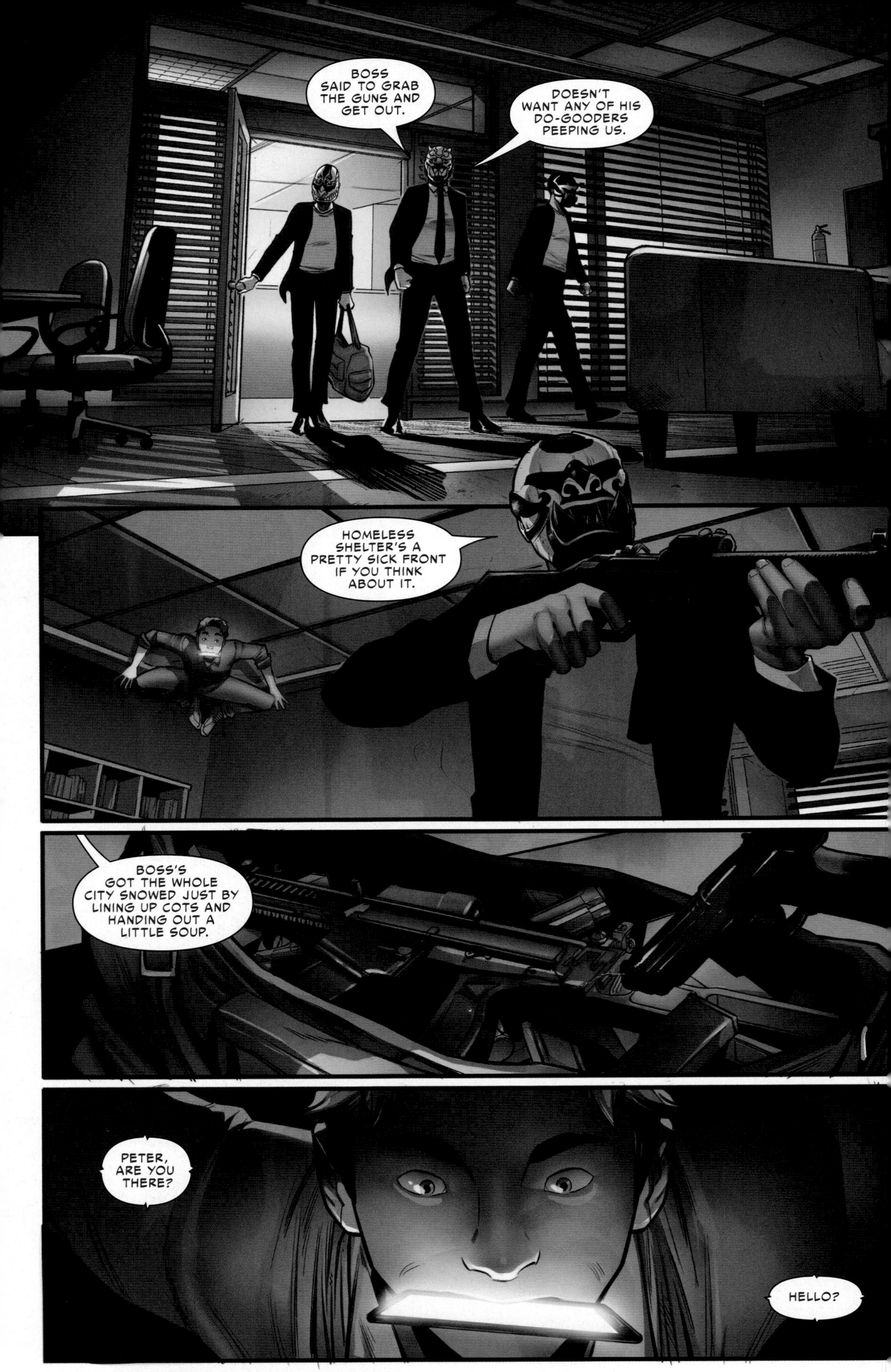
BOSS SAID TO GRAB THE GUNS AND GET OUT.
DOESN'T WANT ANY OF HIS DO-GOODERS PEEPING US.
HOMELESS SHELTER'S A PRETTY SICK FRONT IF YOU THINK ABOUT IT.
BOSS'S GOT THE WHOLE CITY SNOWED JUST BY LINING UP COTS AND HANDING OUT A LITTLE SOUP.
PETER, ARE YOU THERE?
HELLO?

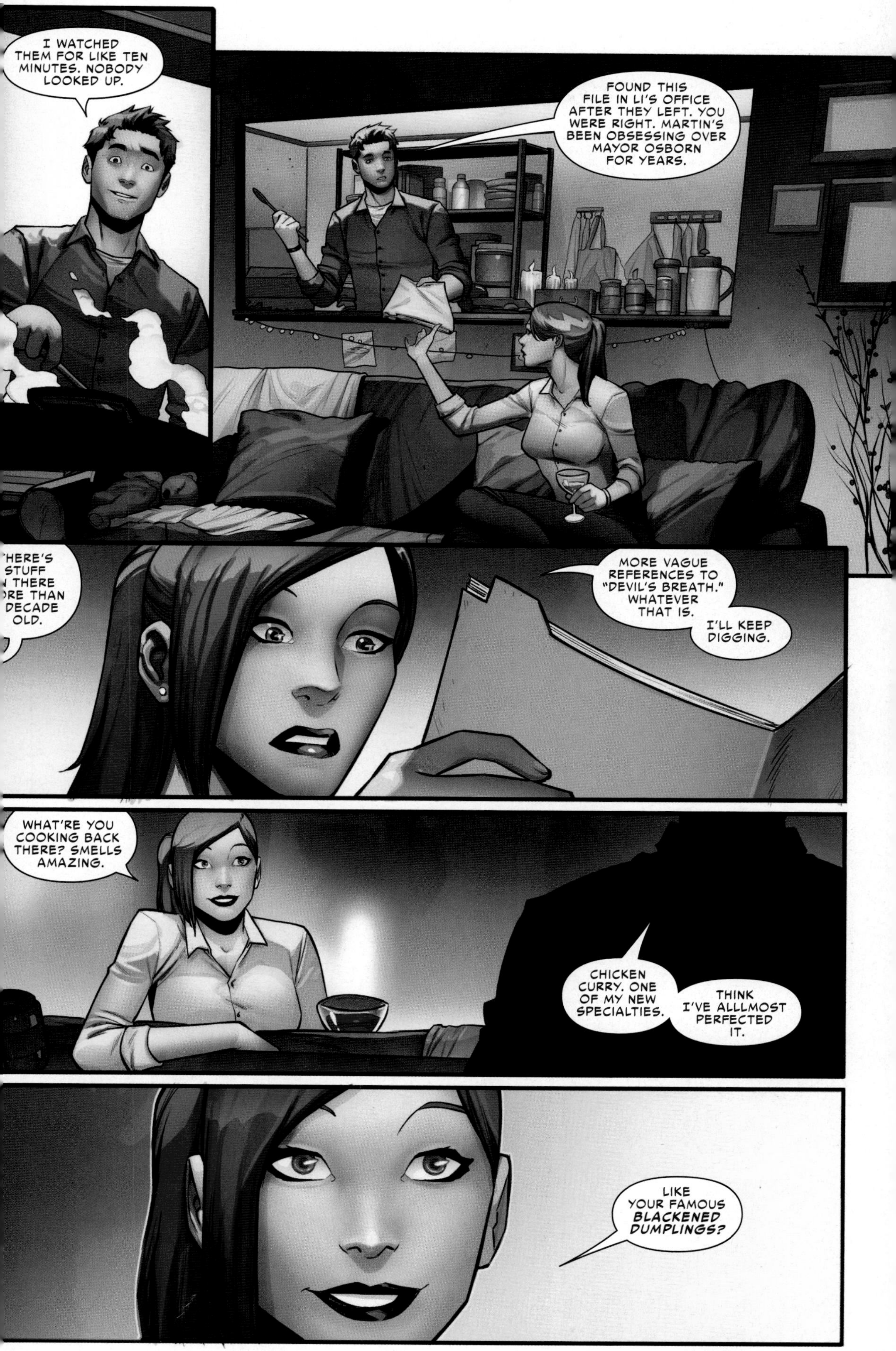
I WATCHED THEM FOR LIKE TEN MINUTES. NOBODY LOOKED UP.
FOUND THIS FILE IN LI'S OFFICE AFTER THEY LEFT. YOU WERE RIGHT. MARTIN'S BEEN OBSESSING OVER MAYOR OSBORN FOR YEARS.
HERE'S STUFF N THERE ORE THAN DECADE OLD.
MORE VAGUE REFERENCES TO "DEVIL'S BREATH." WHATEVER THAT IS.
I'LL KEEP DIGGING.
WHAT'RE YOU COOKING BACK THERE? SMELLS AMAZING.
CHICKEN CURRY. ONE OF MY NEW SPECIALTIES.
THINK I'VE ALLLMOST PERFECTED IT.
LIKE YOUR FAMOUS *BLACKENED DUMPLINGS?*

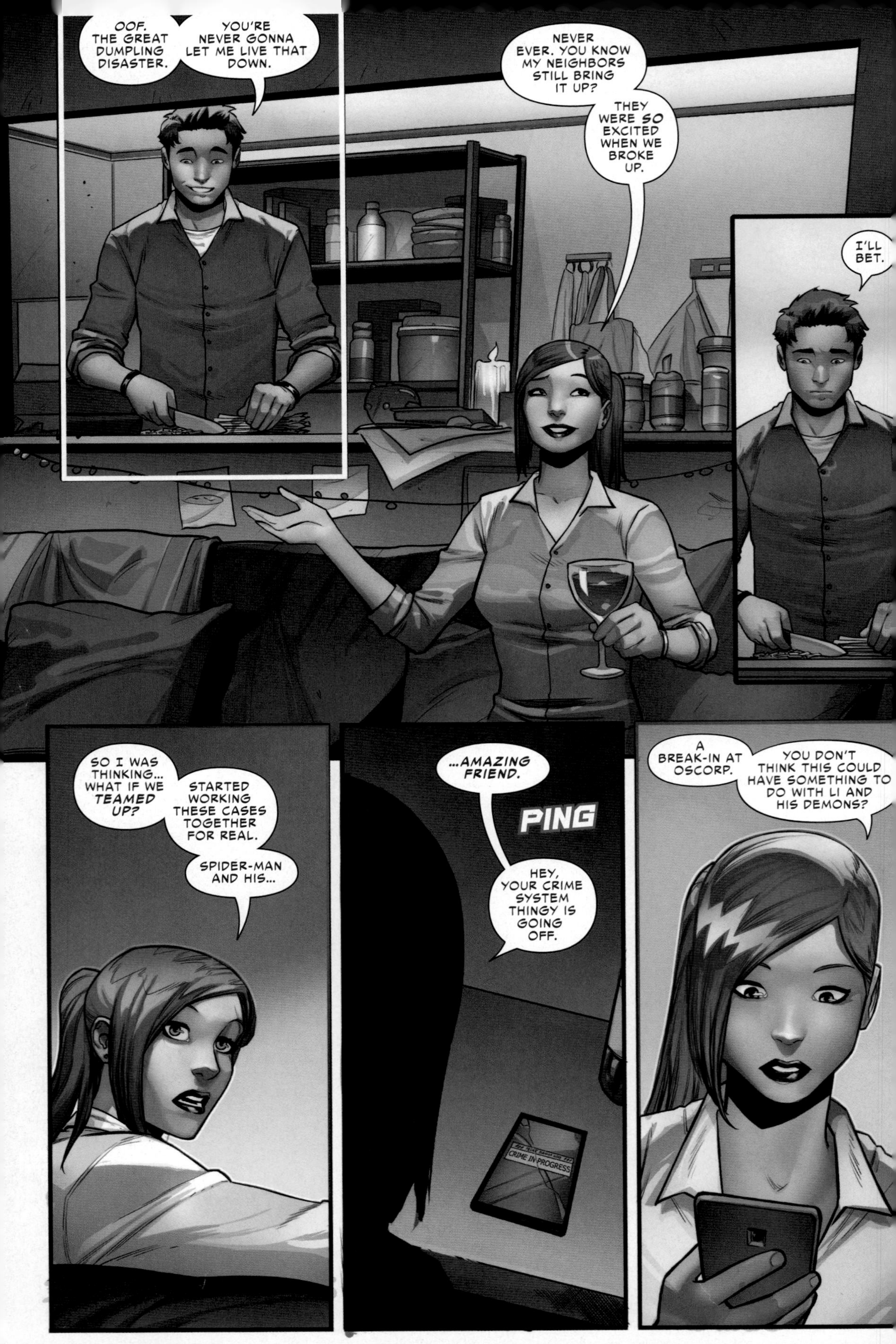

OOF. THE GREAT DUMPLING DISASTER.
YOU'RE NEVER GONNA LET ME LIVE THAT DOWN.
NEVER EVER. YOU KNOW MY NEIGHBORS STILL BRING IT UP?
THEY WERE SO EXCITED WHEN WE BROKE UP.
I'LL BET.
SO I WAS THINKING... WHAT IF WE TEAMED UP?
STARTED WORKING THESE CASES TOGETHER FOR REAL.
SPIDER-MAN AND HIS...
...AMAZING FRIEND.
PING
HEY, YOUR CRIME SYSTEM THINGY IS GOING OFF.
CRIME IN PROGRESS
A BREAK-IN AT OSCORP.
YOU DON'T THINK THIS COULD HAVE SOMETHING TO DO WITH LI AND HIS DEMONS?

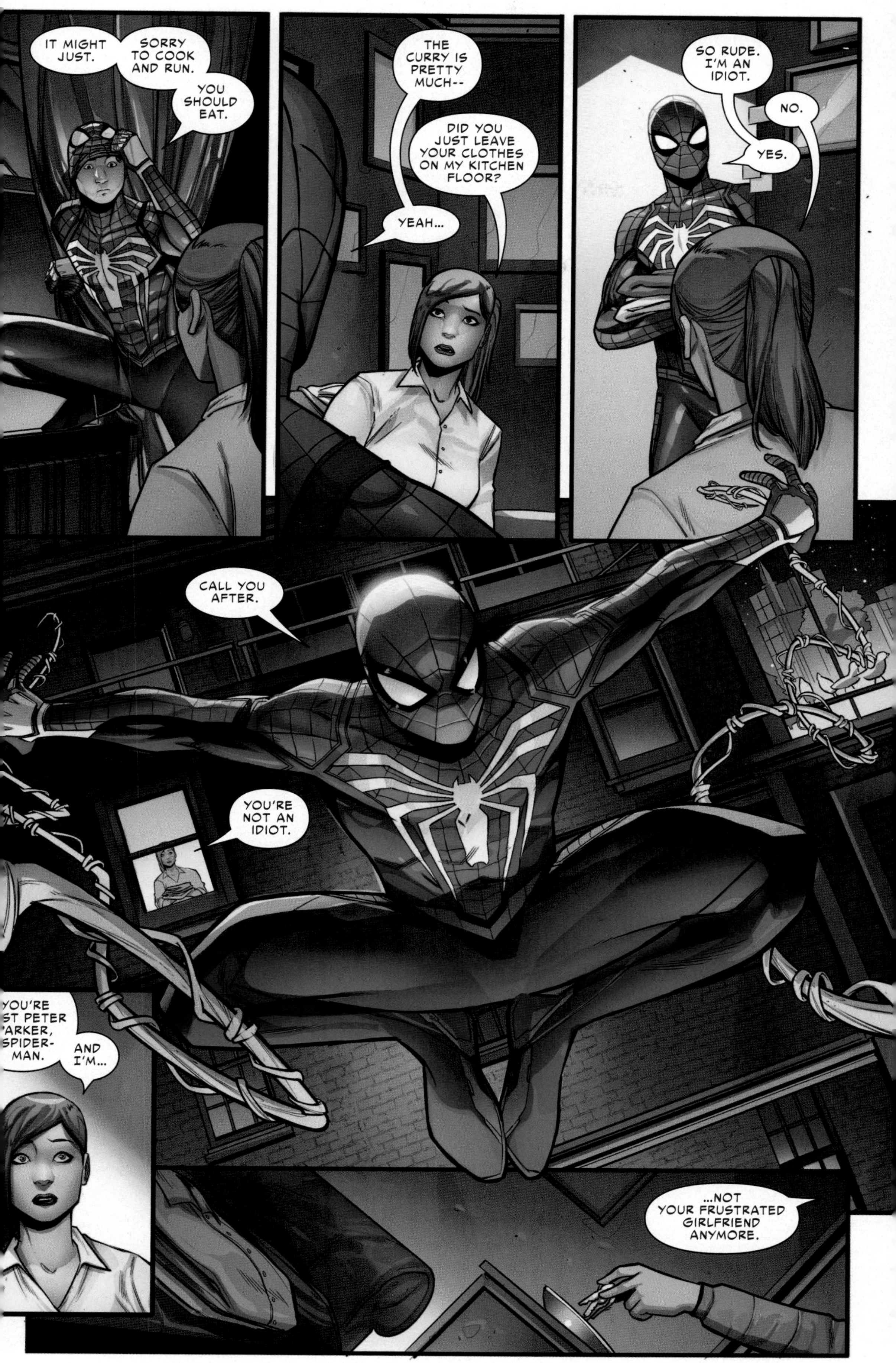
IT MIGHT JUST.
SORRY TO COOK AND RUN.
YOU SHOULD EAT.
THE CURRY IS PRETTY MUCH--
DID YOU JUST LEAVE YOUR CLOTHES ON MY KITCHEN FLOOR?
YEAH...
SO RUDE. I'M AN IDIOT.
NO.
YES.
CALL YOU AFTER.
YOU'RE NOT AN IDIOT.
YOU'RE ST PETER PARKER, SPIDER-MAN.
AND I'M...
...NOT YOUR FRUSTRATED GIRLFRIEND ANYMORE.

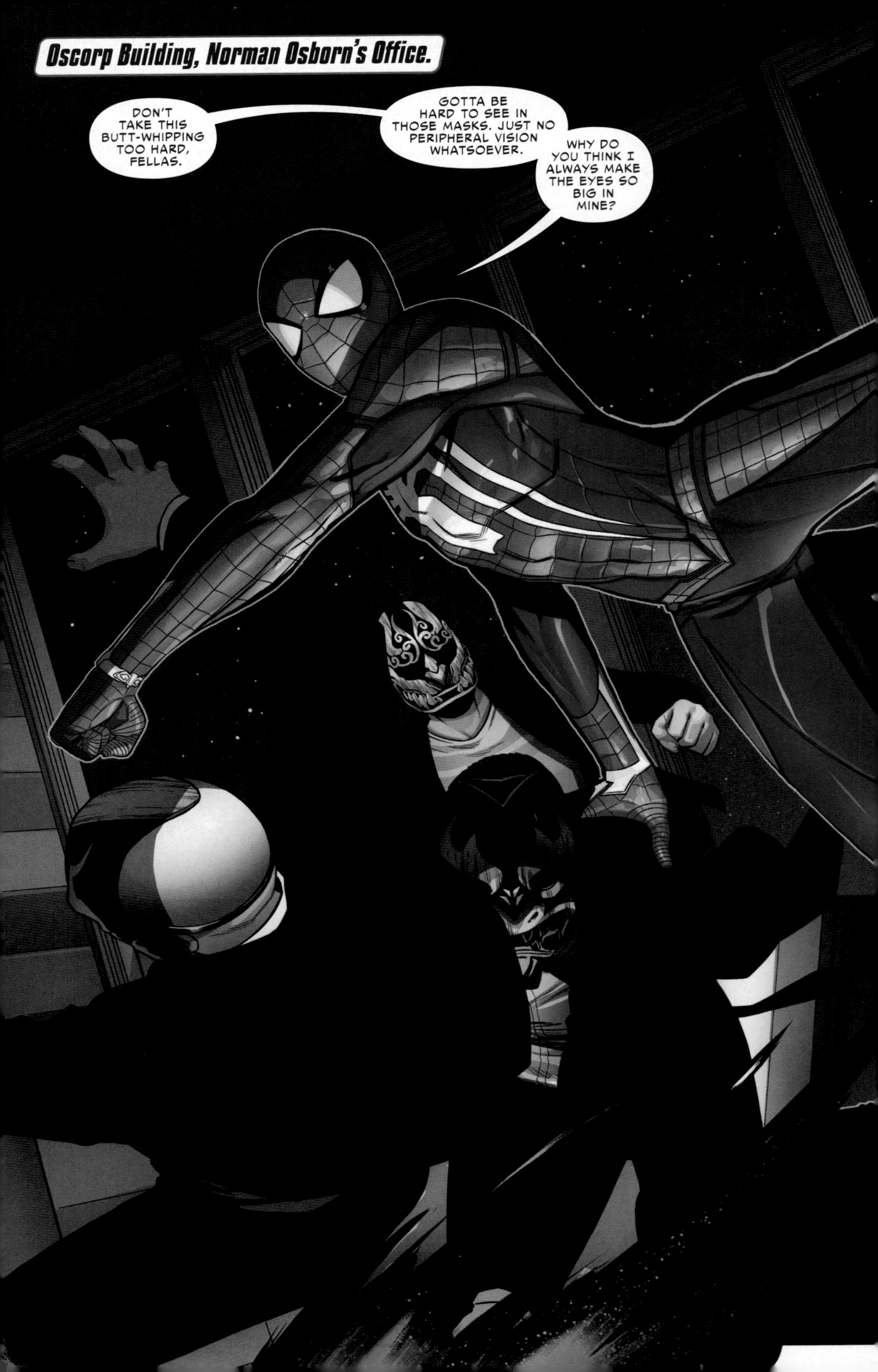
Oscorp Building, Norman Osborn's Office.
DON'T TAKE THIS BUTT-WHIPPING TOO HARD, FELLAS.
GOTTA BE HARD TO SEE IN THOSE MASKS. JUST NO PERIPHERAL VISION WHATSOEVER.
WHY DO YOU THINK I ALWAYS MAKE THE EYES SO BIG IN MINE?

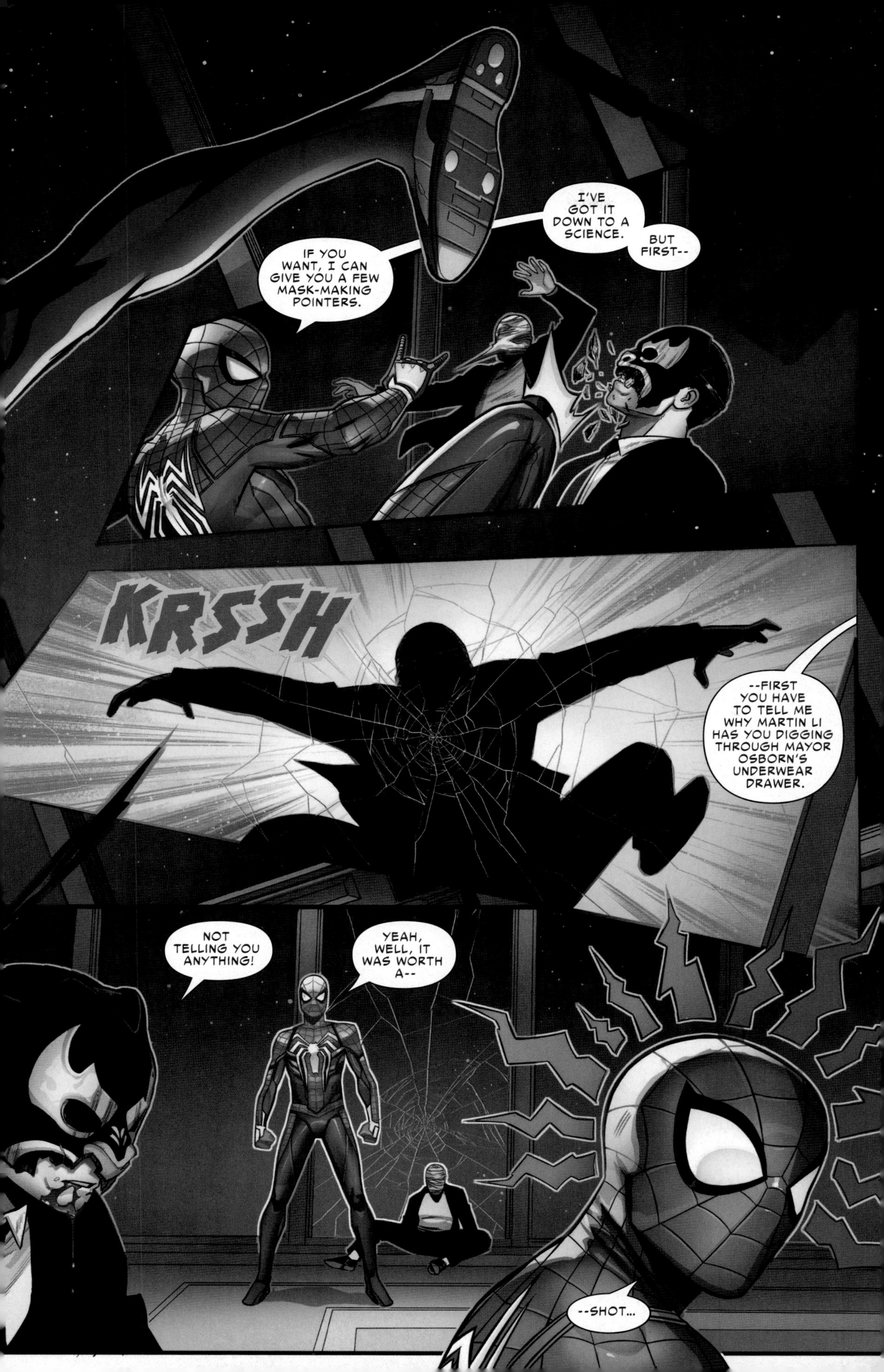
IF YOU WANT, I CAN GIVE YOU A FEW MASK-MAKING POINTERS.
I'VE GOT IT DOWN TO A SCIENCE.
BUT FIRST--
KRSSH
--FIRST YOU HAVE TO TELL ME WHY MARTIN LI HAS YOU DIGGING THROUGH MAYOR OSBORN'S UNDERWEAR DRAWER.
NOT TELLING YOU ANYTHING!
YEAH, WELL, IT WAS WORTH A--
--SHOT...

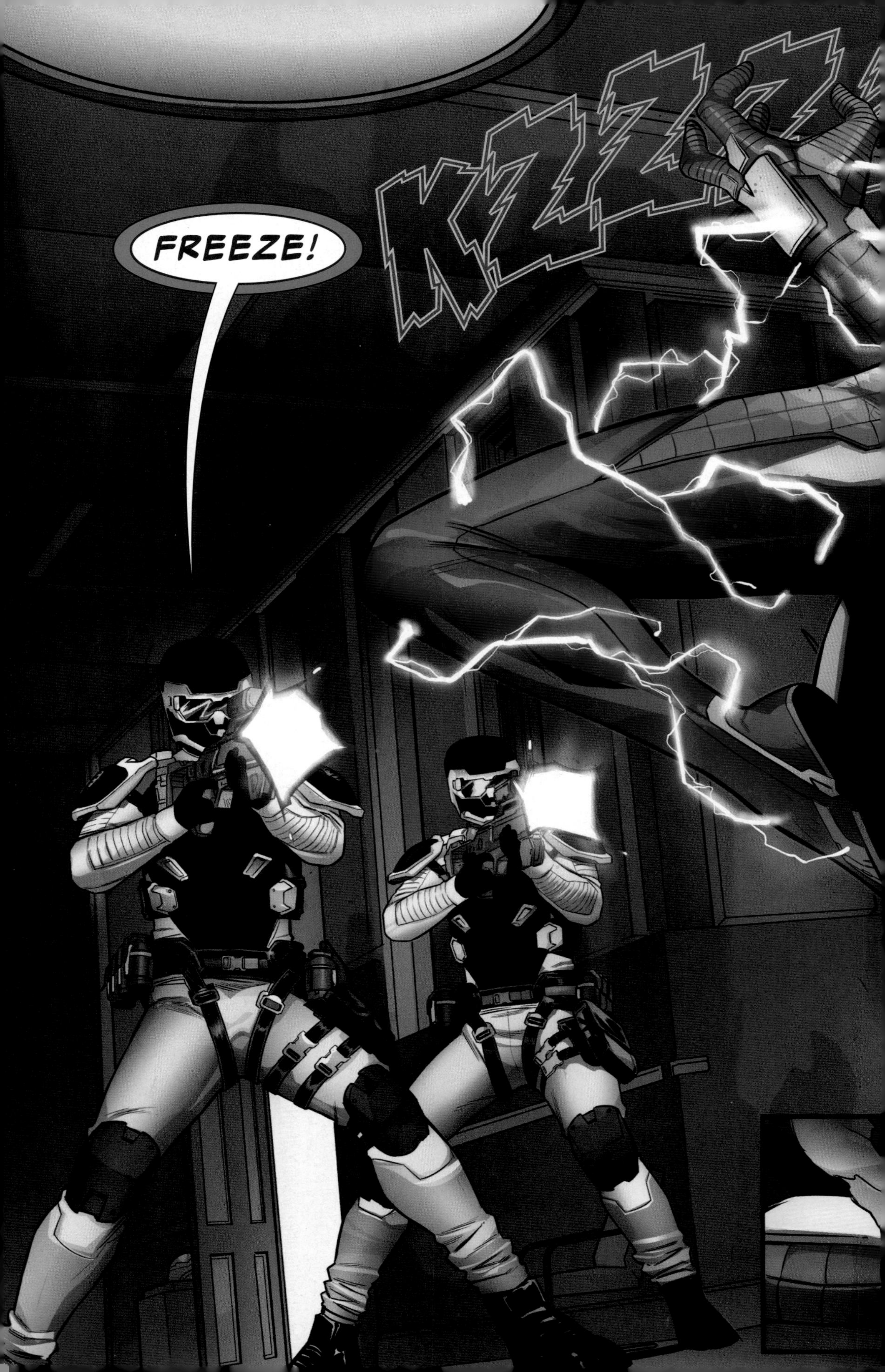
FREEZE!
KZZZZ

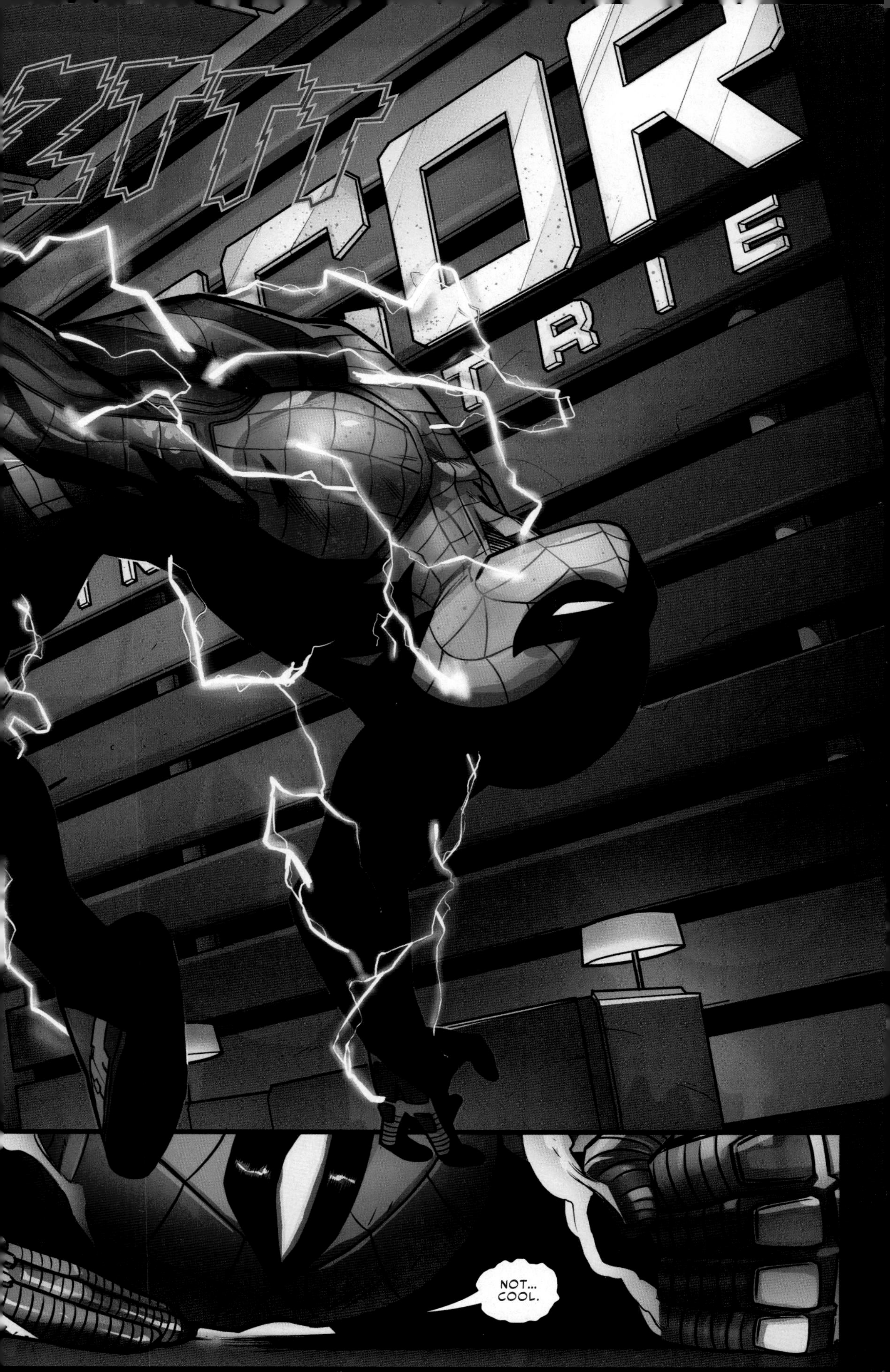
NOT...
COOL.

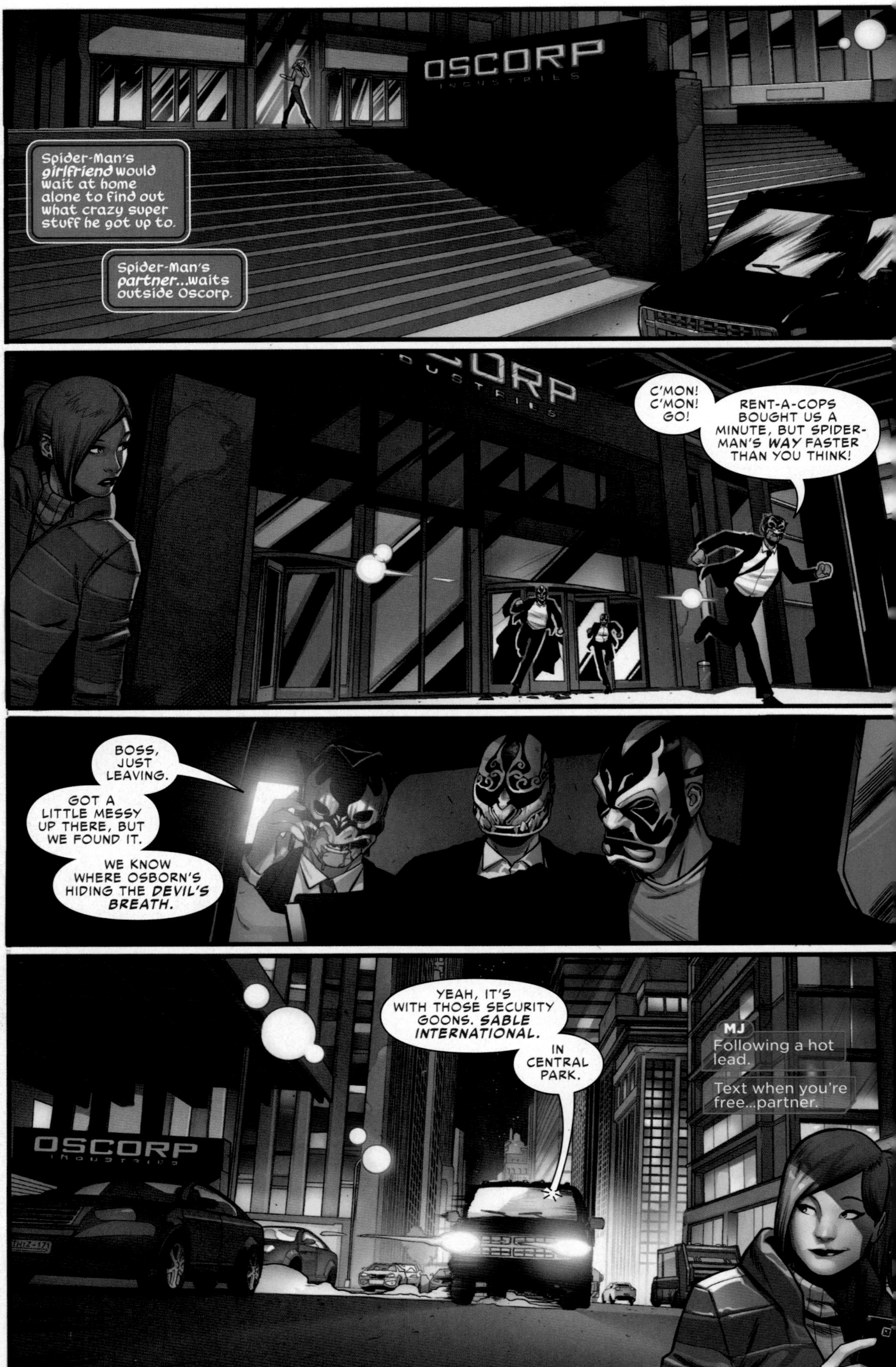
OSCORP INDUSTRIES
Spider-Man's *girlfriend* would wait at home alone to find out what crazy super stuff he got up to.
Spider-Man's *partner*...waits outside Oscorp.
C'MON! C'MON! GO!
RENT-A-COPS BOUGHT US A MINUTE, BUT SPIDER-MAN'S *WAY* FASTER THAN YOU THINK!
BOSS, JUST LEAVING.
GOT A LITTLE MESSY UP THERE, BUT WE FOUND IT.
WE KNOW WHERE OSBORN'S HIDING THE *DEVIL'S BREATH*.
OSCORP INDUSTRIES
YEAH, IT'S WITH THOSE SECURITY GOONS. *SABLE INTERNATIONAL*.
IN CENTRAL PARK.
MJ
Following a hot lead.
Text when you're free...partner.

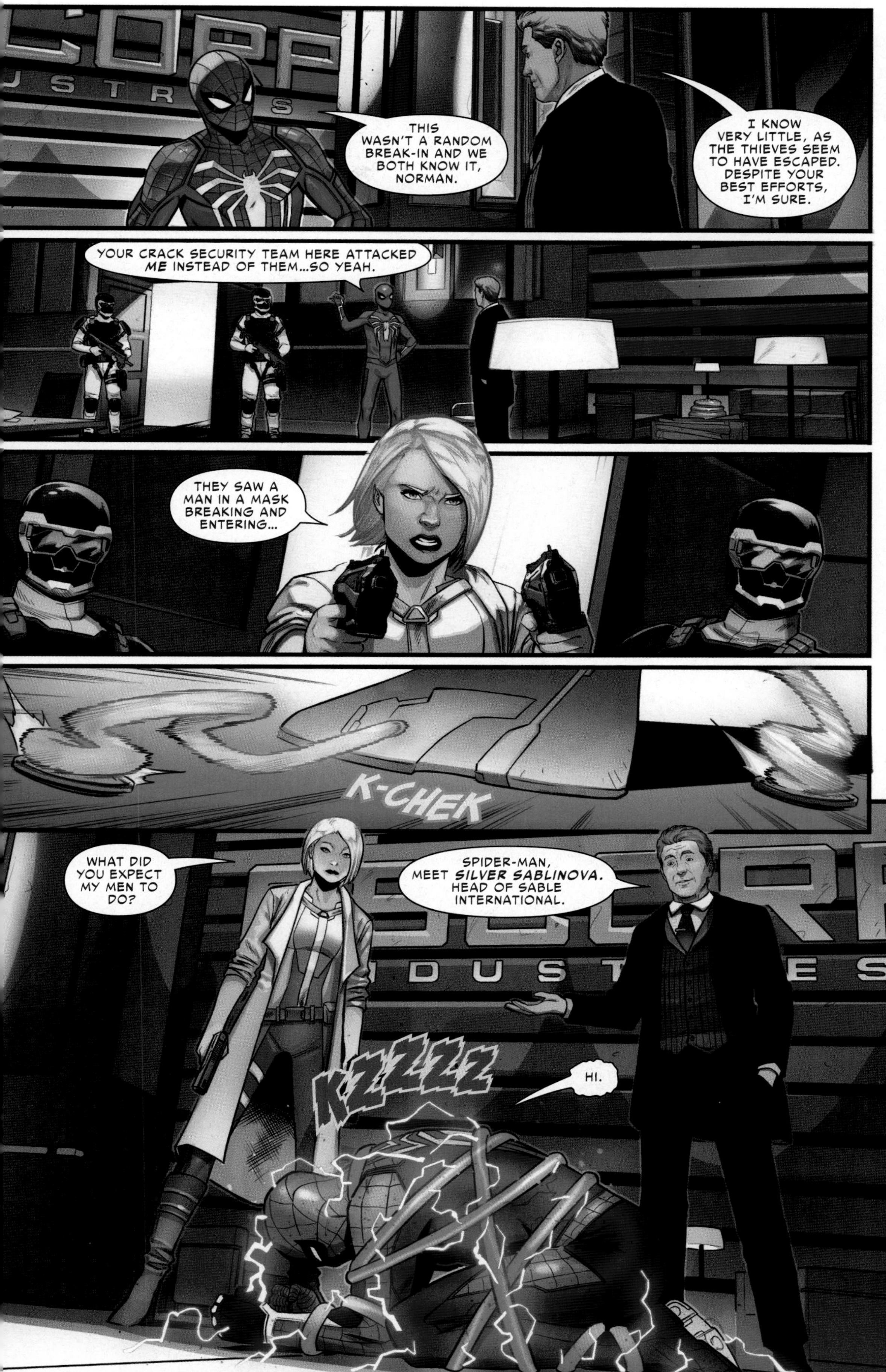
THIS WASN'T A RANDOM BREAK-IN AND WE BOTH KNOW IT, NORMAN.
I KNOW VERY LITTLE, AS THE THIEVES SEEM TO HAVE ESCAPED. DESPITE YOUR BEST EFFORTS, I'M SURE.
YOUR CRACK SECURITY TEAM HERE ATTACKED ME INSTEAD OF THEM...SO YEAH.
THEY SAW A MAN IN A MASK BREAKING AND ENTERING...
K-CHEK
WHAT DID YOU EXPECT MY MEN TO DO?
SPIDER-MAN, MEET SILVER SABLINOVA. HEAD OF SABLE INTERNATIONAL.
KZZZZZ
HI.

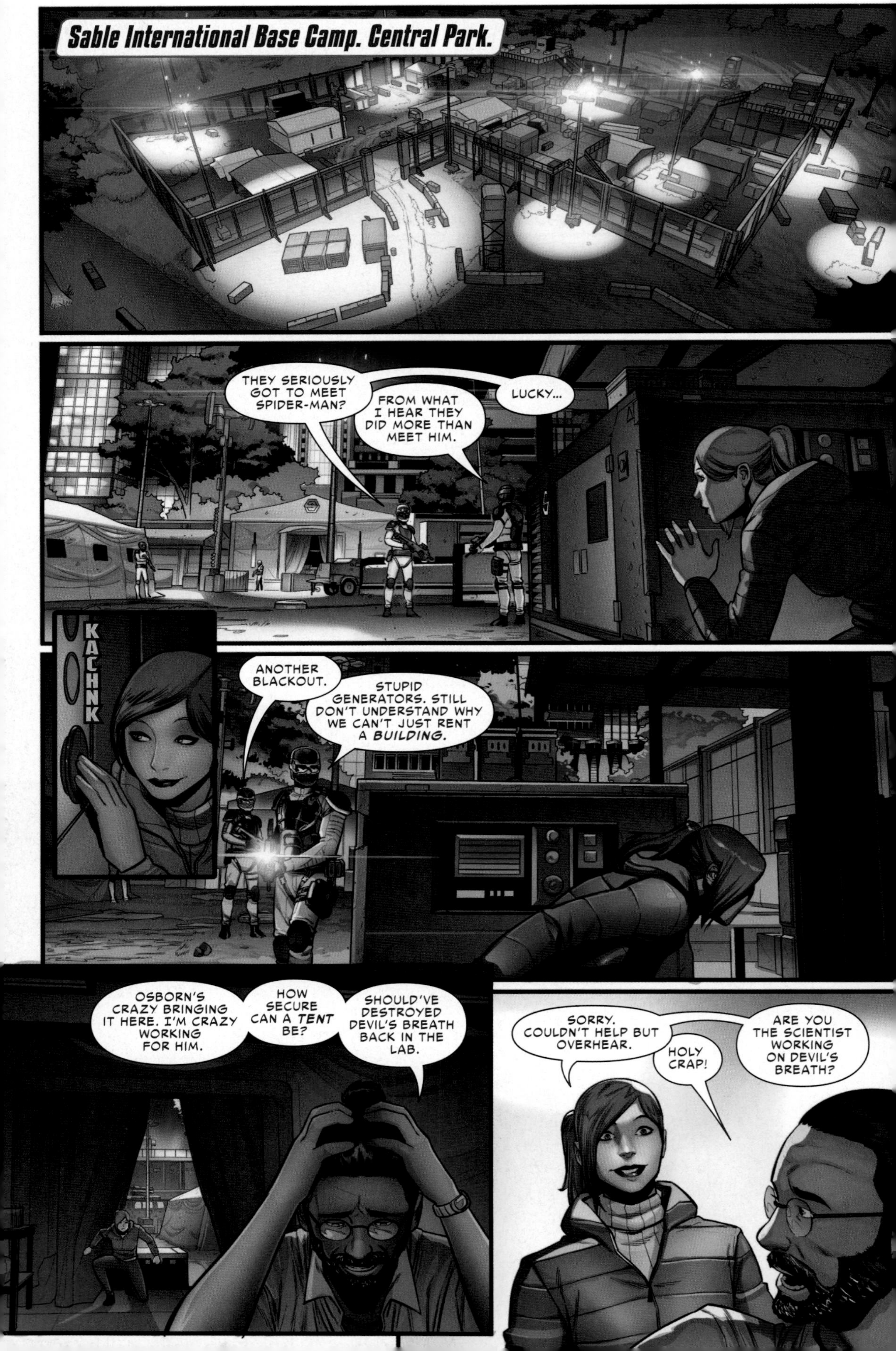
Sable International Base Camp. Central Park.
THEY SERIOUSLY GOT TO MEET SPIDER-MAN?
FROM WHAT I HEAR THEY DID MORE THAN MEET HIM.
LUCKY...
KACHNK
ANOTHER BLACKOUT.
STUPID GENERATORS. STILL DON'T UNDERSTAND WHY WE CAN'T JUST RENT A BUILDING.
OSBORN'S CRAZY BRINGING IT HERE. I'M CRAZY WORKING FOR HIM.
HOW SECURE CAN A TENT BE?
SHOULD'VE DESTROYED DEVIL'S BREATH BACK IN THE LAB.
SORRY. COULDN'T HELP BUT OVERHEAR.
HOLY CRAP!
ARE YOU THE SCIENTIST WORKING ON DEVIL'S BREATH?

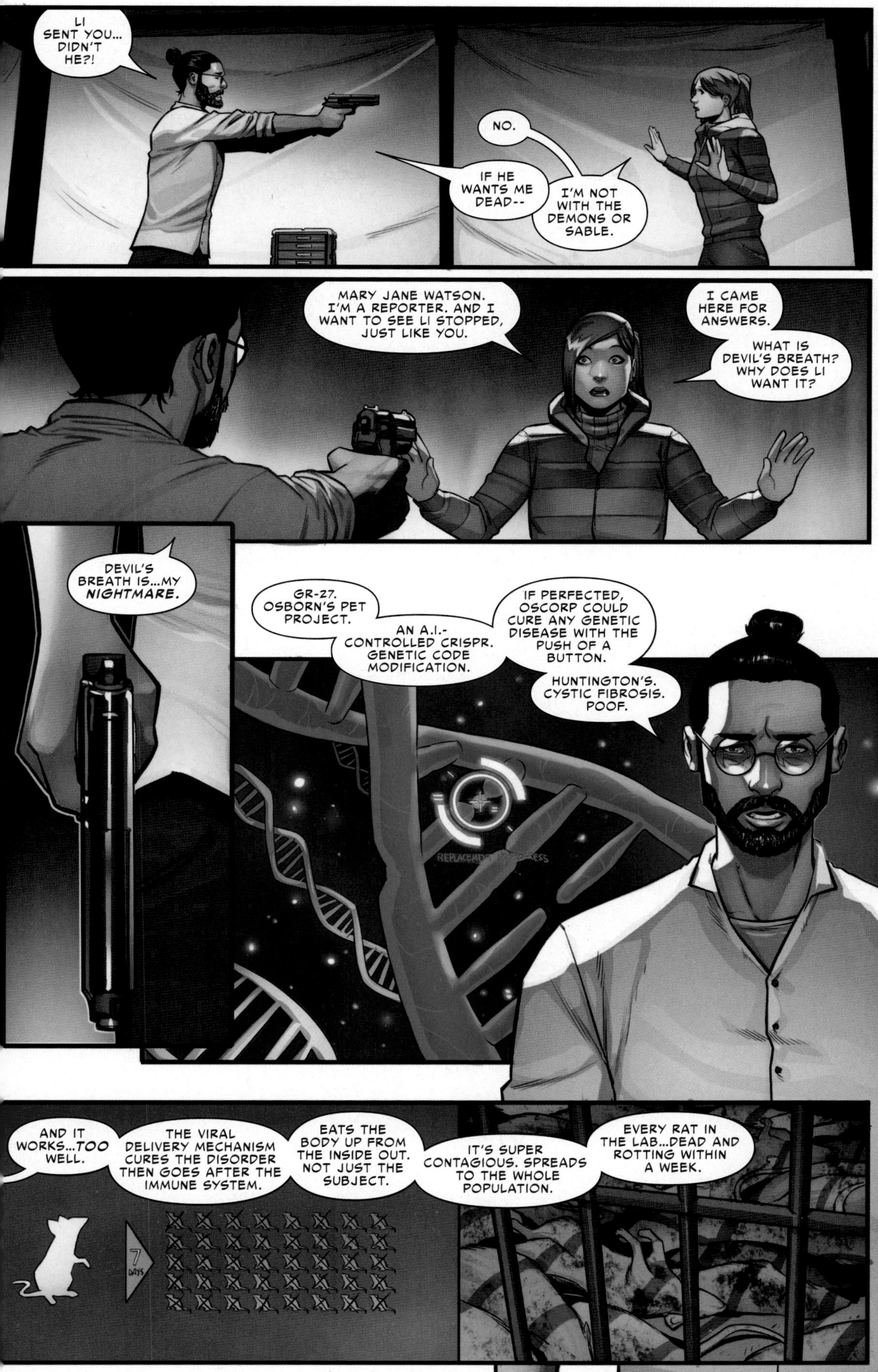
LI SENT YOU... DIDN'T HE?!
NO.
IF HE WANTS ME DEAD--
I'M NOT WITH THE DEMONS OR SABLE.
MARY JANE WATSON. I'M A REPORTER. AND I WANT TO SEE LI STOPPED, JUST LIKE YOU.
I CAME HERE FOR ANSWERS.
WHAT IS DEVIL'S BREATH? WHY DOES LI WANT IT?
DEVIL'S BREATH IS...MY *NIGHTMARE.*
GR-27. OSBORN'S PET PROJECT.
AN A.I.-CONTROLLED CRISPR. GENETIC CODE MODIFICATION.
IF PERFECTED, OSCORP COULD CURE ANY GENETIC DISEASE WITH THE PUSH OF A BUTTON.
HUNTINGTON'S. CYSTIC FIBROSIS. POOF.
AND IT WORKS...*TOO* WELL.
THE VIRAL DELIVERY MECHANISM CURES THE DISORDER THEN GOES AFTER THE IMMUNE SYSTEM.
EATS THE BODY UP FROM THE INSIDE OUT. NOT JUST THE SUBJECT.
IT'S SUPER CONTAGIOUS. SPREADS TO THE WHOLE POPULATION.
EVERY RAT IN THE LAB...DEAD AND ROTTING WITHIN A WEEK.
7 DAYS

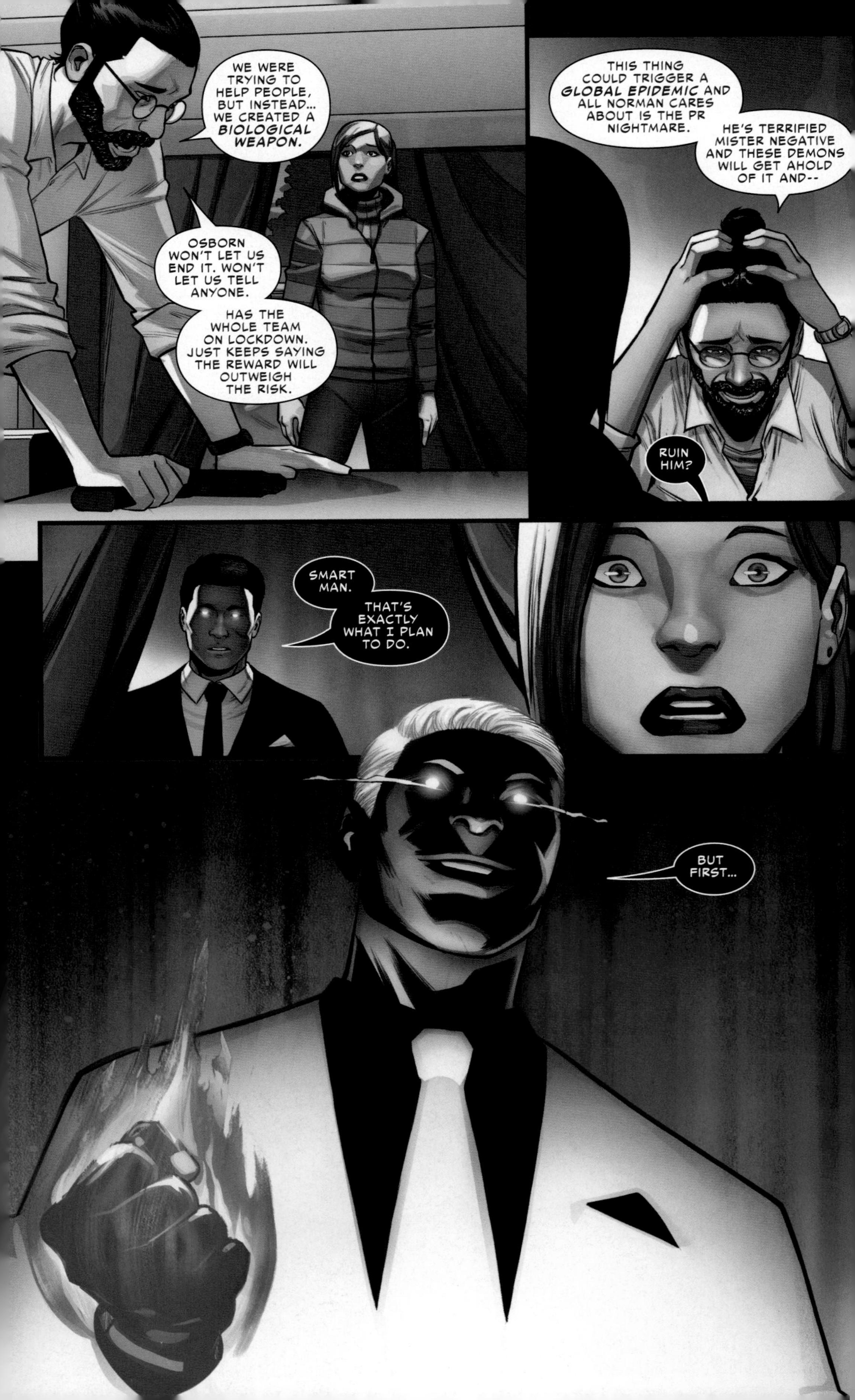
WE WERE TRYING TO HELP PEOPLE, BUT INSTEAD... WE CREATED A *BIOLOGICAL WEAPON*.
OSBORN WON'T LET US END IT. WON'T LET US TELL ANYONE.
HAS THE WHOLE TEAM ON LOCKDOWN. JUST KEEPS SAYING THE REWARD WILL OUTWEIGH THE RISK.
THIS THING COULD TRIGGER A *GLOBAL EPIDEMIC* AND ALL NORMAN CARES ABOUT IS THE PR NIGHTMARE.
HE'S TERRIFIED MISTER NEGATIVE AND THESE DEMONS WILL GET AHOLD OF IT AND--
RUIN HIM?
SMART MAN.
THAT'S EXACTLY WHAT I PLAN TO DO.
BUT FIRST...

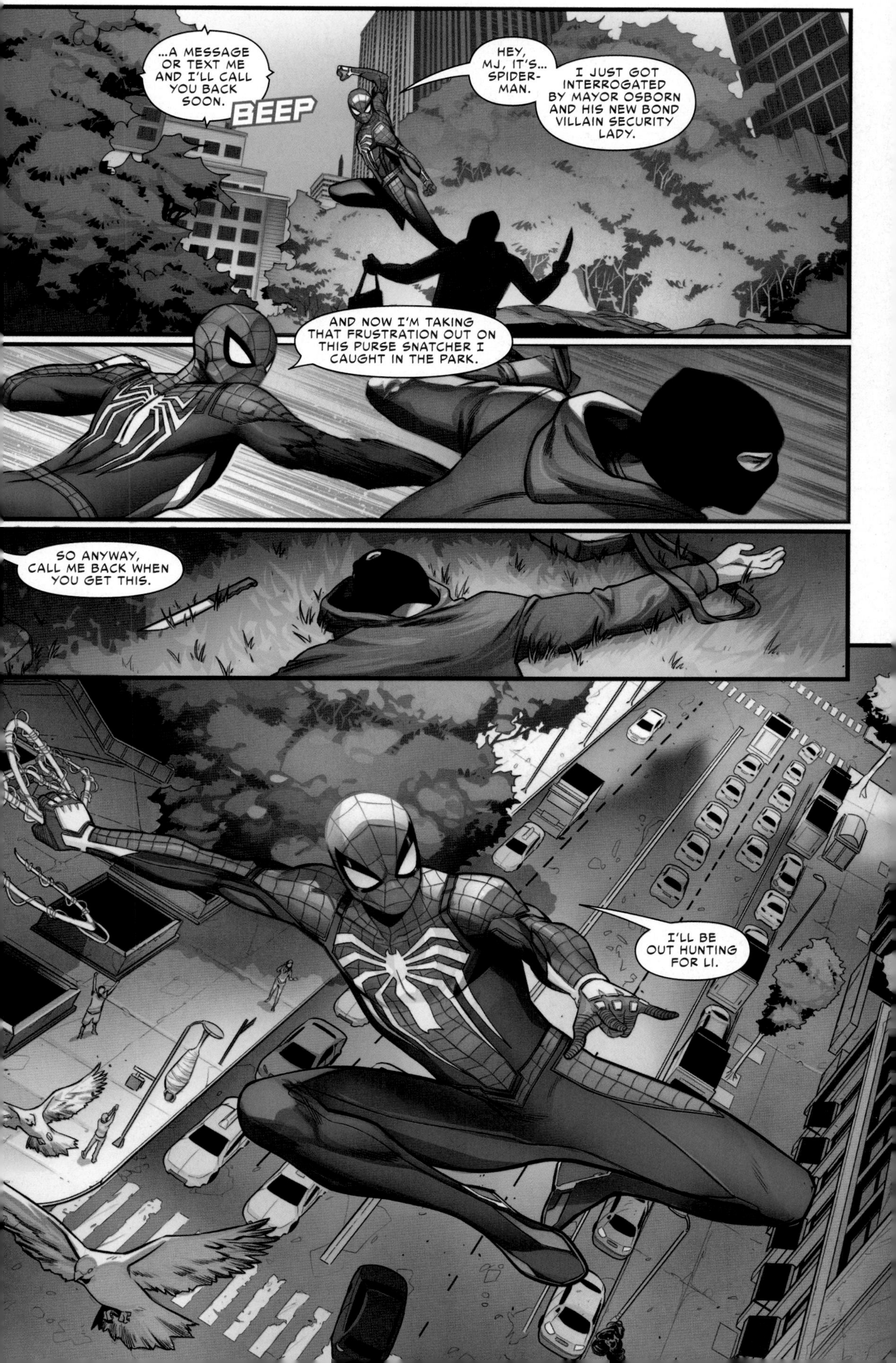
...A MESSAGE OR TEXT ME AND I'LL CALL YOU BACK SOON.
BEEP
HEY, MJ, IT'S... SPIDER-MAN.
I JUST GOT INTERROGATED BY MAYOR OSBORN AND HIS NEW BOND VILLAIN SECURITY LADY.
AND NOW I'M TAKING THAT FRUSTRATION OUT ON THIS PURSE SNATCHER I CAUGHT IN THE PARK.
SO ANYWAY, CALL ME BACK WHEN YOU GET THIS.
I'LL BE OUT HUNTING FOR LI.

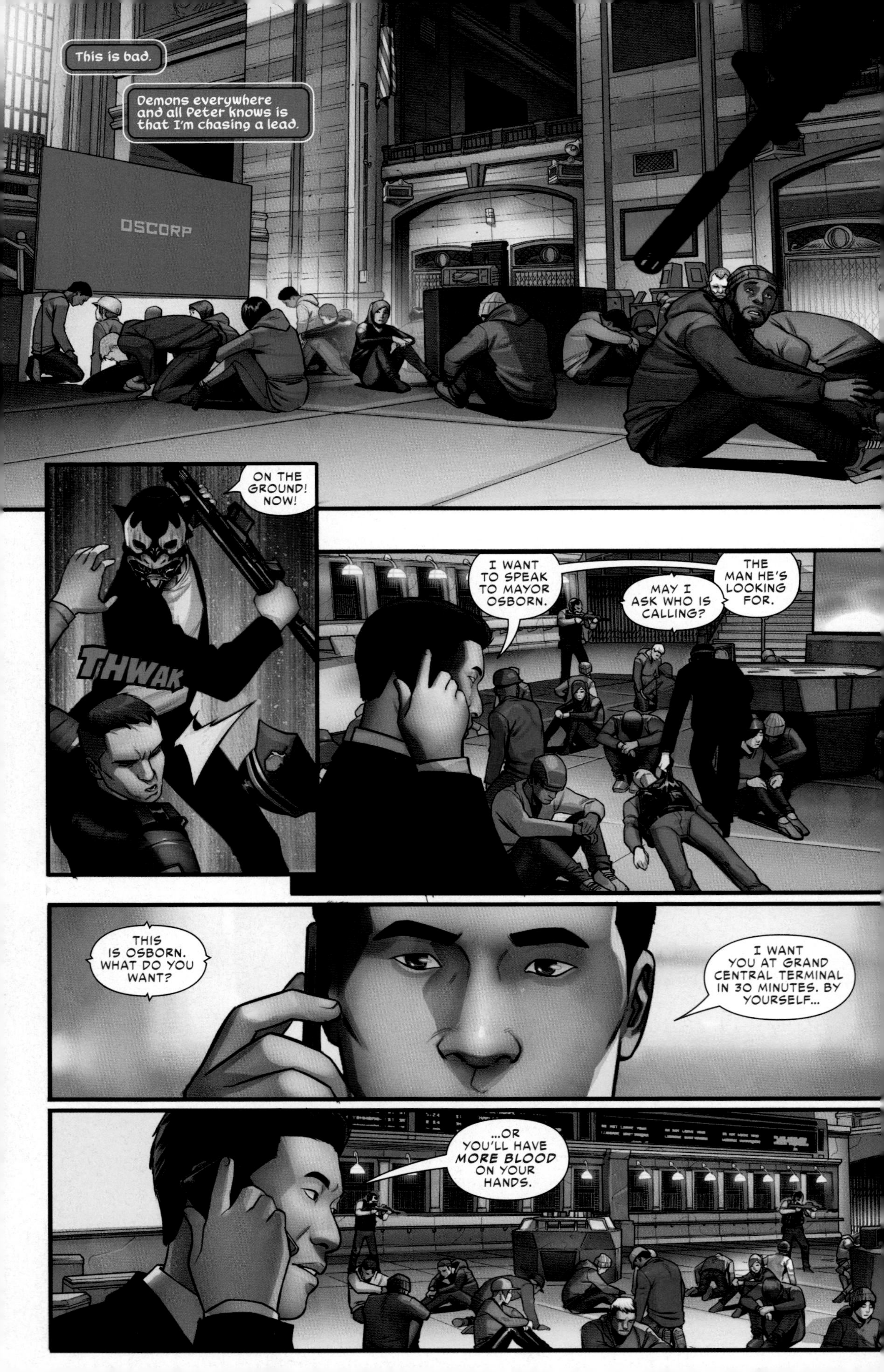
This is bad.
Demons everywhere and all Peter knows is that I'm chasing a lead.
OSCORP
ON THE GROUND! NOW!
THWAK
I WANT TO SPEAK TO MAYOR OSBORN.
MAY I ASK WHO IS CALLING?
THE MAN HE'S LOOKING FOR.
THIS IS OSBORN. WHAT DO YOU WANT?
I WANT YOU AT GRAND CENTRAL TERMINAL IN 30 MINUTES. BY YOURSELF...
...OR YOU'LL HAVE MORE BLOOD ON YOUR HANDS.

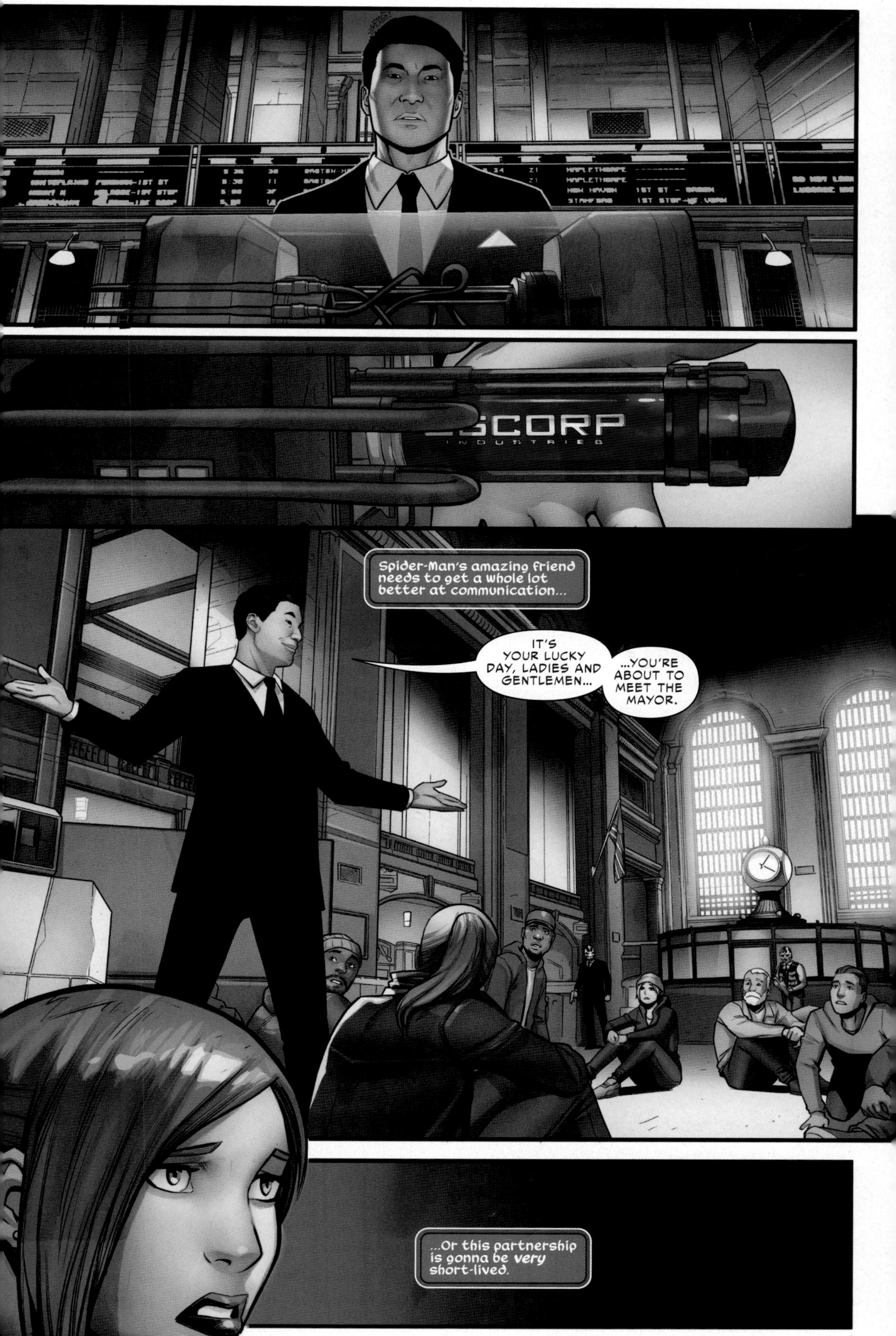
Spider-Man's amazing friend needs to get a whole lot better at communication...
IT'S YOUR LUCKY DAY, LADIES AND GENTLEMEN...
...YOU'RE ABOUT TO MEET THE MAYOR.
...Or this partnership is gonna be *very* short-lived.

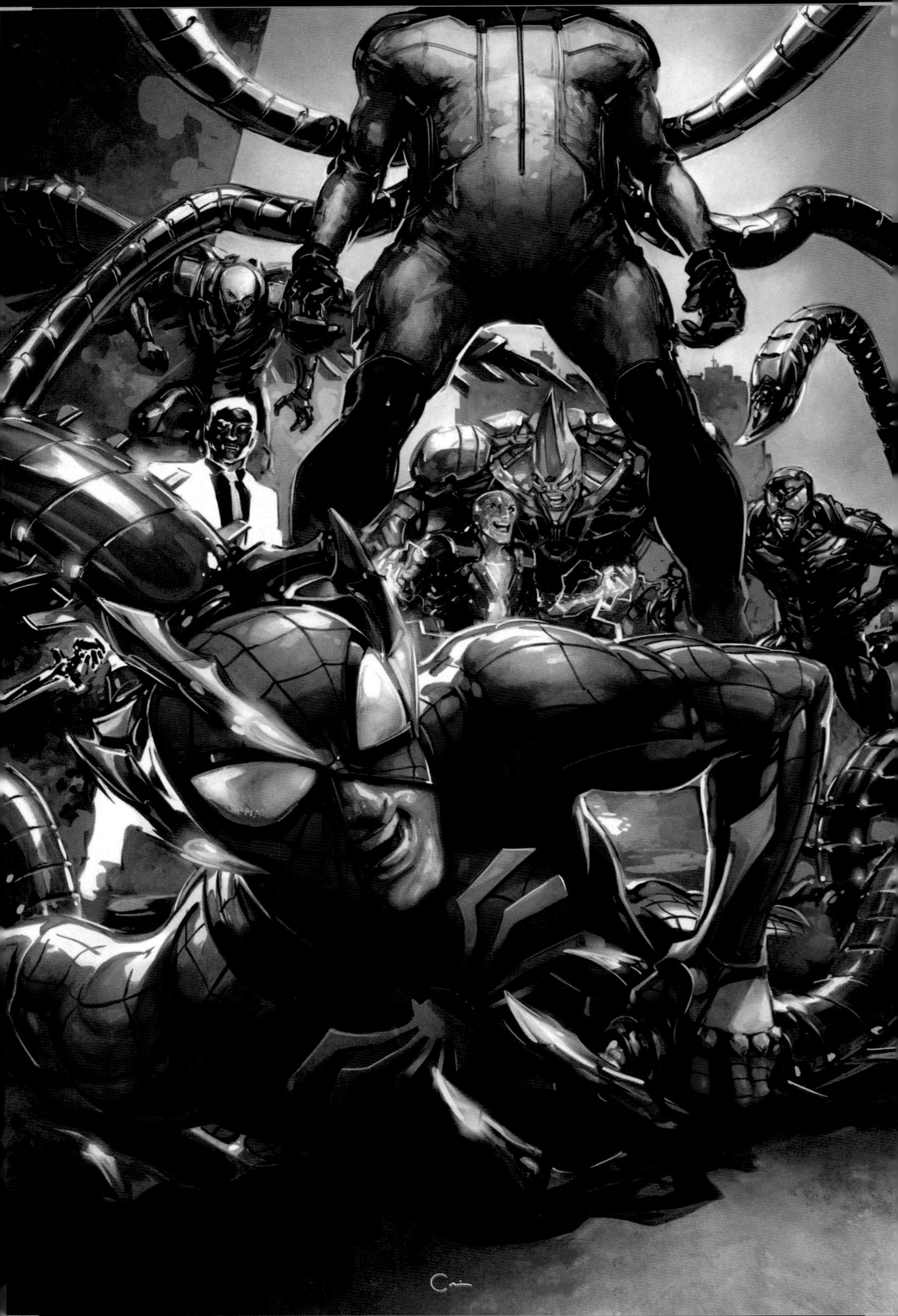

4

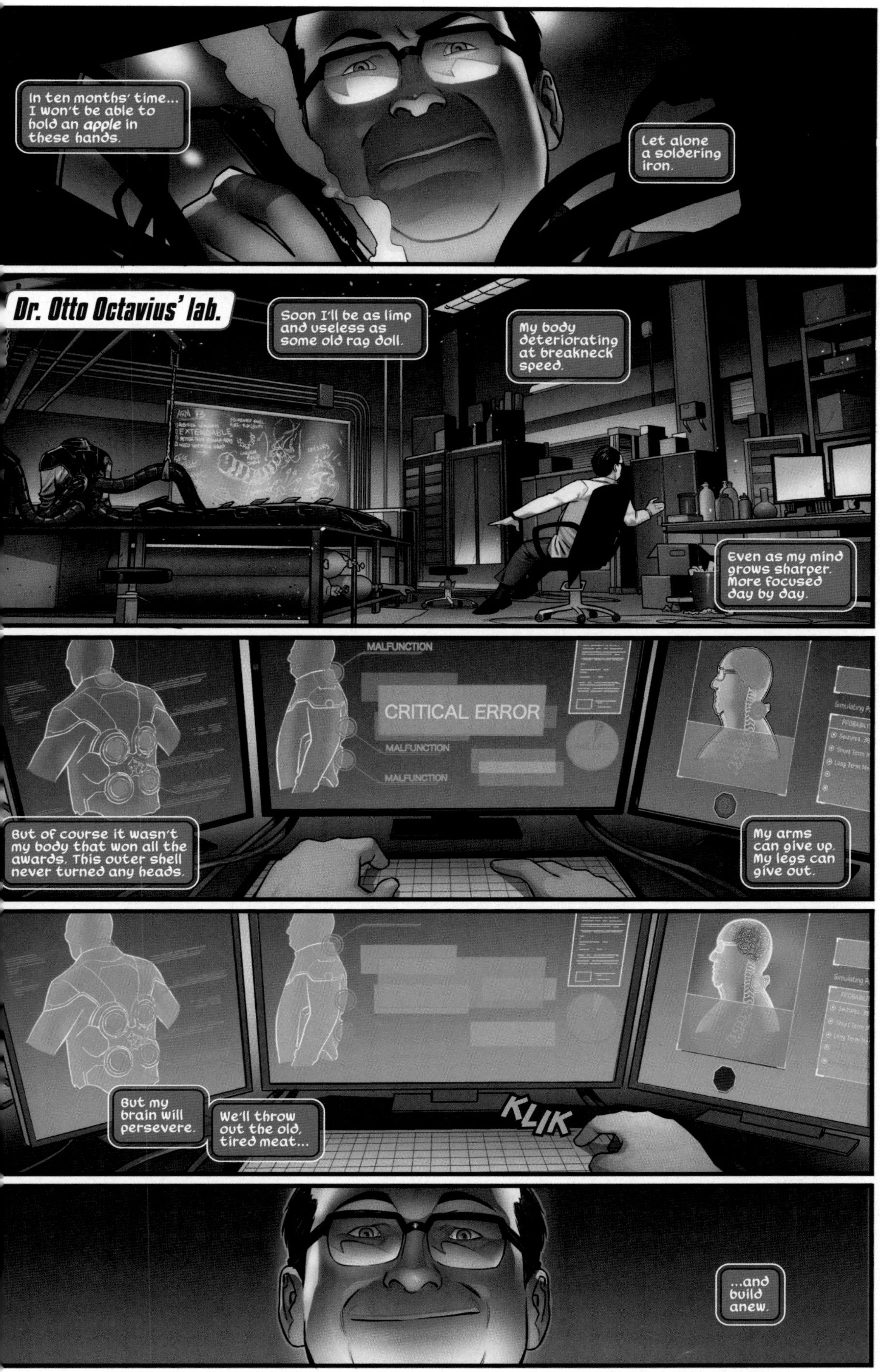
In ten months' time... I won't be able to hold an *apple* in these hands.
Let alone a soldering iron.
Dr. Otto Octavius' lab.
Soon I'll be as limp and useless as some old rag doll.
My body deteriorating at breakneck speed.
Even as my mind grows sharper. More focused day by day.
MALFUNCTION
CRITICAL ERROR
MALFUNCTION
MALFUNCTION
But of course it wasn't my body that won all the awards. This outer shell never turned any heads.
My arms can give up. My legs can give out.
But my brain will persevere.
We'll throw out the old, tired meat...
KLIK
...and build anew.

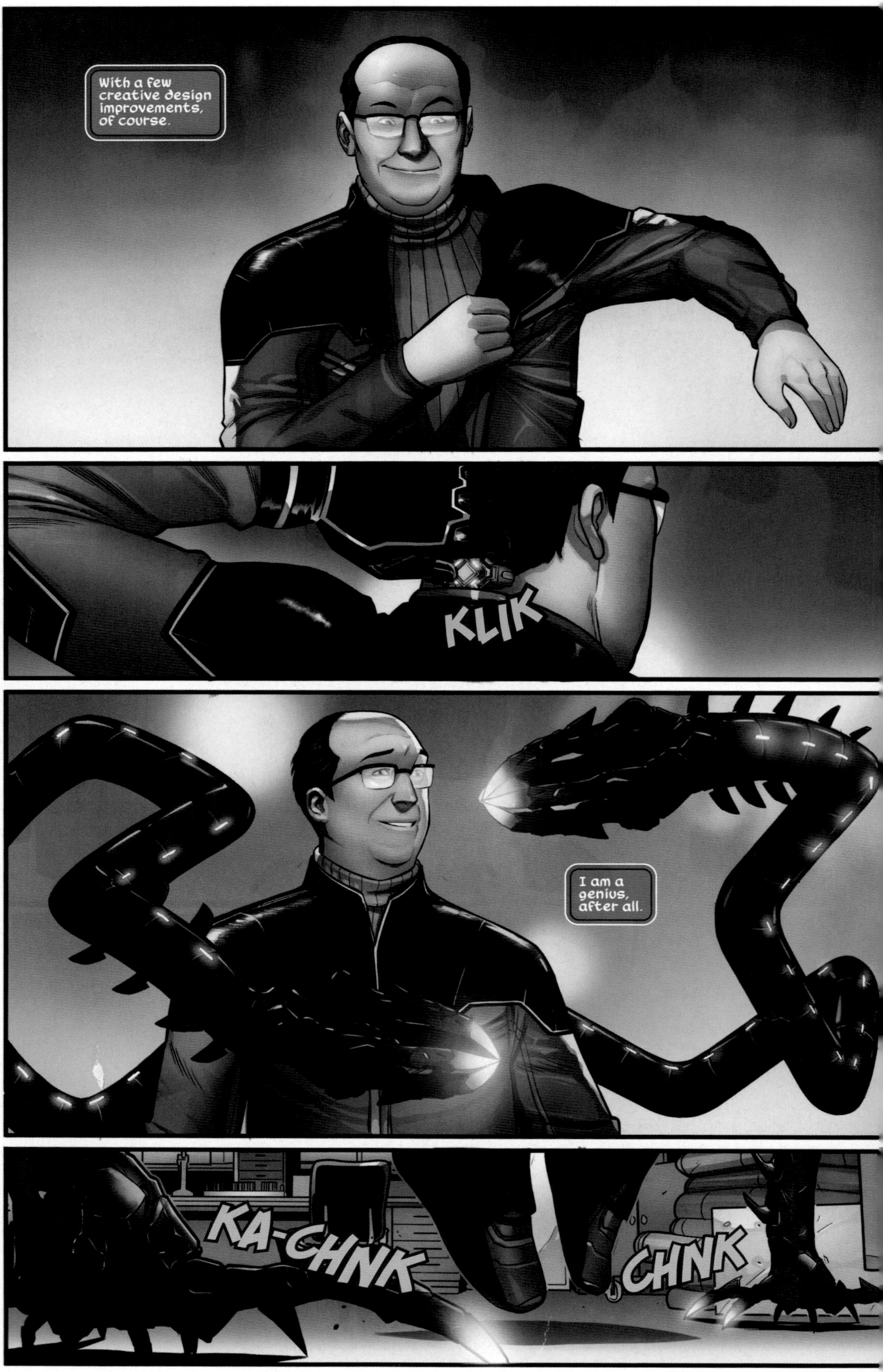
With a few creative design improvements, of course.
KLIK
I am a genius, after all.
KA-CHNK
CHNK

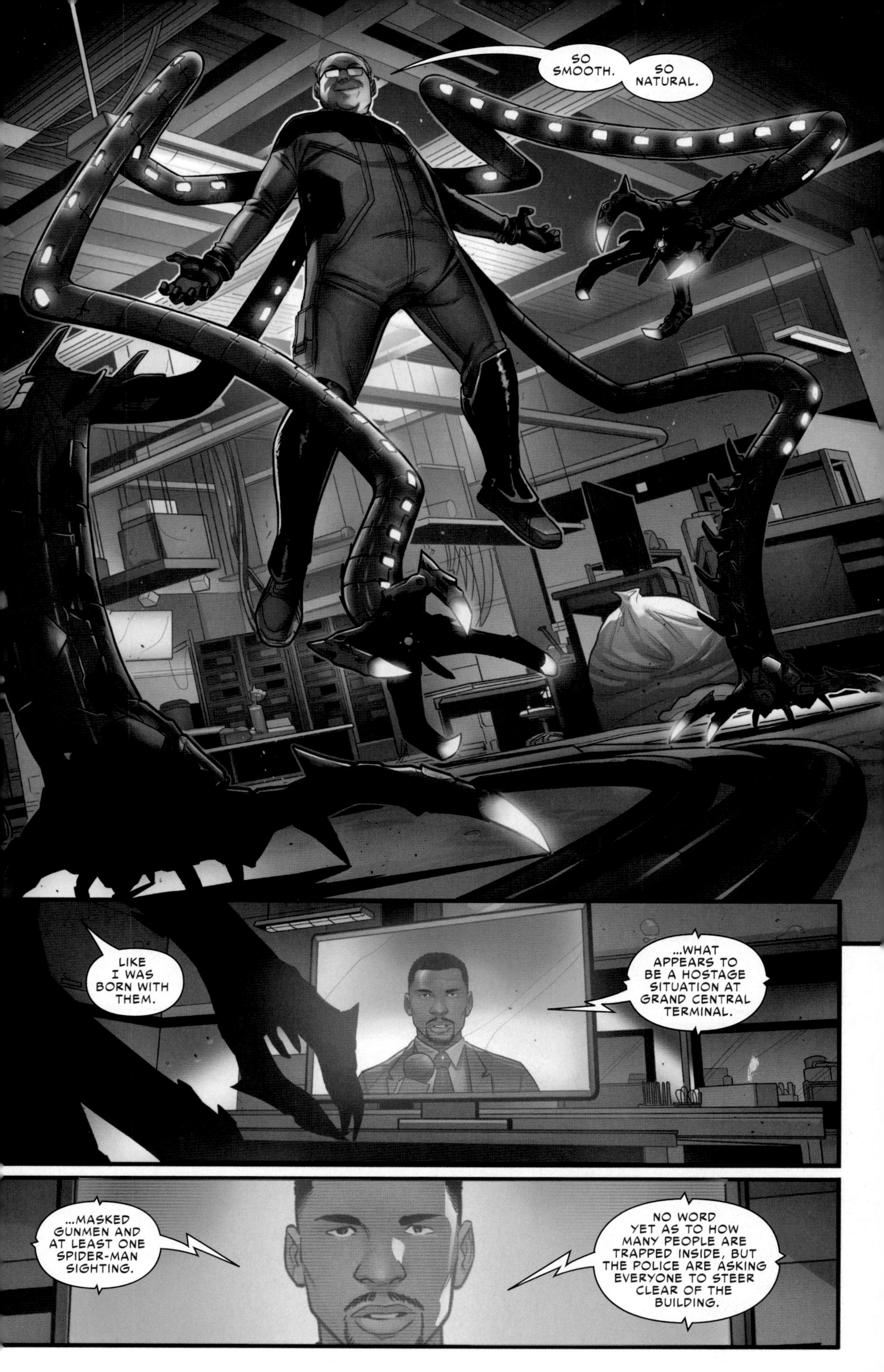
SO SMOOTH.
SO NATURAL.
LIKE I WAS BORN WITH THEM.
...WHAT APPEARS TO BE A HOSTAGE SITUATION AT GRAND CENTRAL TERMINAL.
...MASKED GUNMEN AND AT LEAST ONE SPIDER-MAN SIGHTING.
NO WORD YET AS TO HOW MANY PEOPLE ARE TRAPPED INSIDE, BUT THE POLICE ARE ASKING EVERYONE TO STEER CLEAR OF THE BUILDING.

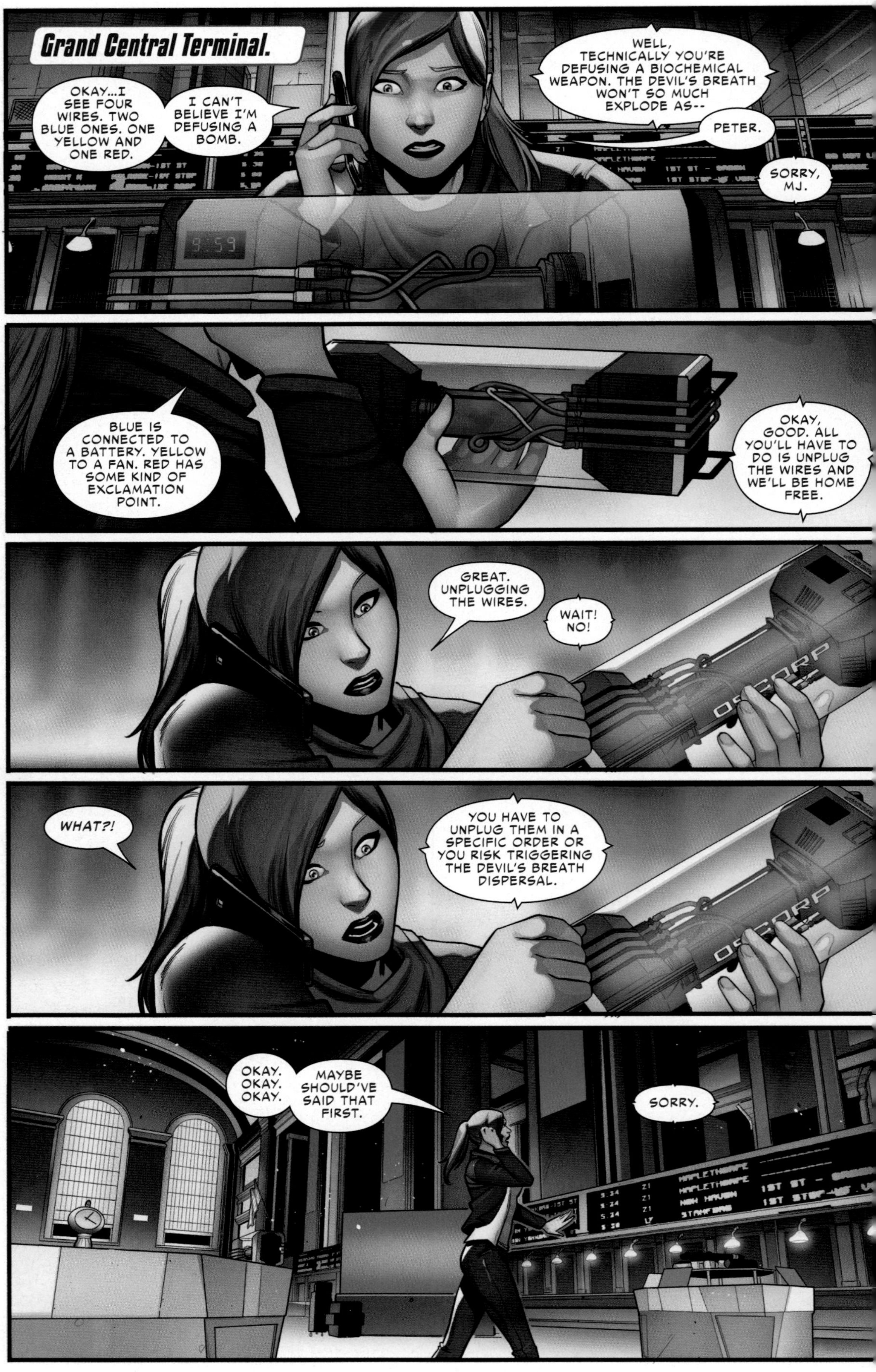
Grand Central Terminal.
OKAY...I SEE FOUR WIRES. TWO BLUE ONES. ONE YELLOW AND ONE RED.
I CAN'T BELIEVE I'M DEFUSING A BOMB.
WELL, TECHNICALLY YOU'RE DEFUSING A BIOCHEMICAL WEAPON. THE DEVIL'S BREATH WON'T SO MUCH EXPLODE AS--
PETER.
SORRY, MJ.
BLUE IS CONNECTED TO A BATTERY. YELLOW TO A FAN. RED HAS SOME KIND OF EXCLAMATION POINT.
OKAY, GOOD. ALL YOU'LL HAVE TO DO IS UNPLUG THE WIRES AND WE'LL BE HOME FREE.
GREAT. UNPLUGGING THE WIRES.
WAIT! NO!
WHAT?!
YOU HAVE TO UNPLUG THEM IN A SPECIFIC ORDER OR YOU RISK TRIGGERING THE DEVIL'S BREATH DISPERSAL.
OKAY. OKAY. OKAY.
MAYBE SHOULD'VE SAID THAT FIRST.
SORRY.

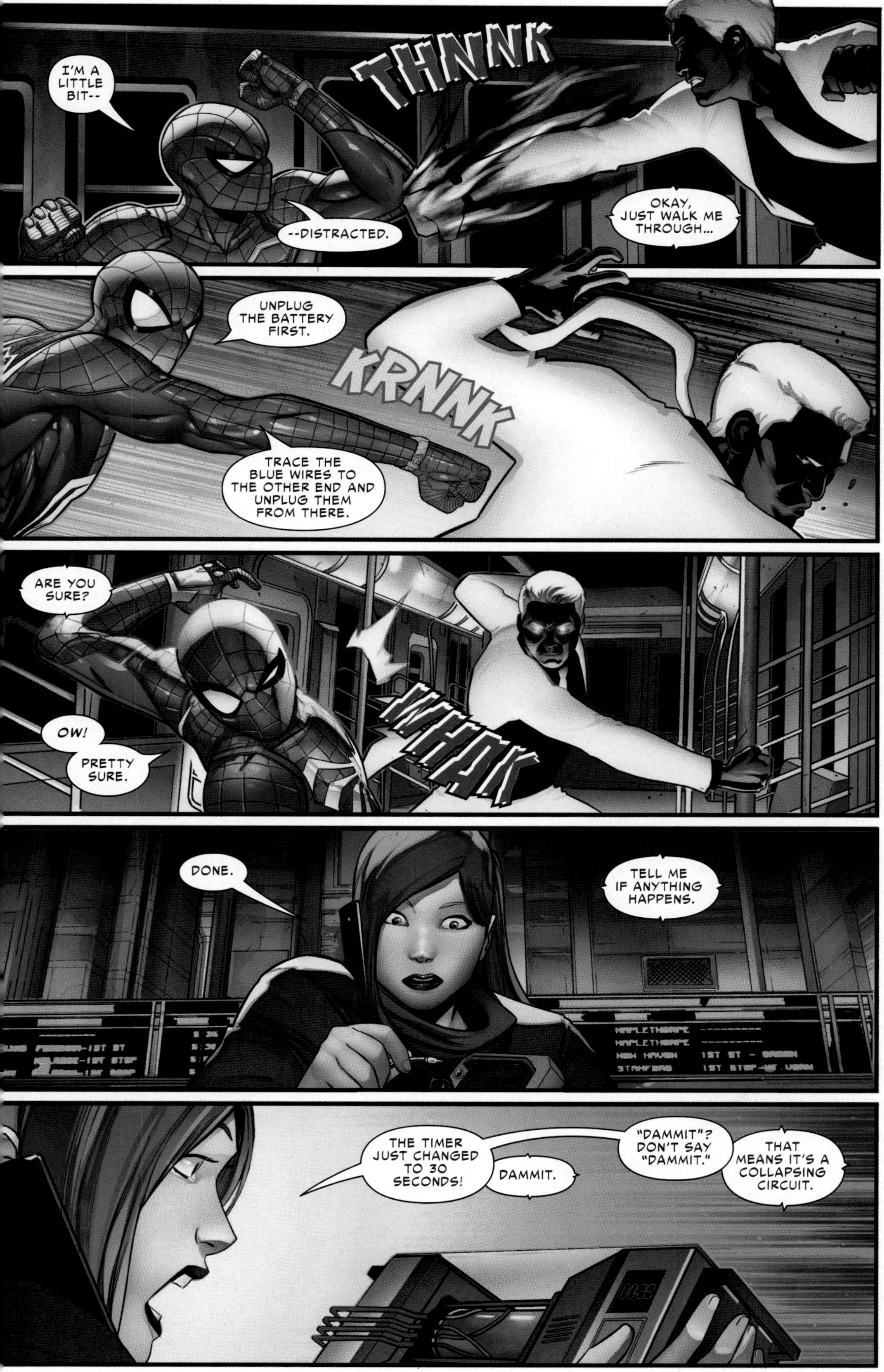
I'M A LITTLE BIT--
THNNK
--DISTRACTED.
OKAY, JUST WALK ME THROUGH...
UNPLUG THE BATTERY FIRST.
KRNNK
TRACE THE BLUE WIRES TO THE OTHER END AND UNPLUG THEM FROM THERE.
ARE YOU SURE?
WHAK
OW!
PRETTY SURE.
DONE.
TELL ME IF ANYTHING HAPPENS.
THE TIMER JUST CHANGED TO 30 SECONDS!
DAMMIT.
"DAMMIT"? DON'T SAY "DAMMIT."
THAT MEANS IT'S A COLLAPSING CIRCUIT.

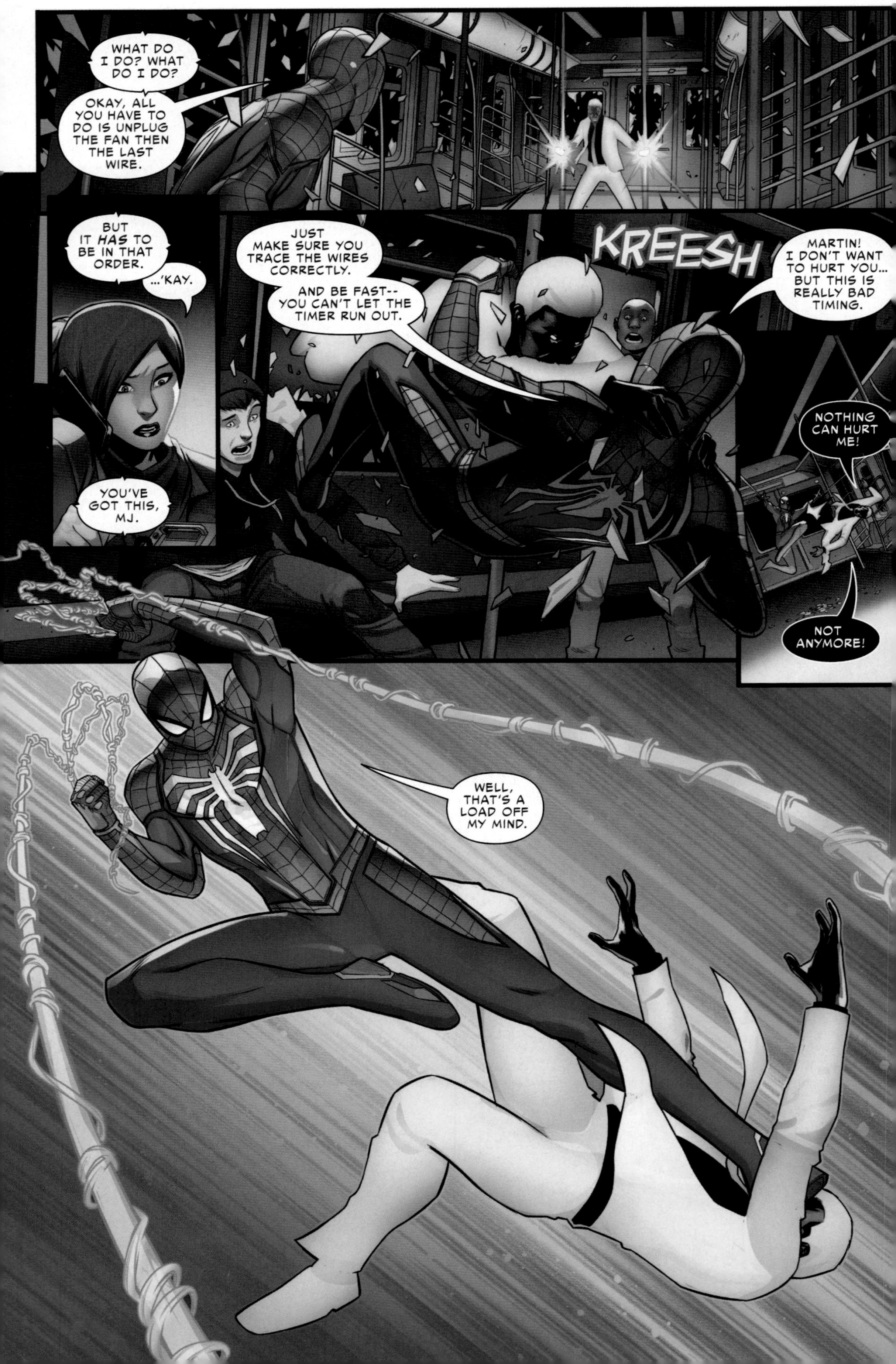
WHAT DO I DO? WHAT DO I DO?
OKAY, ALL YOU HAVE TO DO IS UNPLUG THE FAN THEN THE LAST WIRE.
BUT IT HAS TO BE IN THAT ORDER.
...'KAY.
JUST MAKE SURE YOU TRACE THE WIRES CORRECTLY.
AND BE FAST-- YOU CAN'T LET THE TIMER RUN OUT.
YOU'VE GOT THIS, MJ.
KREESH
MARTIN! I DON'T WANT TO HURT YOU... BUT THIS IS REALLY BAD TIMING.
NOTHING CAN HURT ME!
NOT ANYMORE!
WELL, THAT'S A LOAD OFF MY MIND.

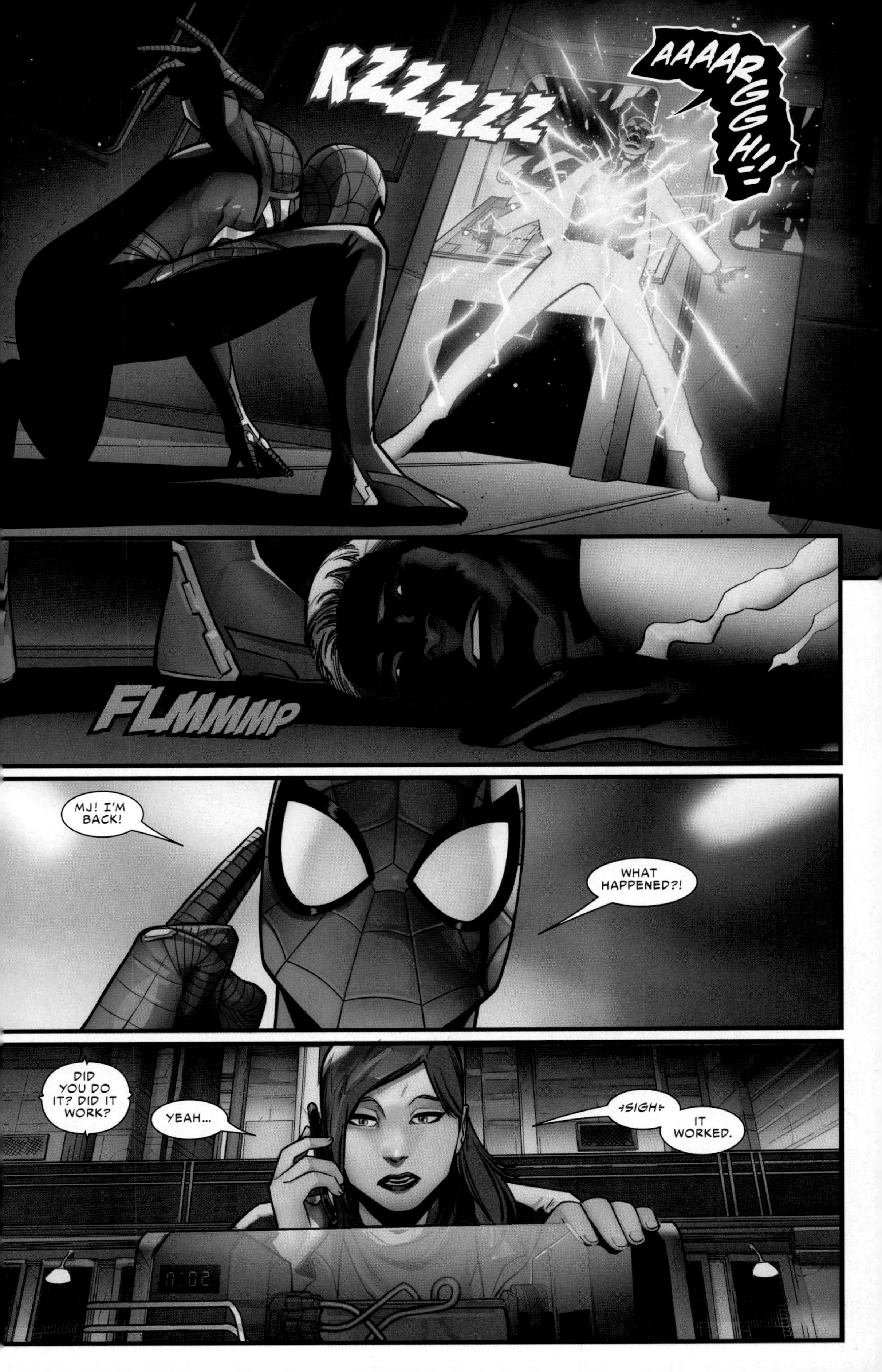
KZZZZZZ
AAAARGGGH!!!
FLMMMP
MJ! I'M BACK!
WHAT HAPPENED?!
DID YOU DO IT? DID IT WORK?
YEAH...
⇉SIGH⇇ IT WORKED.

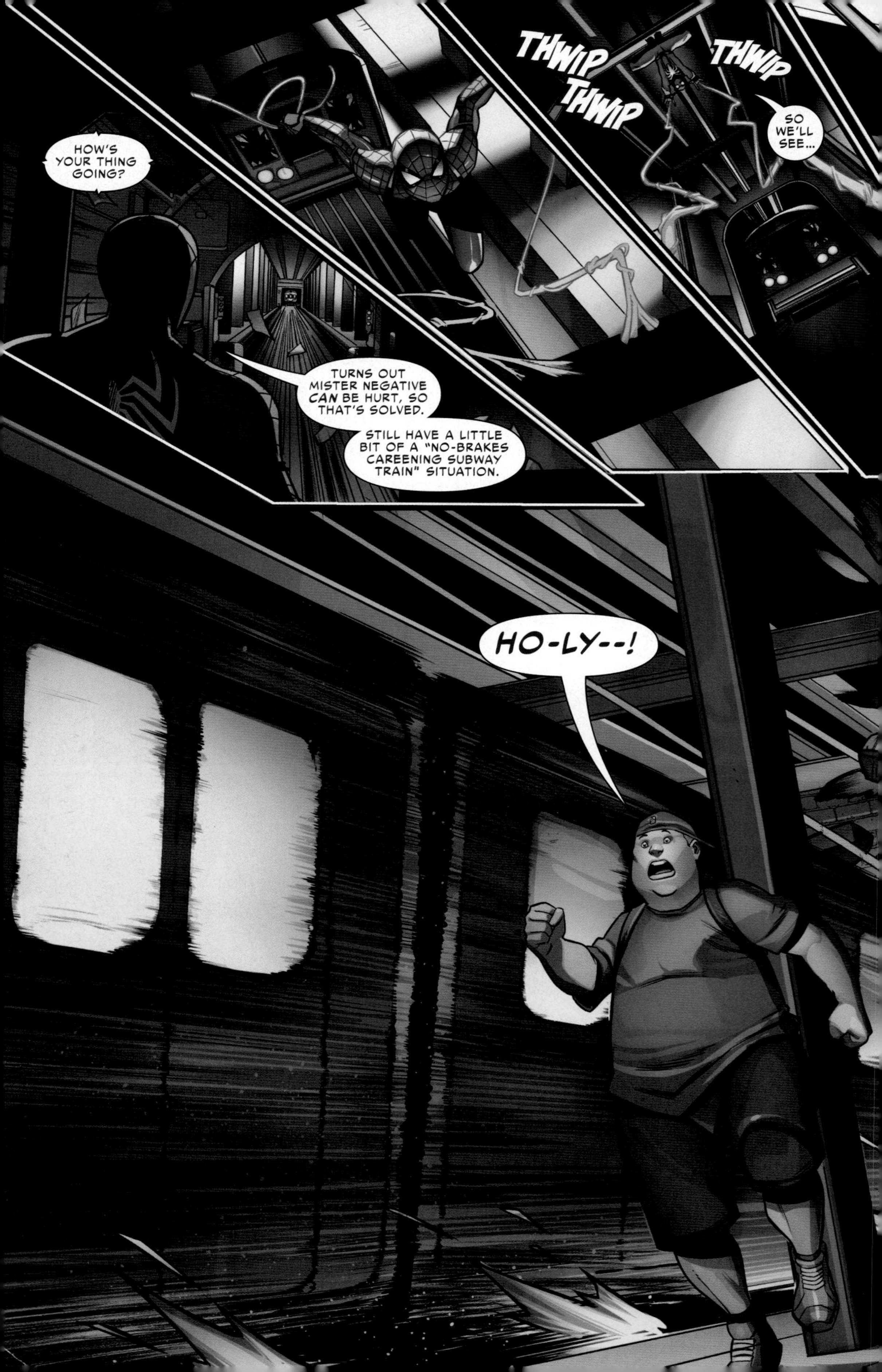
HOW'S YOUR THING GOING?
TURNS OUT MISTER NEGATIVE CAN BE HURT, SO THAT'S SOLVED.
STILL HAVE A LITTLE BIT OF A "NO-BRAKES CAREENING SUBWAY TRAIN" SITUATION.
THWIP
THWIP
THWIP
SO WE'LL SEE...
HO-LY--!

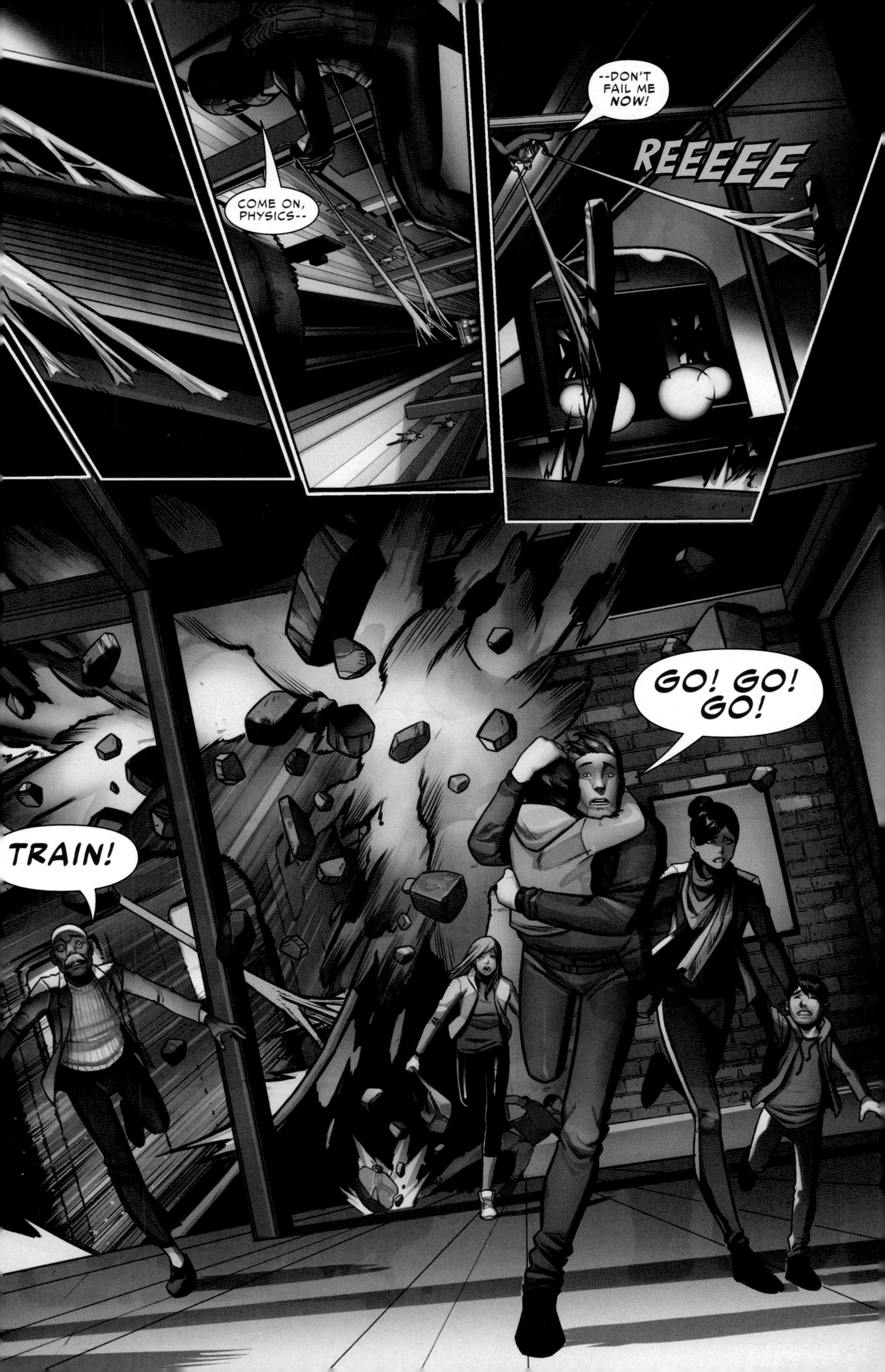
COME ON, PHYSICS--
--DON'T FAIL ME NOW!
REEEEE
TRAIN!
GO! GO! GO!

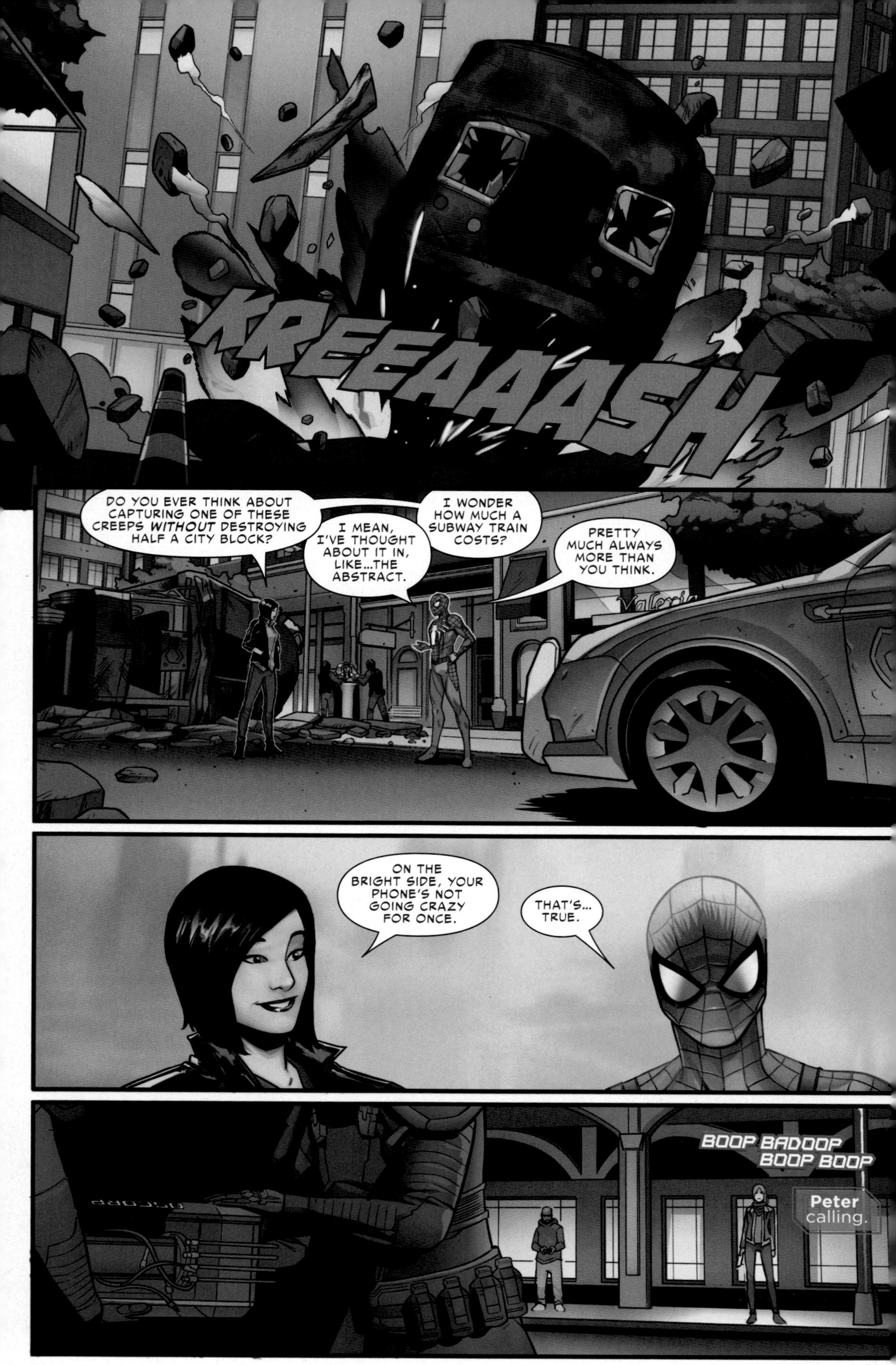
KREEAAAASH
DO YOU EVER THINK ABOUT CAPTURING ONE OF THESE CREEPS WITHOUT DESTROYING HALF A CITY BLOCK?
I MEAN, I'VE THOUGHT ABOUT IT IN, LIKE...THE ABSTRACT.
I WONDER HOW MUCH A SUBWAY TRAIN COSTS?
PRETTY MUCH ALWAYS MORE THAN YOU THINK.
ON THE BRIGHT SIDE, YOUR PHONE'S NOT GOING CRAZY FOR ONCE.
THAT'S... TRUE.
BOOP BADOOP BOOP BOOP
Peter calling.

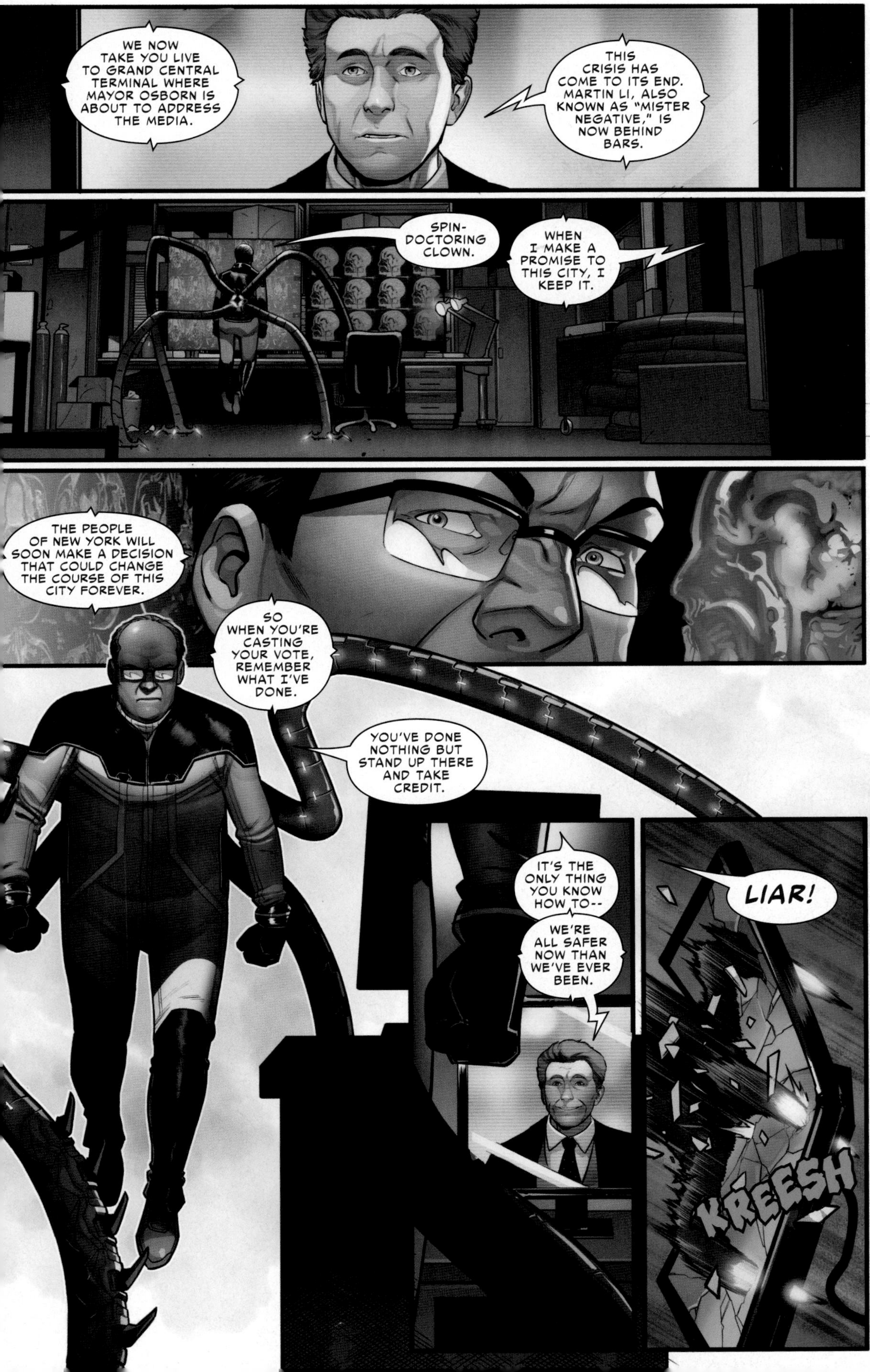
WE NOW TAKE YOU LIVE TO GRAND CENTRAL TERMINAL WHERE MAYOR OSBORN IS ABOUT TO ADDRESS THE MEDIA.
THIS CRISIS HAS COME TO ITS END. MARTIN LI, ALSO KNOWN AS "MISTER NEGATIVE," IS NOW BEHIND BARS.
SPIN-DOCTORING CLOWN.
WHEN I MAKE A PROMISE TO THIS CITY, I KEEP IT.
THE PEOPLE OF NEW YORK WILL SOON MAKE A DECISION THAT COULD CHANGE THE COURSE OF THIS CITY FOREVER.
SO WHEN YOU'RE CASTING YOUR VOTE, REMEMBER WHAT I'VE DONE.
YOU'VE DONE NOTHING BUT STAND UP THERE AND TAKE CREDIT.
IT'S THE ONLY THING YOU KNOW HOW TO--
WE'RE ALL SAFER NOW THAN WE'VE EVER BEEN.
LIAR!
KREESH

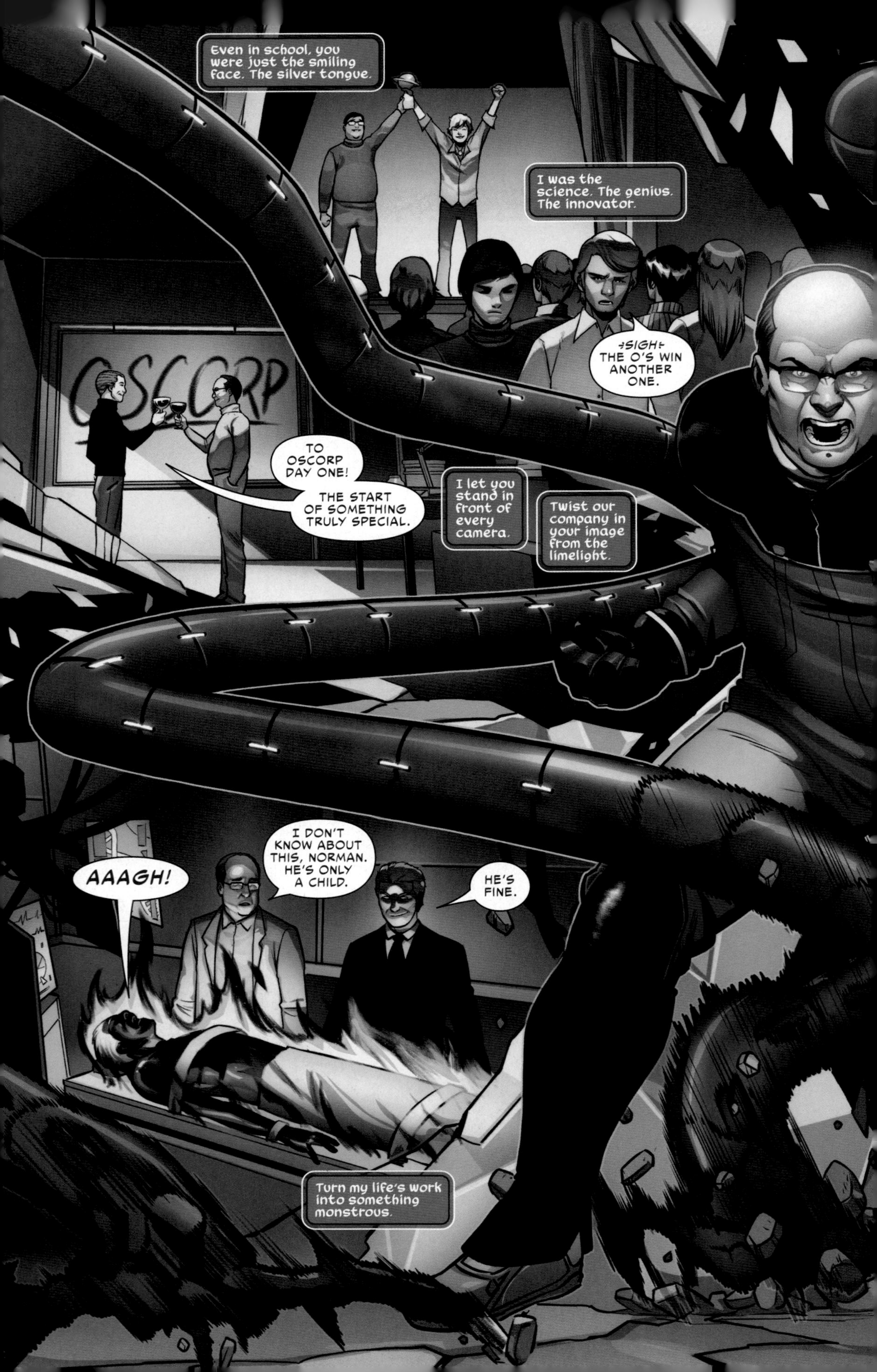
Even in school, you were just the smiling face. The silver tongue.
I was the science. The genius. The innovator.
SIGH THE O'S WIN ANOTHER ONE.
TO OSCORP DAY ONE!
THE START OF SOMETHING TRULY SPECIAL.
I let you stand in front of every camera.
Twist our company in your image from the limelight.
AAAGH!
I DON'T KNOW ABOUT THIS, NORMAN. HE'S ONLY A CHILD.
HE'S FINE.
Turn my life's work into something monstrous.

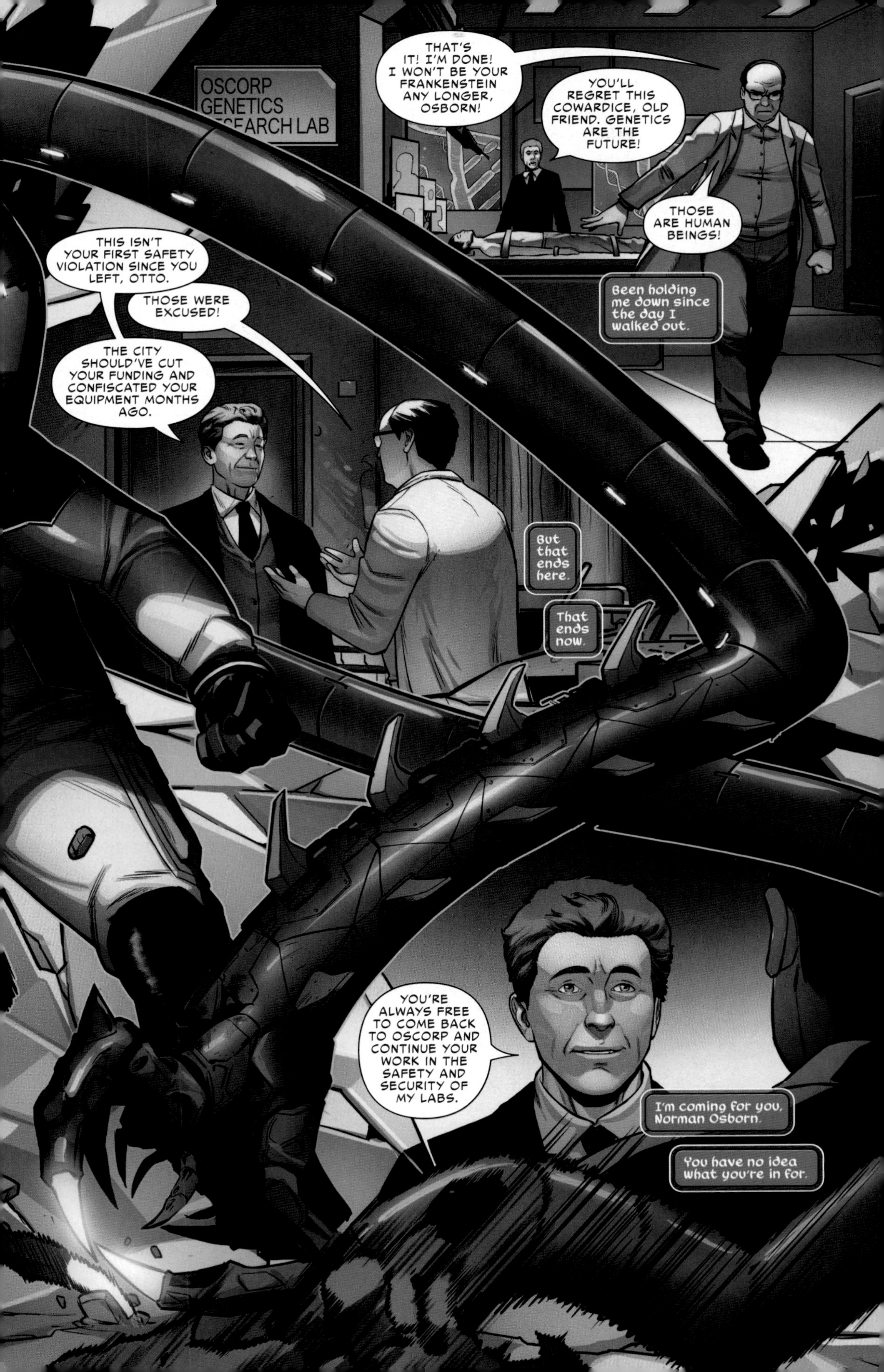
OSCORP GENETICS RESEARCH LAB
THAT'S IT! I'M DONE! I WON'T BE YOUR FRANKENSTEIN ANY LONGER, OSBORN!
YOU'LL REGRET THIS COWARDICE, OLD FRIEND. GENETICS ARE THE FUTURE!
THOSE ARE HUMAN BEINGS!
Been holding me down since the day I walked out.
THIS ISN'T YOUR FIRST SAFETY VIOLATION SINCE YOU LEFT, OTTO.
THOSE WERE EXCUSED!
THE CITY SHOULD'VE CUT YOUR FUNDING AND CONFISCATED YOUR EQUIPMENT MONTHS AGO.
But that ends here.
That ends now.
YOU'RE ALWAYS FREE TO COME BACK TO OSCORP AND CONTINUE YOUR WORK IN THE SAFETY AND SECURITY OF MY LABS.
I'm coming for you, Norman Osborn.
You have no idea what you're in for.

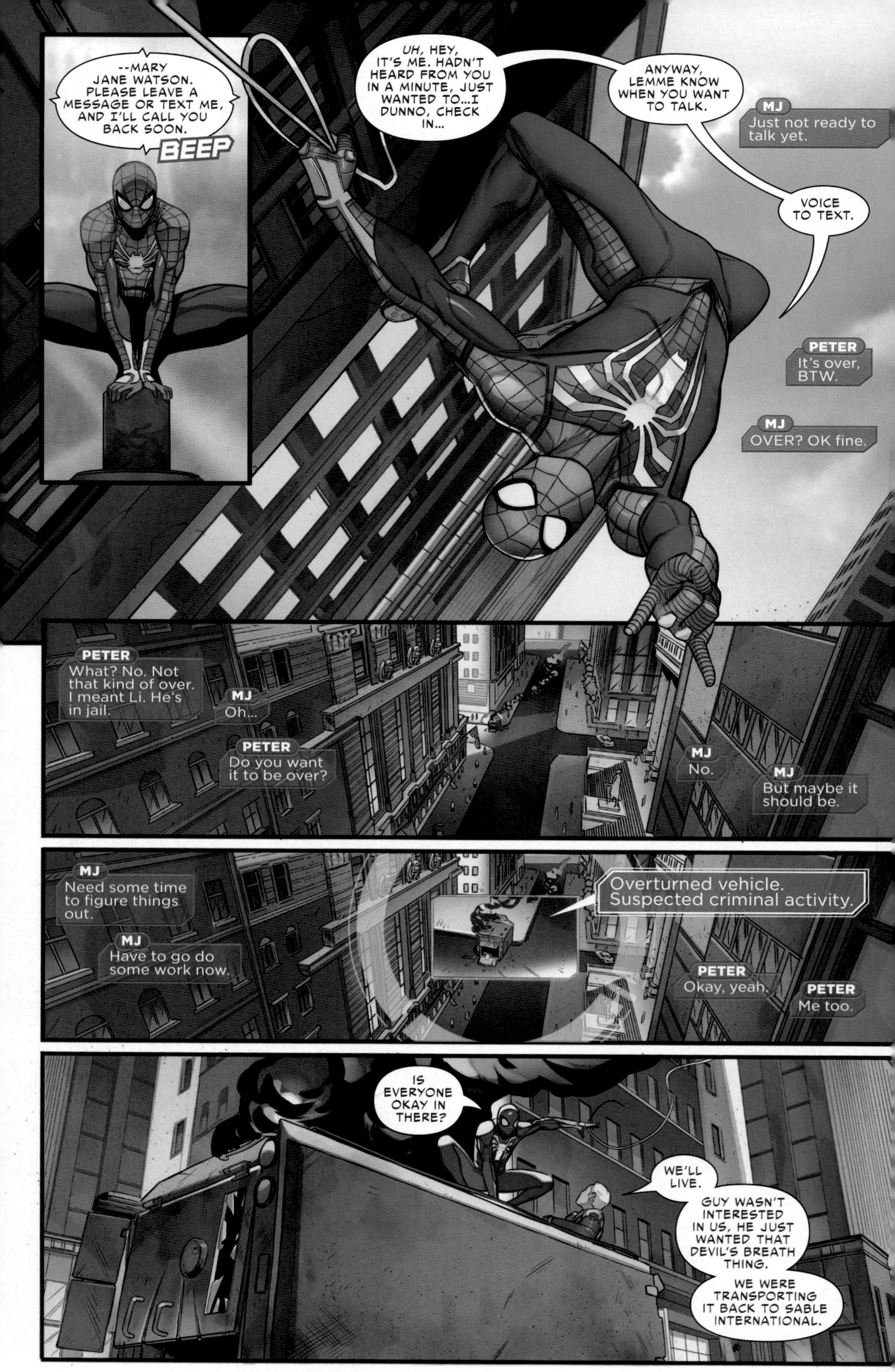

--MARY JANE WATSON. PLEASE LEAVE A MESSAGE OR TEXT ME, AND I'LL CALL YOU BACK SOON.
BEEP
UH, HEY, IT'S ME. HADN'T HEARD FROM YOU IN A MINUTE, JUST WANTED TO...I DUNNO, CHECK IN...
ANYWAY, LEMME KNOW WHEN YOU WANT TO TALK.
MJ
Just not ready to talk yet.
VOICE TO TEXT.
PETER
It's over, BTW.
MJ
OVER? OK fine.
PETER
What? No. Not that kind of over. I meant Li. He's in jail.
MJ
Oh...
PETER
Do you want it to be over?
MJ
No.
MJ
But maybe it should be.
MJ
Need some time to figure things out.
MJ
Have to go do some work now.
Overturned vehicle. Suspected criminal activity.
PETER
Okay, yeah.
PETER
Me too.
IS EVERYONE OKAY IN THERE?
WE'LL LIVE.
GUY WASN'T INTERESTED IN US, HE JUST WANTED THAT DEVIL'S BREATH THING.
WE WERE TRANSPORTING IT BACK TO SABLE INTERNATIONAL.

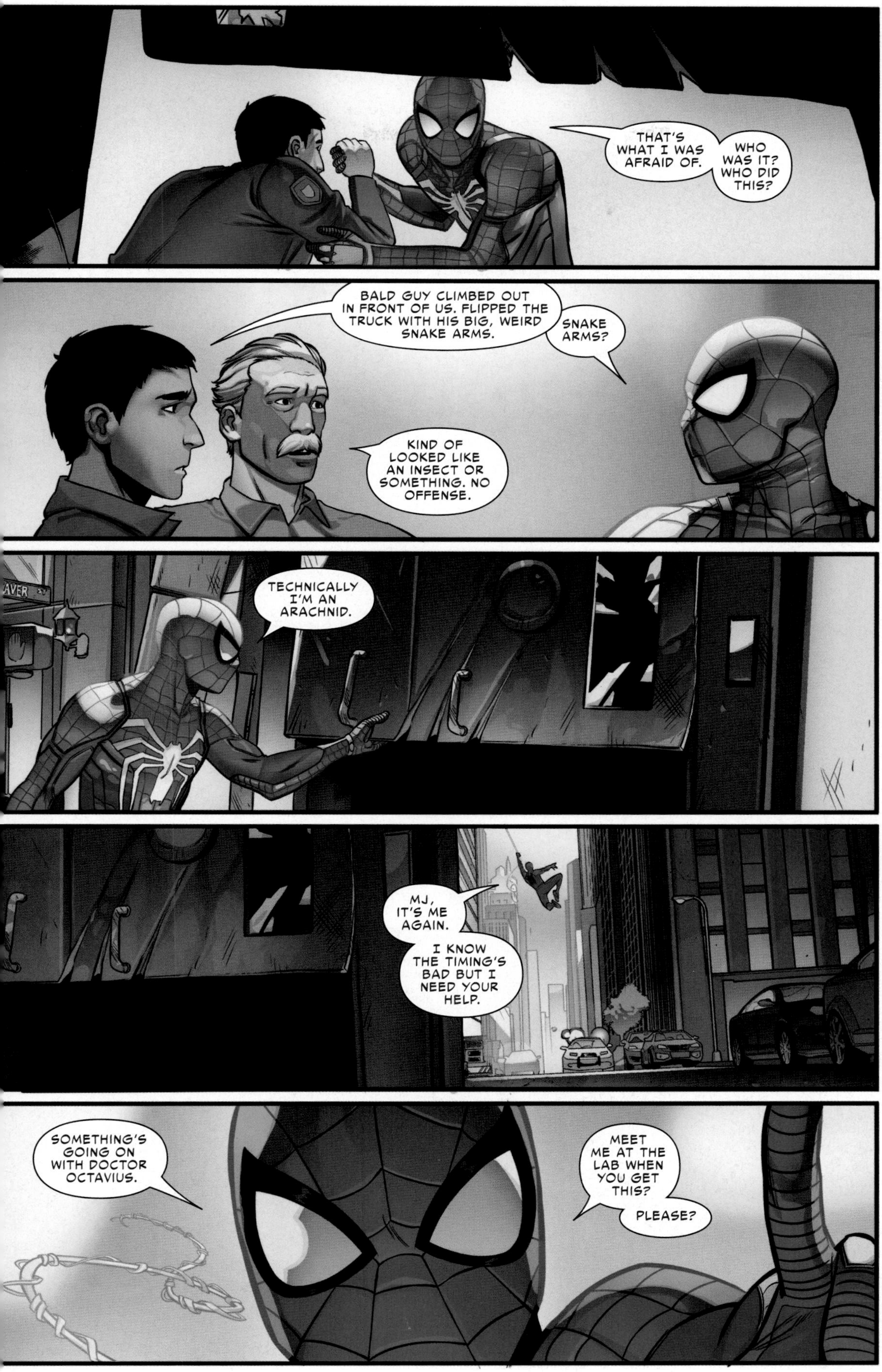
THAT'S WHAT I WAS AFRAID OF.
WHO WAS IT? WHO DID THIS?
BALD GUY CLIMBED OUT IN FRONT OF US. FLIPPED THE TRUCK WITH HIS BIG, WEIRD SNAKE ARMS.
SNAKE ARMS?
KIND OF LOOKED LIKE AN INSECT OR SOMETHING. NO OFFENSE.
TECHNICALLY I'M AN ARACHNID.
MJ, IT'S ME AGAIN.
I KNOW THE TIMING'S BAD BUT I NEED YOUR HELP.
SOMETHING'S GOING ON WITH DOCTOR OCTAVIUS.
MEET ME AT THE LAB WHEN YOU GET THIS?
PLEASE?

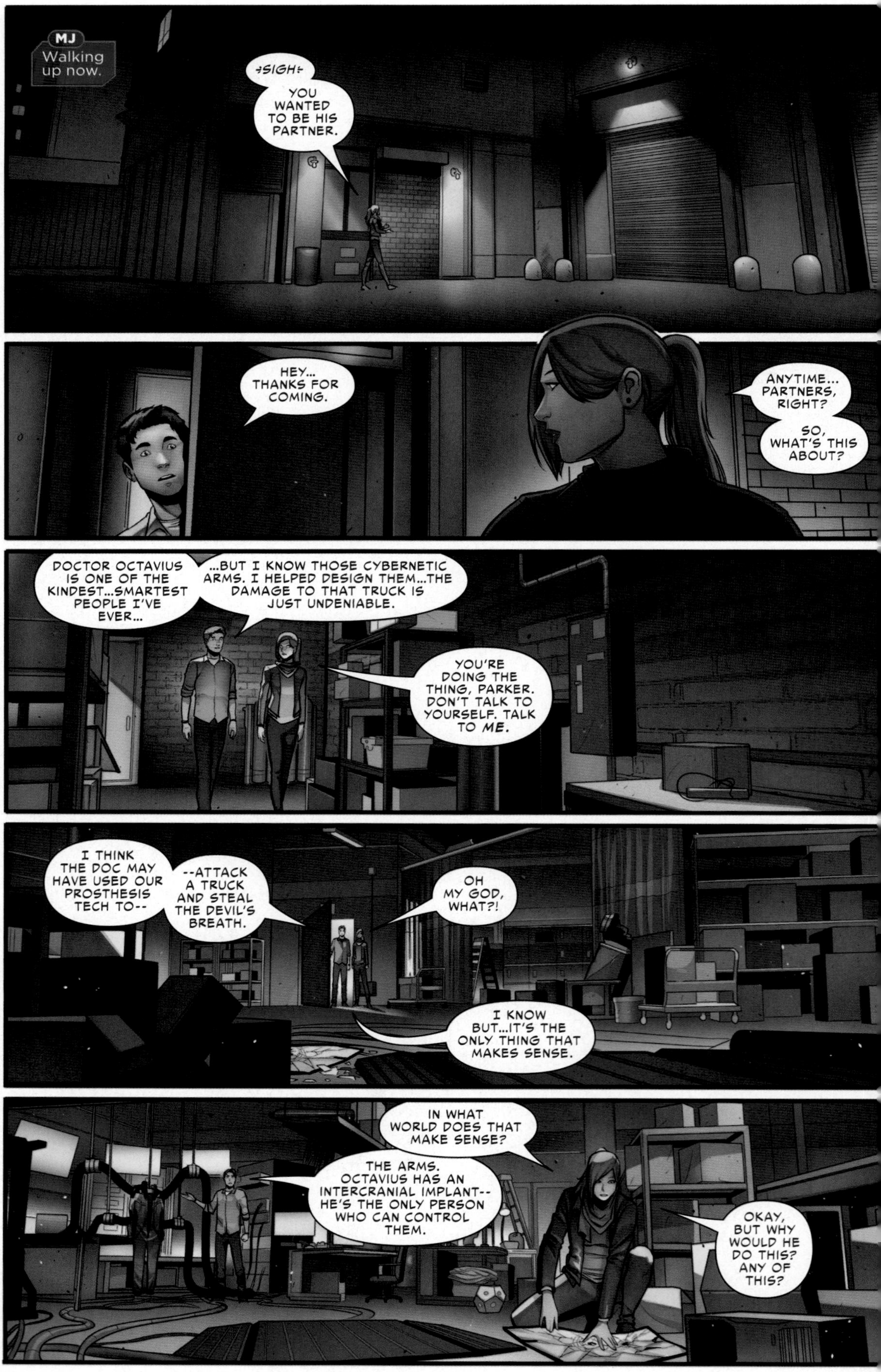
MJ
Walking up now.
≠SIGH≠
YOU WANTED TO BE HIS PARTNER.
HEY... THANKS FOR COMING.
ANYTIME... PARTNERS, RIGHT?
SO, WHAT'S THIS ABOUT?
DOCTOR OCTAVIUS IS ONE OF THE KINDEST...SMARTEST PEOPLE I'VE EVER...
...BUT I KNOW THOSE CYBERNETIC ARMS. I HELPED DESIGN THEM...THE DAMAGE TO THAT TRUCK IS JUST UNDENIABLE.
YOU'RE DOING THE THING, PARKER. DON'T TALK TO YOURSELF. TALK TO *ME*.
I THINK THE DOC MAY HAVE USED OUR PROSTHESIS TECH TO--
--ATTACK A TRUCK AND STEAL THE DEVIL'S BREATH.
OH MY GOD, WHAT?!
I KNOW BUT...IT'S THE ONLY THING THAT MAKES SENSE.
IN WHAT WORLD DOES THAT MAKE SENSE?
THE ARMS. OCTAVIUS HAS AN INTERCRANIAL IMPLANT--HE'S THE ONLY PERSON WHO CAN CONTROL THEM.
OKAY, BUT WHY WOULD HE DO THIS? ANY OF THIS?

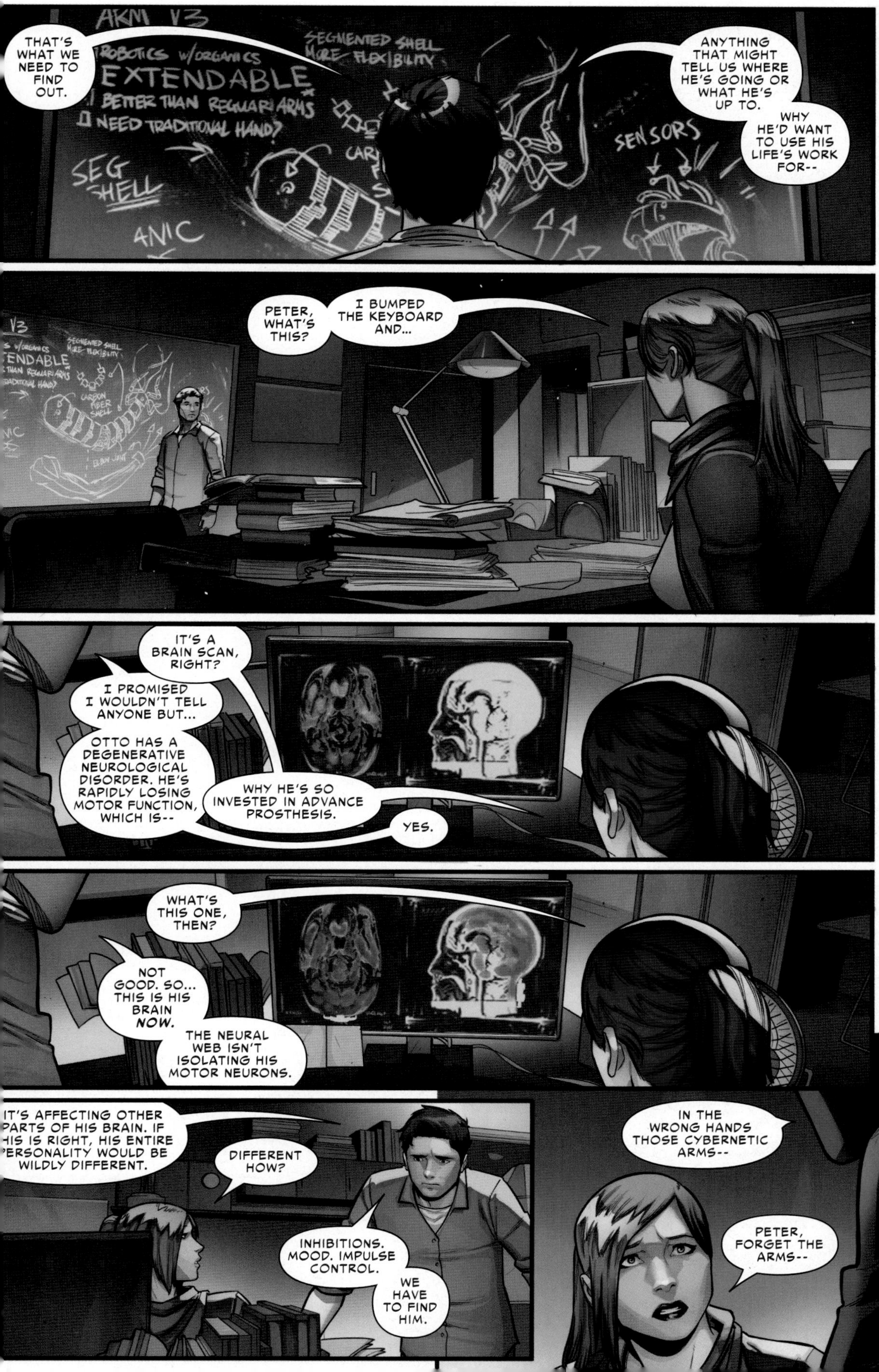

AKM V3
ROBOTICS w/ORGANICS
EXTENDABLE
BETTER THAN REGULAR ARMS
NEED TRADITIONAL HAND?
SEGMENTED SHELL MORE FLEXIBILITY
SEG SHELL
SENSORS
THAT'S WHAT WE NEED TO FIND OUT.
ANYTHING THAT MIGHT TELL US WHERE HE'S GOING OR WHAT HE'S UP TO.
WHY HE'D WANT TO USE HIS LIFE'S WORK FOR--
PETER, WHAT'S THIS?
I BUMPED THE KEYBOARD AND...
CARBON FIBER SHELL
IT'S A BRAIN SCAN, RIGHT?
I PROMISED I WOULDN'T TELL ANYONE BUT...
OTTO HAS A DEGENERATIVE NEUROLOGICAL DISORDER. HE'S RAPIDLY LOSING MOTOR FUNCTION, WHICH IS--
WHY HE'S SO INVESTED IN ADVANCE PROSTHESIS.
YES.
WHAT'S THIS ONE, THEN?
NOT GOOD. SO... THIS IS HIS BRAIN *NOW.*
THE NEURAL WEB ISN'T ISOLATING HIS MOTOR NEURONS.
IT'S AFFECTING OTHER PARTS OF HIS BRAIN. IF THIS IS RIGHT, HIS ENTIRE PERSONALITY WOULD BE WILDLY DIFFERENT.
DIFFERENT HOW?
INHIBITIONS. MOOD. IMPULSE CONTROL.
WE HAVE TO FIND HIM.
IN THE WRONG HANDS THOSE CYBERNETIC ARMS--
PETER, FORGET THE ARMS--

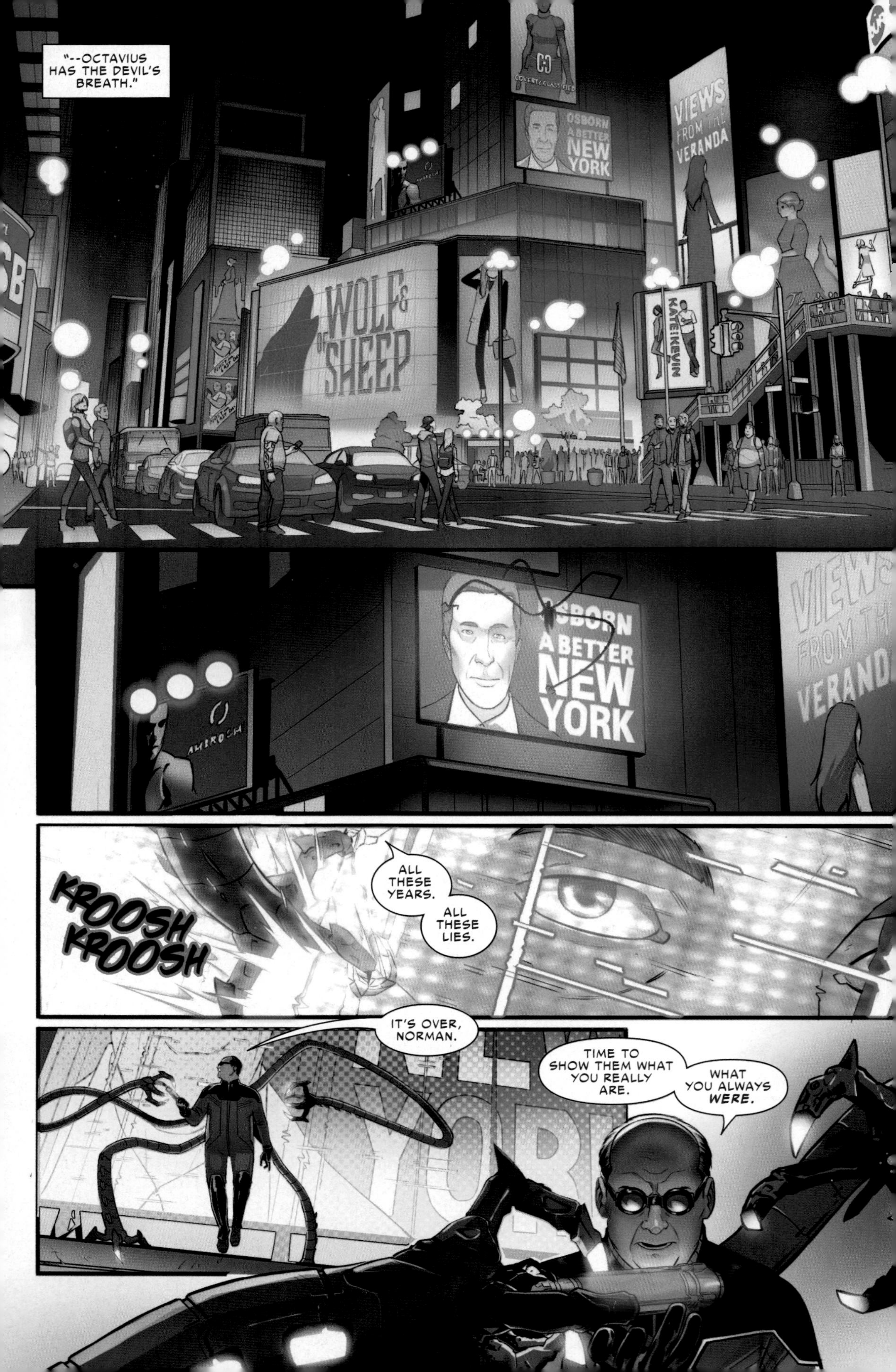
"--OCTAVIUS HAS THE DEVIL'S BREATH."
COVERT & CLASSIFIED
OSBORN A BETTER NEW YORK
VIEWS FROM THE VERANDA
WOLF & SHEEP
KATE & KEVIN
AMBROSH
OSBORN A BETTER NEW YORK
VIEWS FROM THE VERANDA
KROOSH KROOSH
ALL THESE YEARS.
ALL THESE LIES.
IT'S OVER, NORMAN.
TIME TO SHOW THEM WHAT YOU REALLY ARE.
WHAT YOU ALWAYS *WERE.*

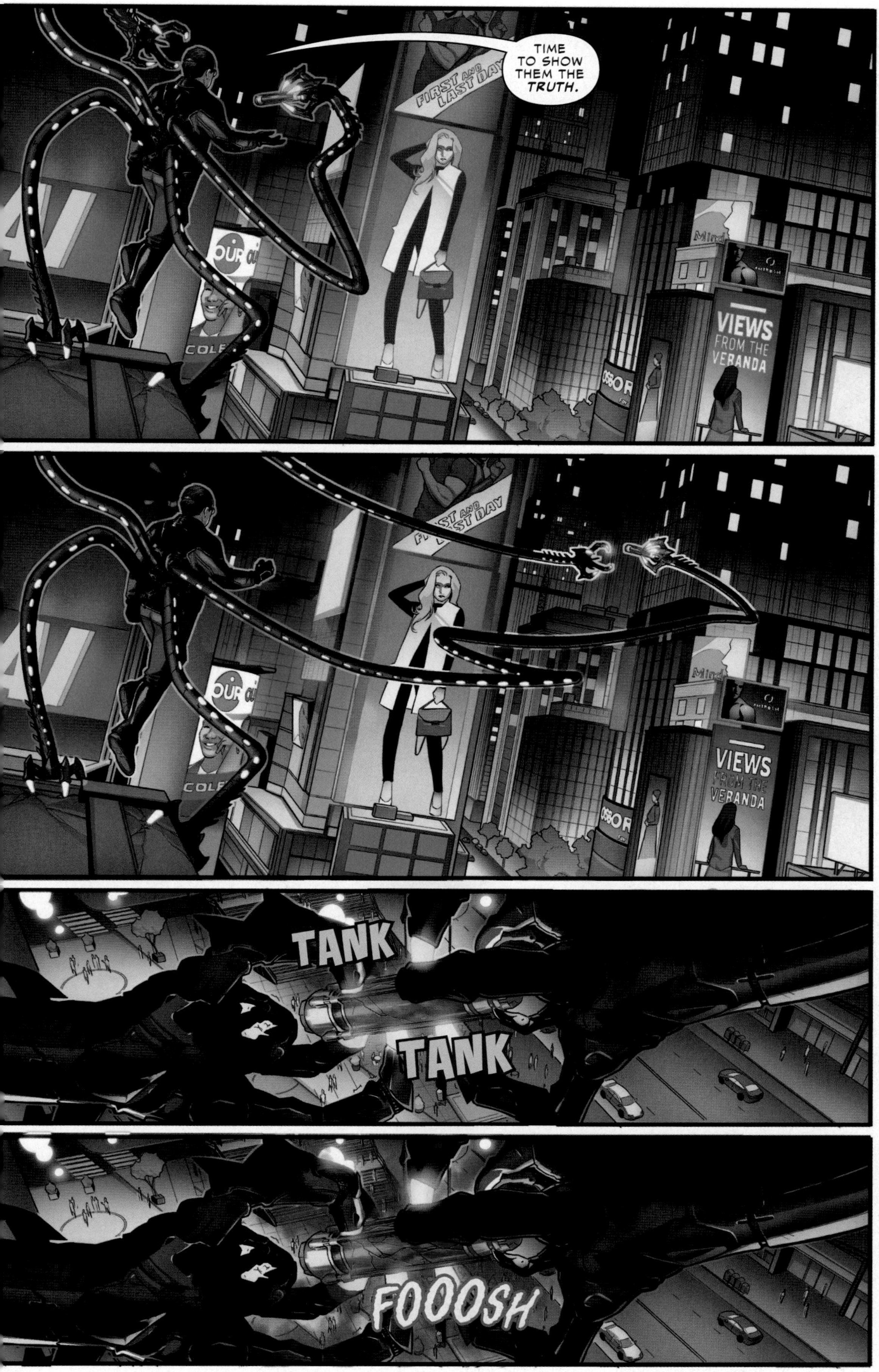
TIME TO SHOW THEM THE *TRUTH.*
FIRST AND LAST DAY
VIEWS FROM THE VERANDA
FIRST AND LAST DAY
VIEWS FROM THE VERANDA
TANK
TANK
FOOOSH

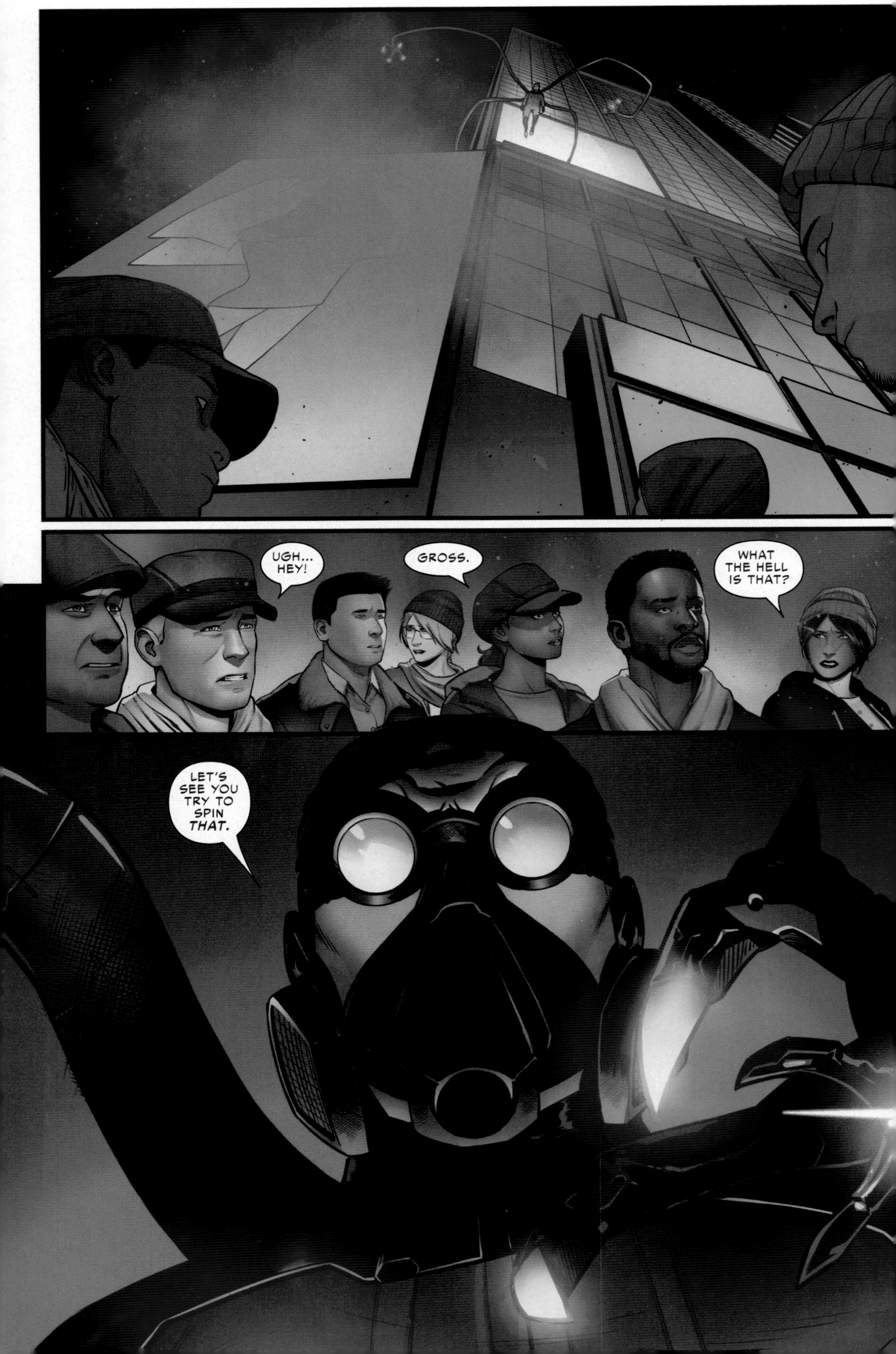
UGH... HEY!
GROSS.
WHAT THE HELL IS THAT?
LET'S SEE YOU TRY TO SPIN *THAT.*

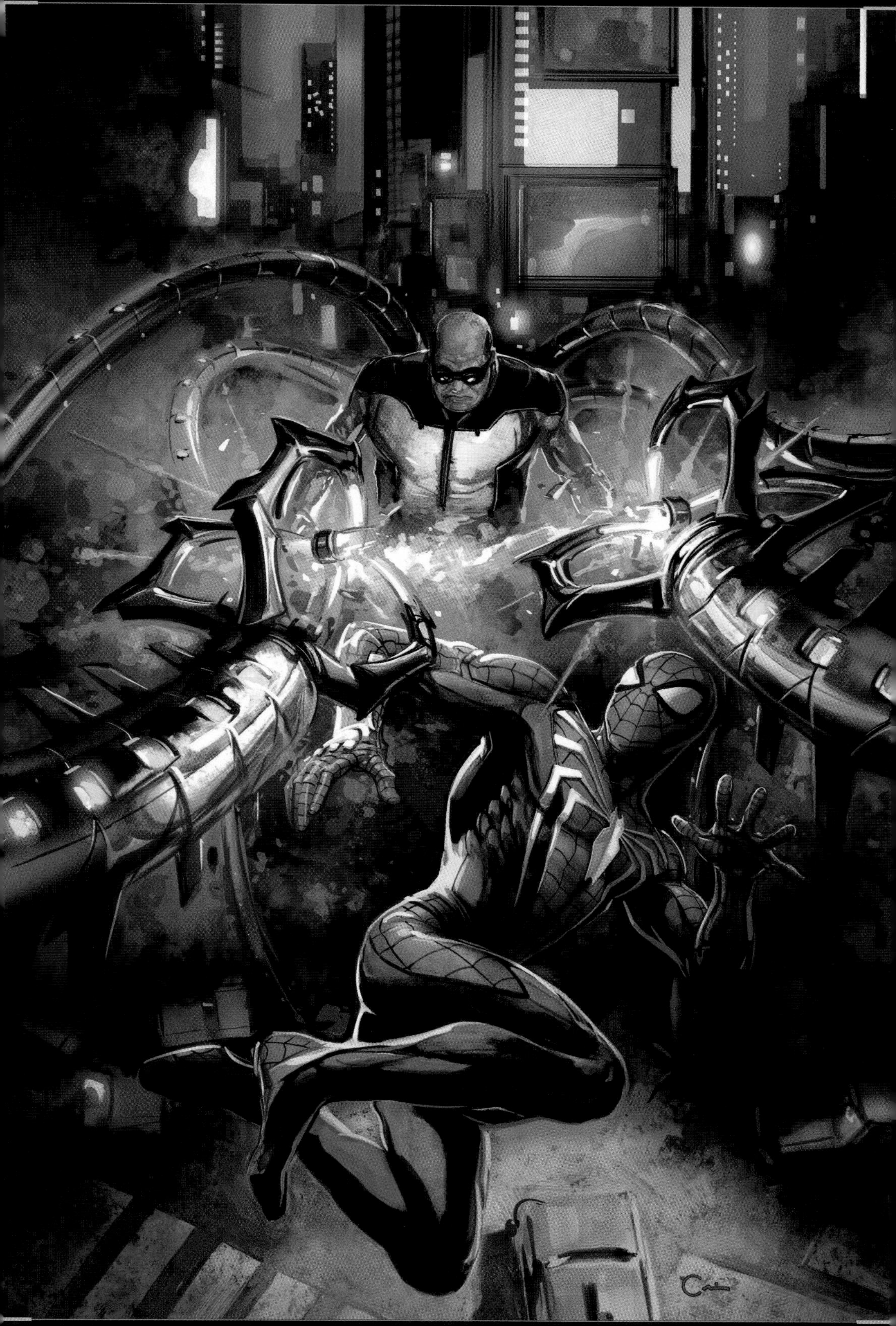

5

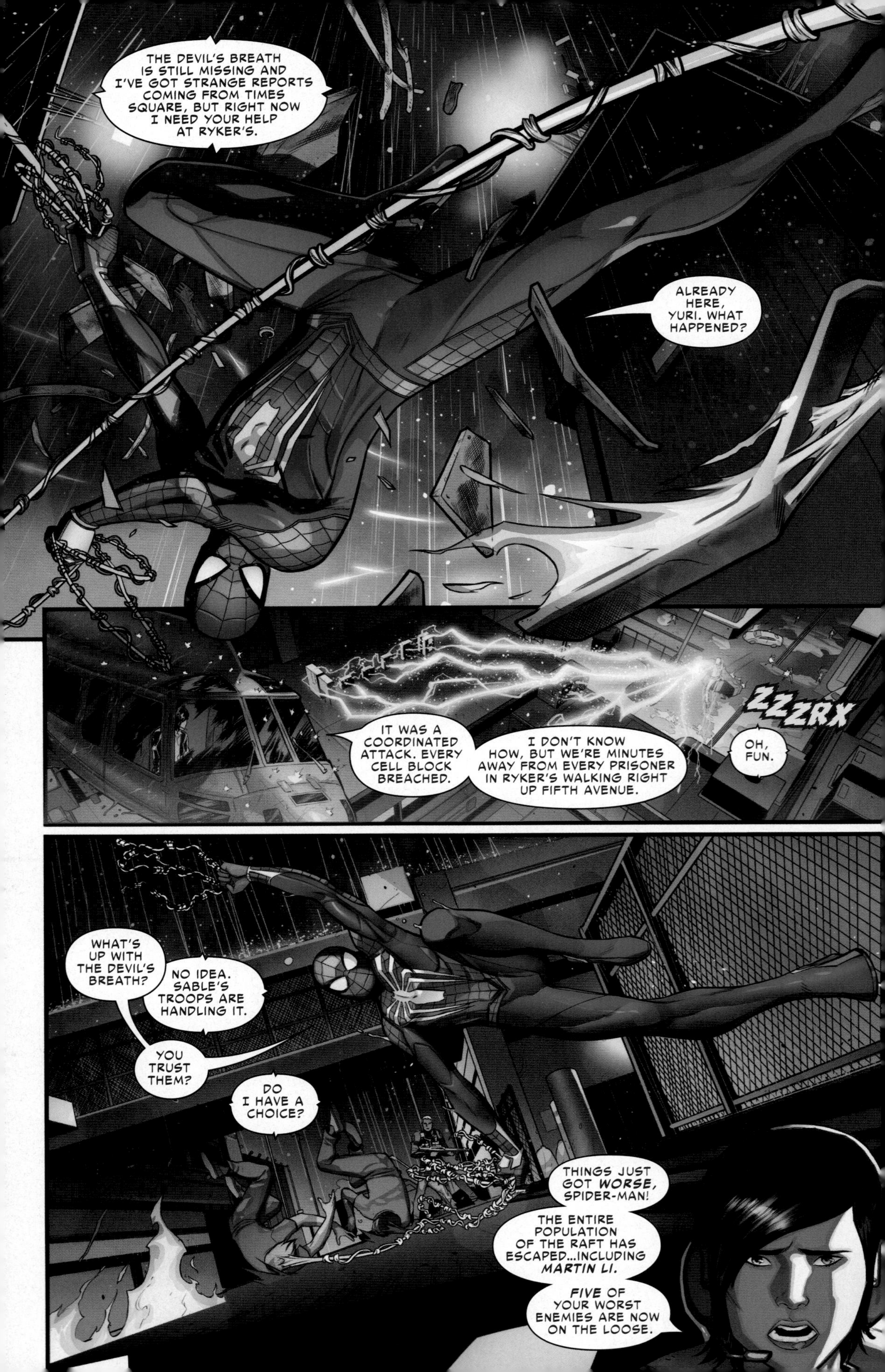
THE DEVIL'S BREATH IS STILL MISSING AND I'VE GOT STRANGE REPORTS COMING FROM TIMES SQUARE, BUT RIGHT NOW I NEED YOUR HELP AT RYKER'S.
ALREADY HERE, YURI. WHAT HAPPENED?
ZZZRX
IT WAS A COORDINATED ATTACK. EVERY CELL BLOCK BREACHED.
I DON'T KNOW HOW, BUT WE'RE MINUTES AWAY FROM EVERY PRISONER IN RYKER'S WALKING RIGHT UP FIFTH AVENUE.
OH, FUN.
WHAT'S UP WITH THE DEVIL'S BREATH?
NO IDEA. SABLE'S TROOPS ARE HANDLING IT.
YOU TRUST THEM?
DO I HAVE A CHOICE?
THINGS JUST GOT *WORSE*, SPIDER-MAN!
THE ENTIRE POPULATION OF THE RAFT HAS ESCAPED...INCLUDING *MARTIN LI*.
FIVE OF YOUR WORST ENEMIES ARE NOW ON THE LOOSE.

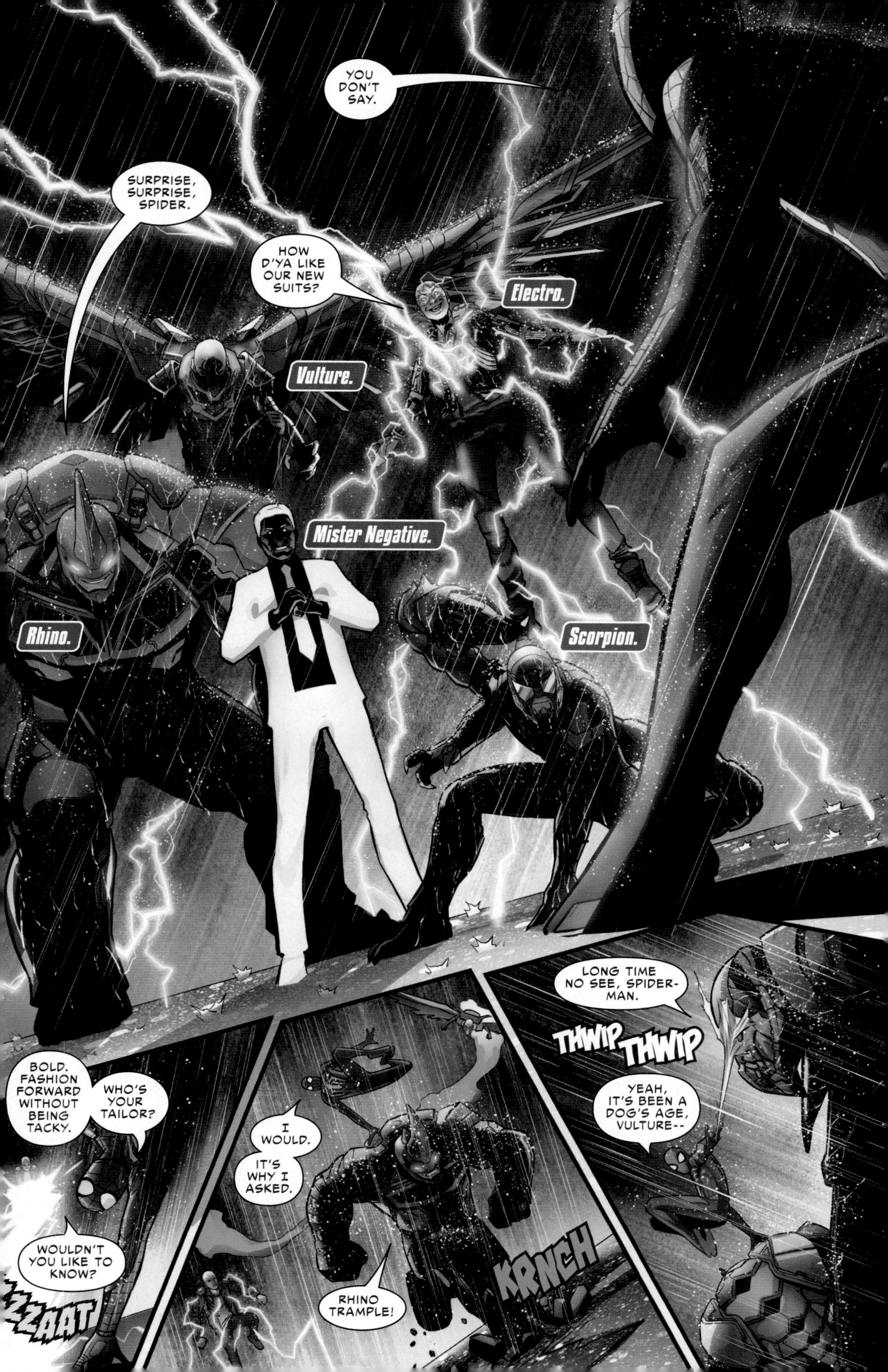

YOU DON'T SAY.
SURPRISE, SURPRISE, SPIDER.
HOW D'YA LIKE OUR NEW SUITS?
Electro.
Vulture.
Mister Negative.
Rhino.
Scorpion.
BOLD. FASHION FORWARD WITHOUT BEING TACKY.
WHO'S YOUR TAILOR?
WOULDN'T YOU LIKE TO KNOW?
ZZAAT
I WOULD.
IT'S WHY I ASKED.
RHINO TRAMPLE!
KRNCH
LONG TIME NO SEE, SPIDER-MAN.
THWIP THWIP
YEAH, IT'S BEEN A DOG'S AGE, VULTURE--

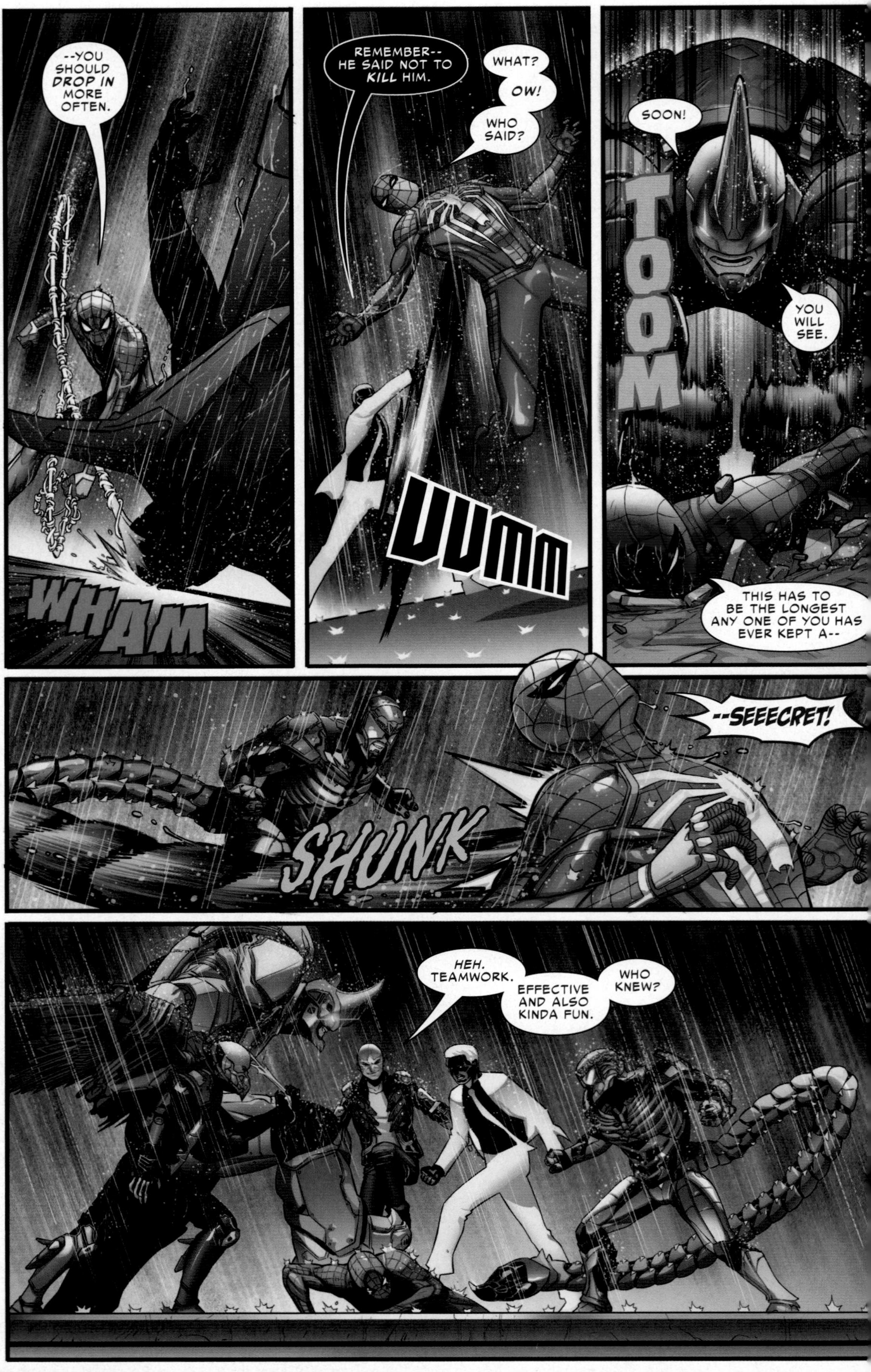

--YOU SHOULD DROP IN MORE OFTEN.
WHAM
REMEMBER-- HE SAID NOT TO KILL HIM.
WHAT?
OW!
WHO SAID?
VVMM
SOON!
TOOM
YOU WILL SEE.
THIS HAS TO BE THE LONGEST ANY ONE OF YOU HAS EVER KEPT A--
--SEEECRET!
SHUNK
HEH. TEAMWORK.
EFFECTIVE AND ALSO KINDA FUN.
WHO KNEW?

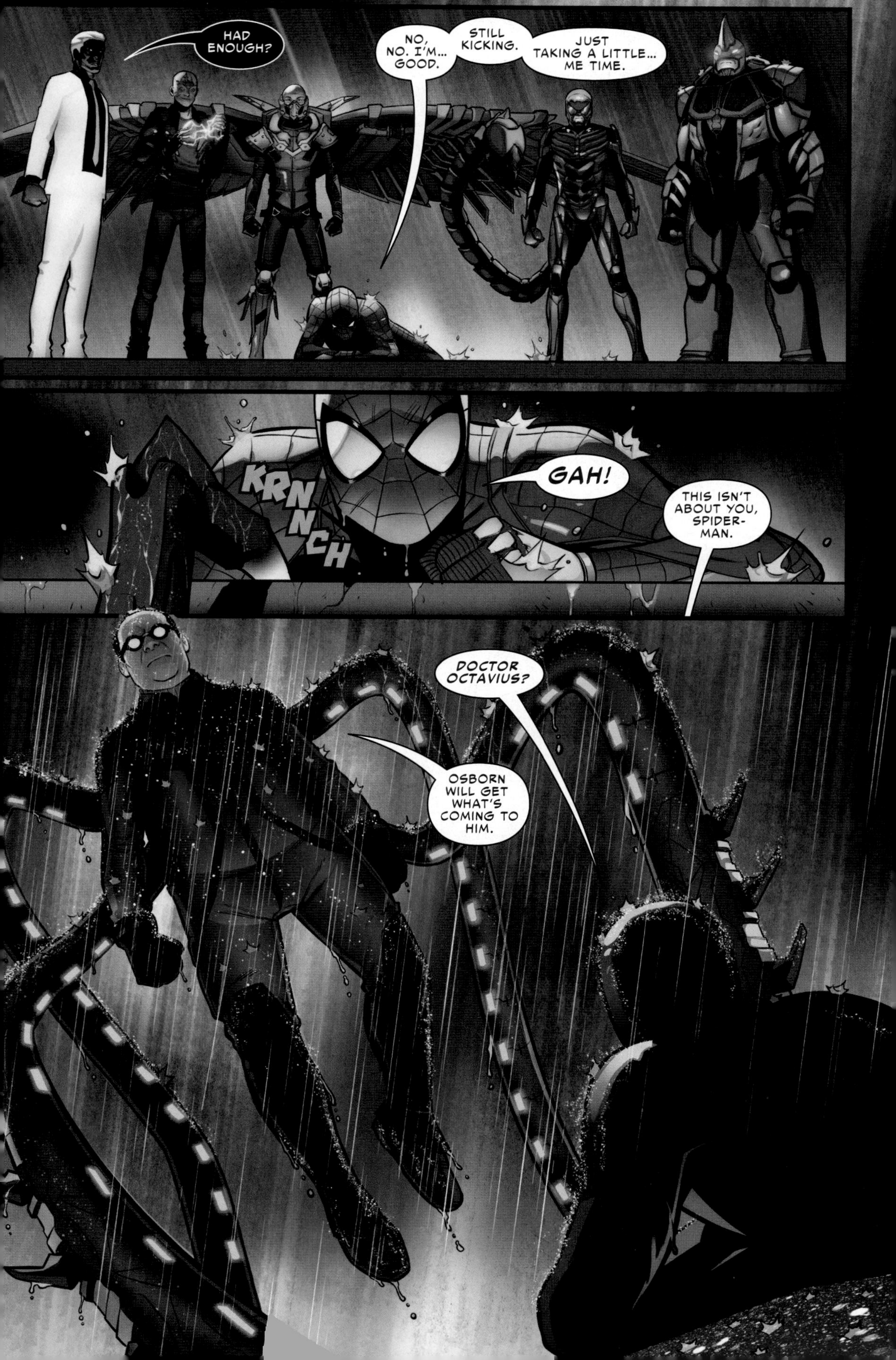
HAD ENOUGH?
NO, NO. I'M... GOOD.
STILL KICKING.
JUST TAKING A LITTLE... ME TIME.
KRNNCH
GAH!
THIS ISN'T ABOUT YOU, SPIDER-MAN.
DOCTOR OCTAVIUS?
OSBORN WILL GET WHAT'S COMING TO HIM.

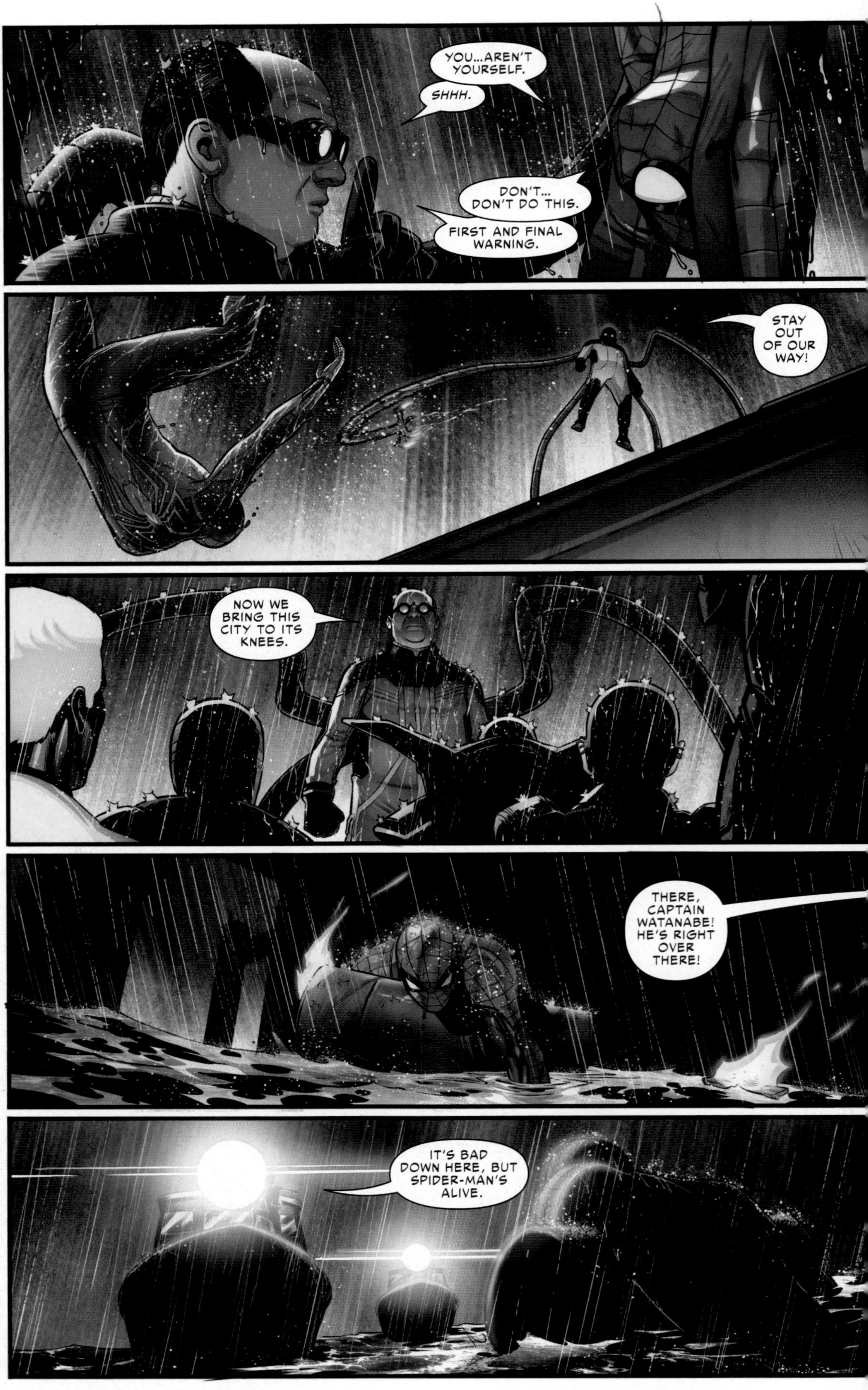
YOU...AREN'T YOURSELF.
SHHH.
DON'T... DON'T DO THIS.
FIRST AND FINAL WARNING.
STAY OUT OF OUR WAY!
NOW WE BRING THIS CITY TO ITS KNEES.
THERE, CAPTAIN WATANABE! HE'S RIGHT OVER THERE!
IT'S BAD DOWN HERE, BUT SPIDER-MAN'S ALIVE.

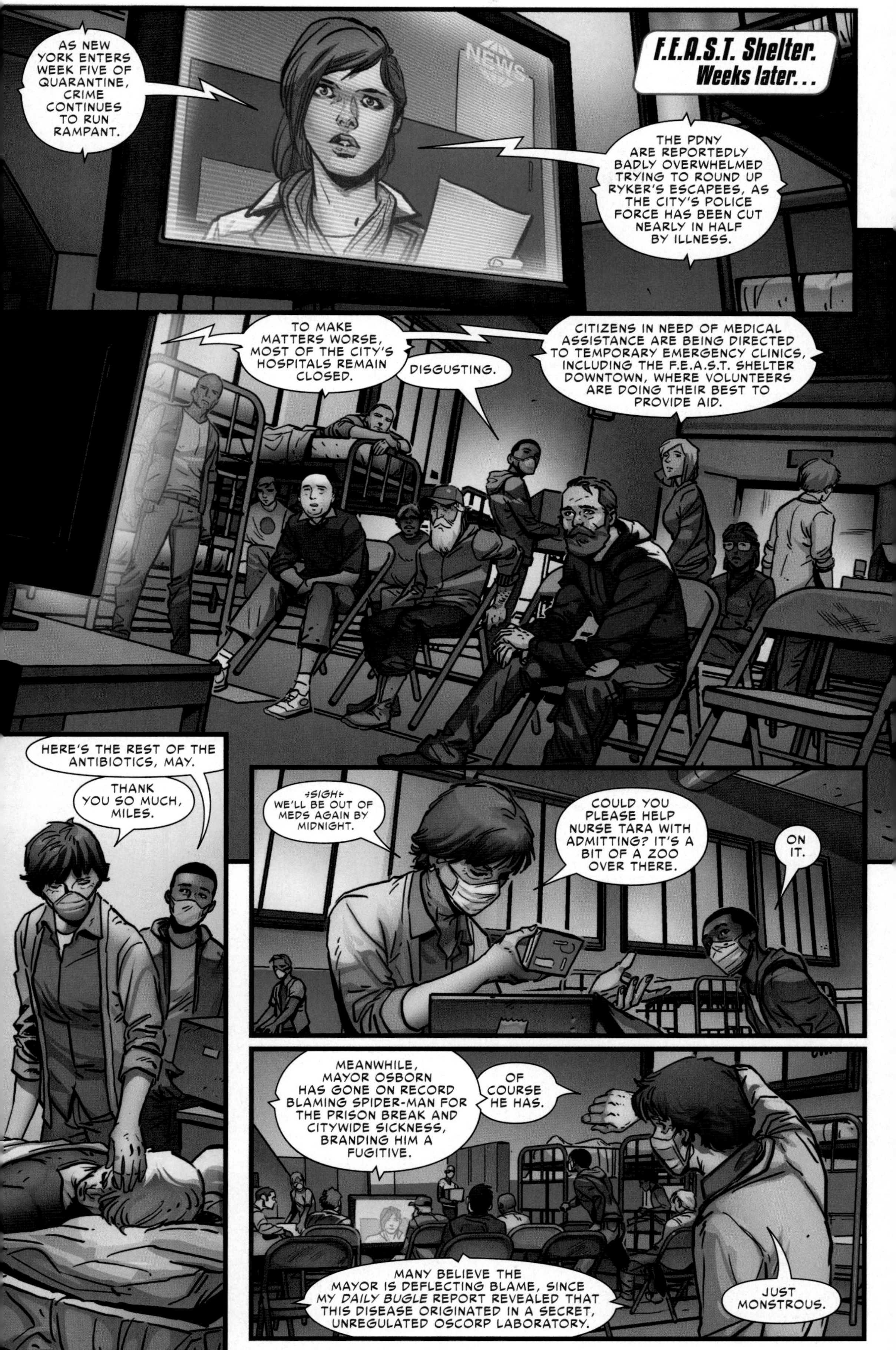
F.E.A.S.T. Shelter. Weeks later. . .
AS NEW YORK ENTERS WEEK FIVE OF QUARANTINE, CRIME CONTINUES TO RUN RAMPANT.
NEWS
THE PDNY ARE REPORTEDLY BADLY OVERWHELMED TRYING TO ROUND UP RYKER'S ESCAPEES, AS THE CITY'S POLICE FORCE HAS BEEN CUT NEARLY IN HALF BY ILLNESS.
TO MAKE MATTERS WORSE, MOST OF THE CITY'S HOSPITALS REMAIN CLOSED.
CITIZENS IN NEED OF MEDICAL ASSISTANCE ARE BEING DIRECTED TO TEMPORARY EMERGENCY CLINICS, INCLUDING THE F.E.A.S.T. SHELTER DOWNTOWN, WHERE VOLUNTEERS ARE DOING THEIR BEST TO PROVIDE AID.
DISGUSTING.
HERE'S THE REST OF THE ANTIBIOTICS, MAY.
THANK YOU SO MUCH, MILES.
SIGH WE'LL BE OUT OF MEDS AGAIN BY MIDNIGHT.
COULD YOU PLEASE HELP NURSE TARA WITH ADMITTING? IT'S A BIT OF A ZOO OVER THERE.
ON IT.
MEANWHILE, MAYOR OSBORN HAS GONE ON RECORD BLAMING SPIDER-MAN FOR THE PRISON BREAK AND CITYWIDE SICKNESS, BRANDING HIM A FUGITIVE.
OF COURSE HE HAS.
MANY BELIEVE THE MAYOR IS DEFLECTING BLAME, SINCE MY DAILY BUGLE REPORT REVEALED THAT THIS DISEASE ORIGINATED IN A SECRET, UNREGULATED OSCORP LABORATORY.
JUST MONSTROUS.

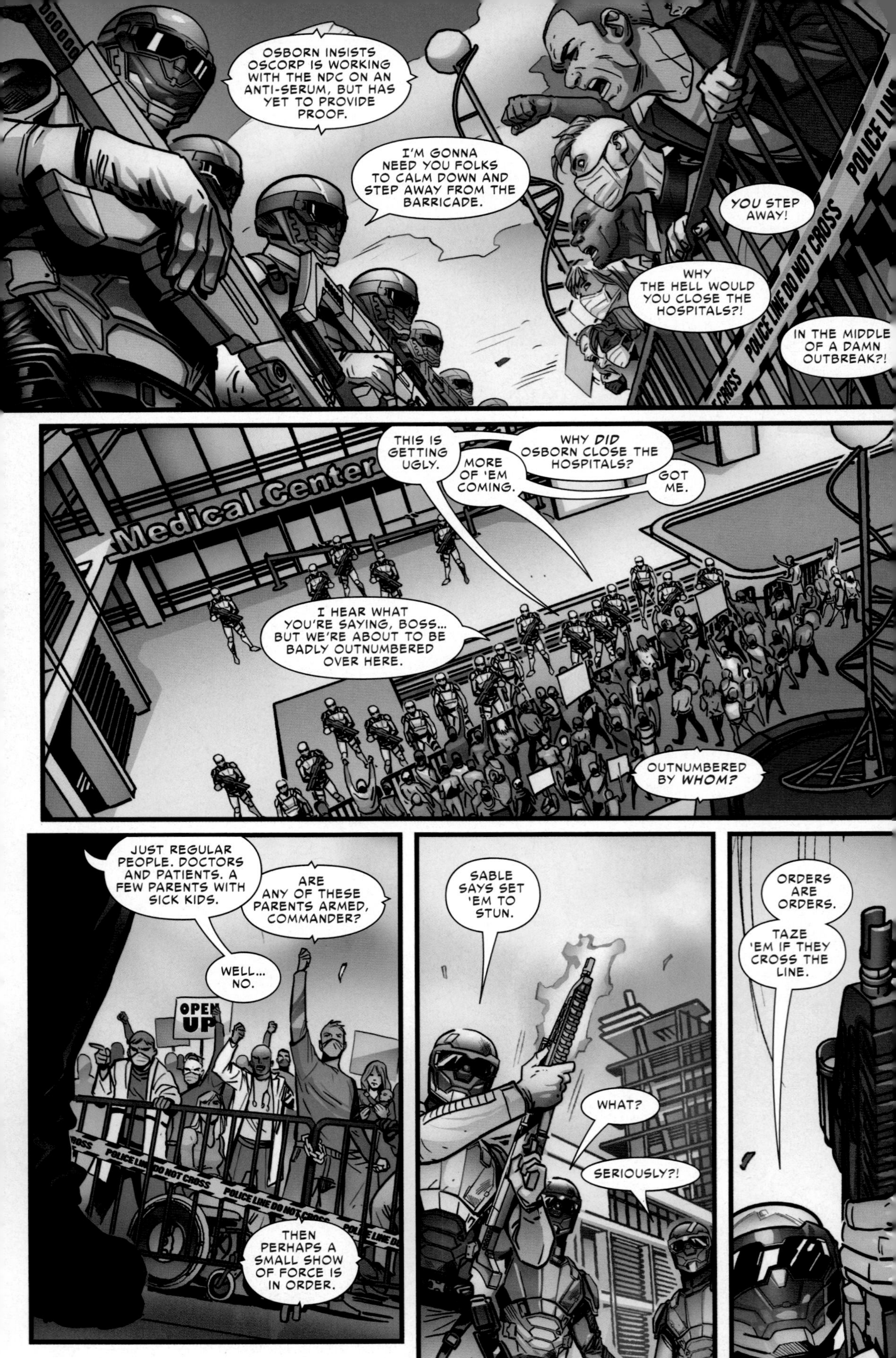
OSBORN INSISTS OSCORP IS WORKING WITH THE NDC ON AN ANTI-SERUM, BUT HAS YET TO PROVIDE PROOF.
I'M GONNA NEED YOU FOLKS TO CALM DOWN AND STEP AWAY FROM THE BARRICADE.
YOU STEP AWAY!
WHY THE HELL WOULD YOU CLOSE THE HOSPITALS?!
IN THE MIDDLE OF A DAMN OUTBREAK?!
POLICE LINE DO NOT CROSS
Medical Center
THIS IS GETTING UGLY.
MORE OF 'EM COMING.
WHY *DID* OSBORN CLOSE THE HOSPITALS?
GOT ME.
I HEAR WHAT YOU'RE SAYING, BOSS... BUT WE'RE ABOUT TO BE BADLY OUTNUMBERED OVER HERE.
OUTNUMBERED BY *WHOM?*
JUST REGULAR PEOPLE. DOCTORS AND PATIENTS. A FEW PARENTS WITH SICK KIDS.
ARE ANY OF THESE PARENTS ARMED, COMMANDER?
WELL... NO.
OPEN UP
THEN PERHAPS A SMALL SHOW OF FORCE IS IN ORDER.
SABLE SAYS SET 'EM TO STUN.
WHAT?
SERIOUSLY?!
ORDERS ARE ORDERS.
TAZE 'EM IF THEY CROSS THE LINE.

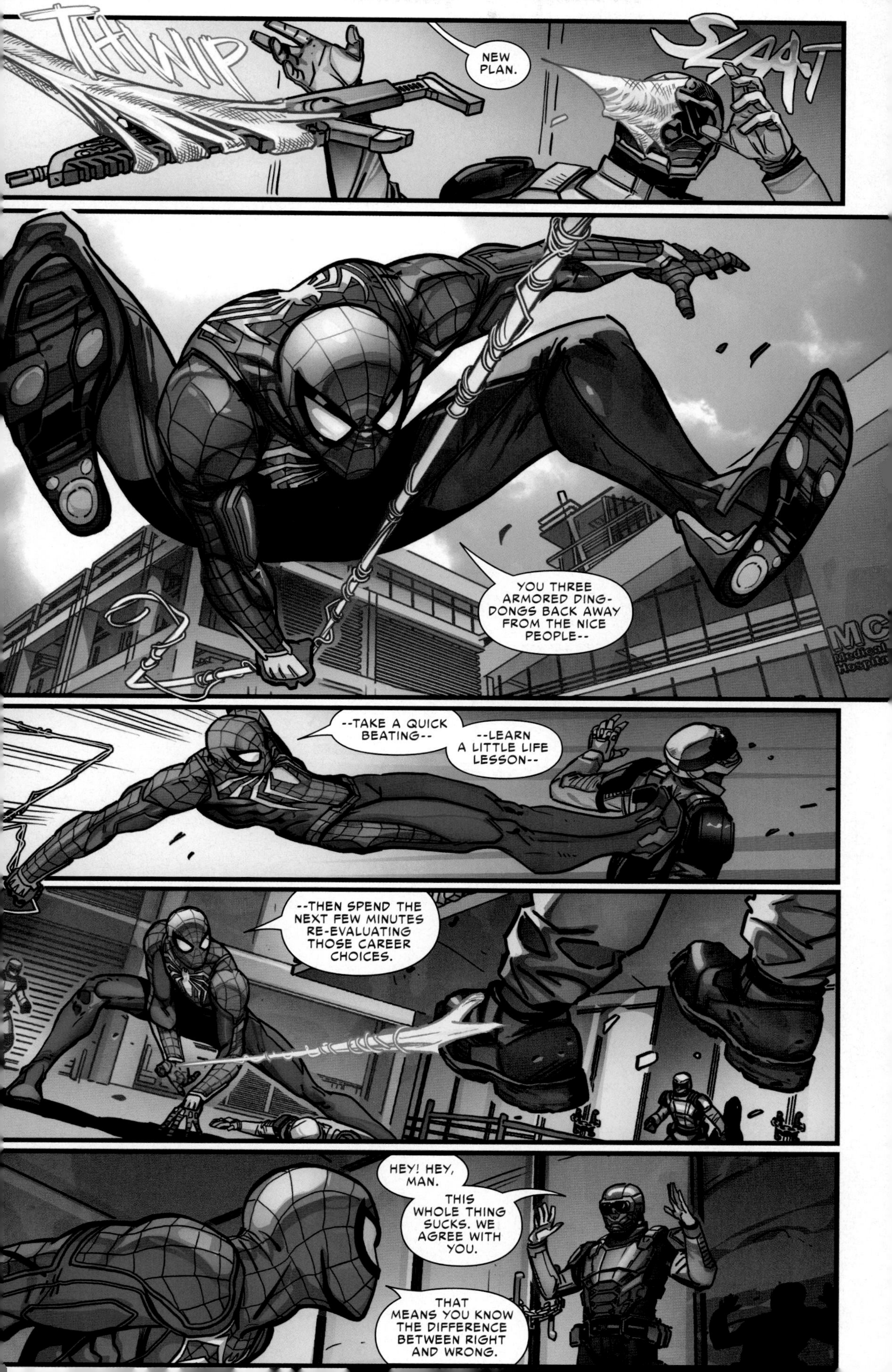
THWIP
NEW PLAN.
ZAAT
YOU THREE ARMORED DING-DONGS BACK AWAY FROM THE NICE PEOPLE--
MC
Medical
Hospita
--TAKE A QUICK BEATING--
--LEARN A LITTLE LIFE LESSON--
--THEN SPEND THE NEXT FEW MINUTES RE-EVALUATING THOSE CAREER CHOICES.
HEY! HEY, MAN.
THIS WHOLE THING SUCKS. WE AGREE WITH YOU.
THAT MEANS YOU KNOW THE DIFFERENCE BETWEEN RIGHT AND WRONG.

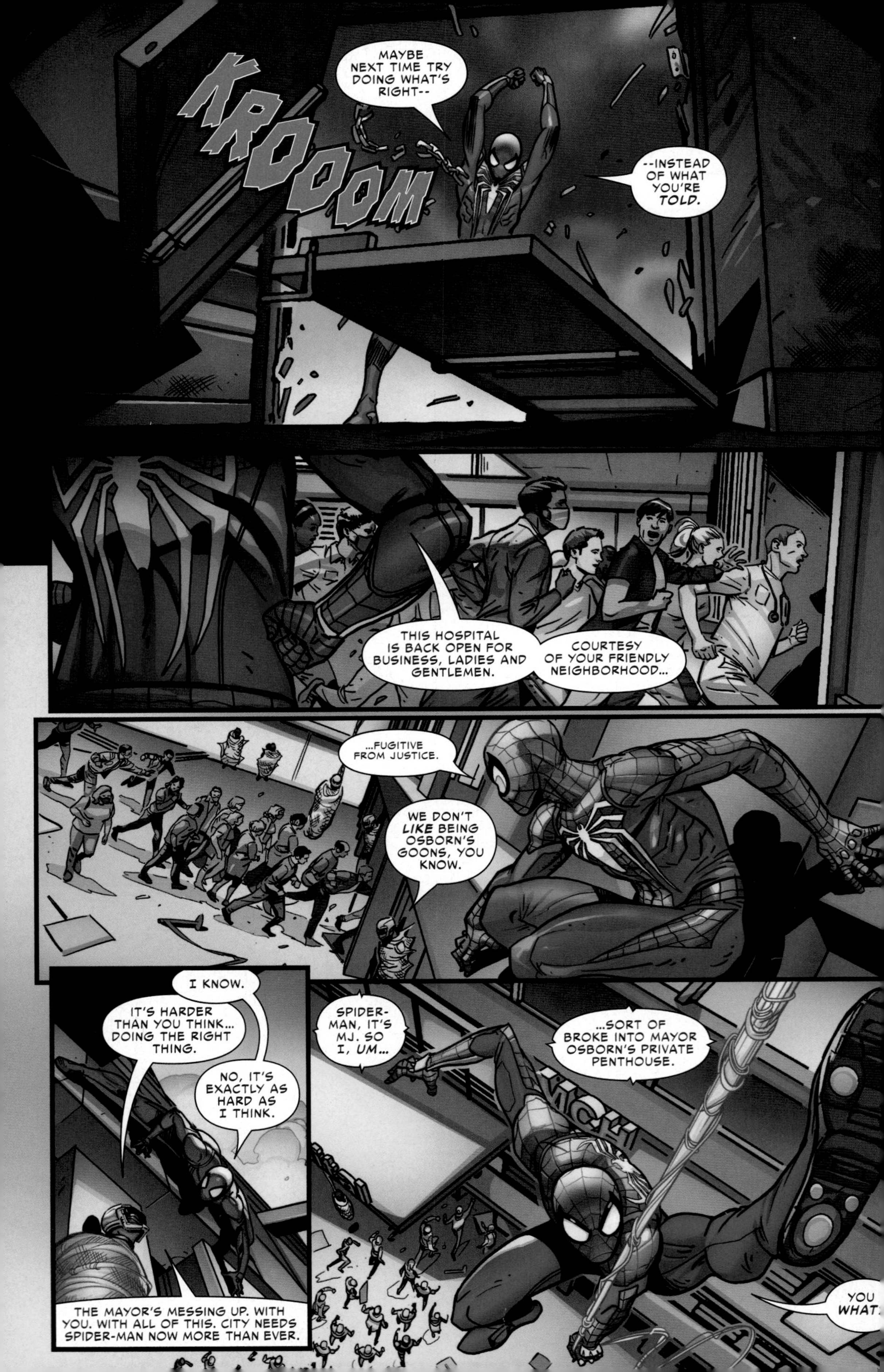
KROOOM
MAYBE NEXT TIME TRY DOING WHAT'S RIGHT--
--INSTEAD OF WHAT YOU'RE TOLD.
THIS HOSPITAL IS BACK OPEN FOR BUSINESS, LADIES AND GENTLEMEN.
COURTESY OF YOUR FRIENDLY NEIGHBORHOOD...
...FUGITIVE FROM JUSTICE.
WE DON'T LIKE BEING OSBORN'S GOONS, YOU KNOW.
I KNOW.
IT'S HARDER THAN YOU THINK... DOING THE RIGHT THING.
NO, IT'S EXACTLY AS HARD AS I THINK.
THE MAYOR'S MESSING UP. WITH YOU. WITH ALL OF THIS. CITY NEEDS SPIDER-MAN NOW MORE THAN EVER.
SPIDER-MAN, IT'S MJ. SO I, UM...
...SORT OF BROKE INTO MAYOR OSBORN'S PRIVATE PENTHOUSE.
YOU WHAT.

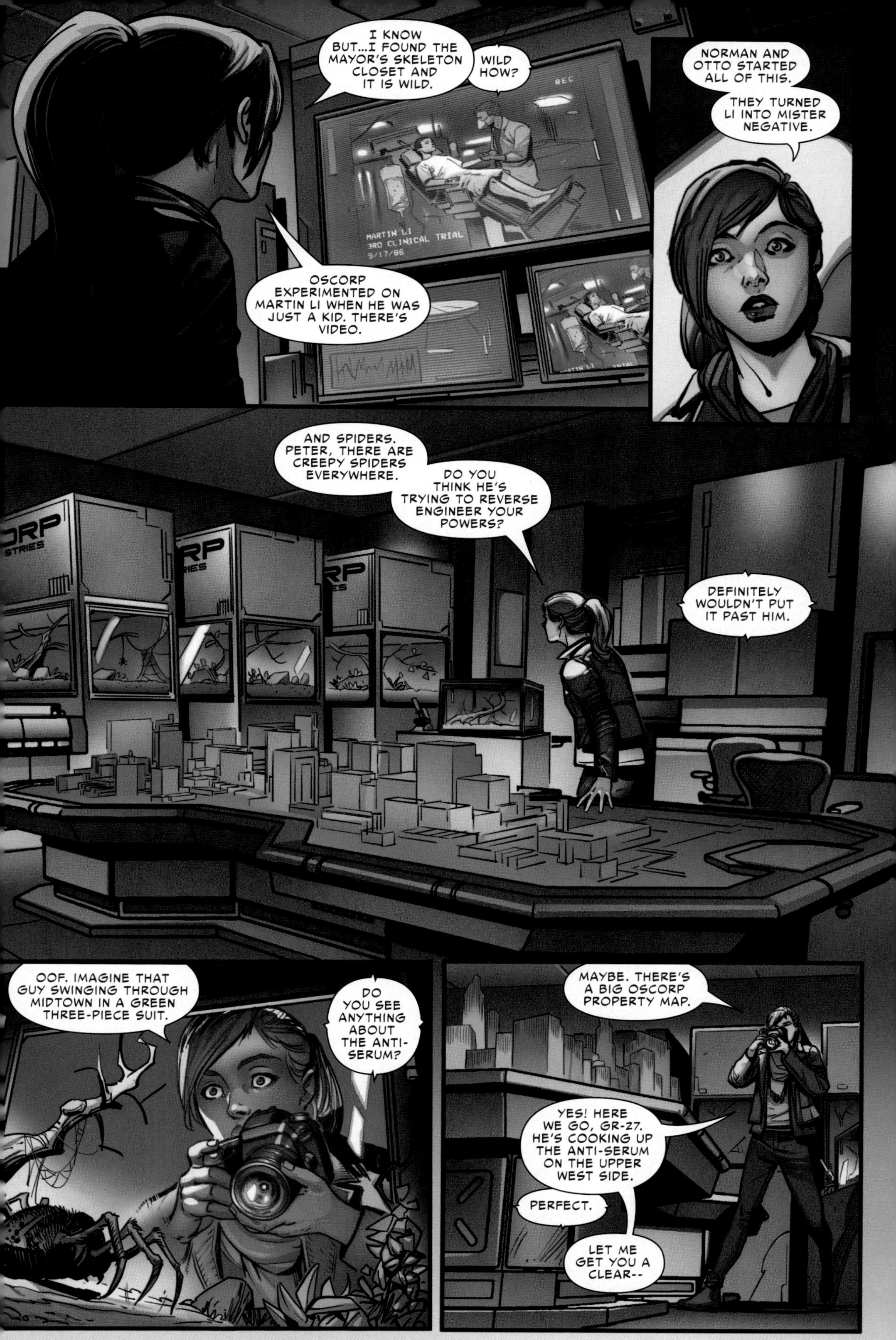
I KNOW BUT...I FOUND THE MAYOR'S SKELETON CLOSET AND IT IS WILD.
WILD HOW?
REC
MARTIN LI
3RD CLINICAL TRIAL
9/17/86
OSCORP EXPERIMENTED ON MARTIN LI WHEN HE WAS JUST A KID. THERE'S VIDEO.
NORMAN AND OTTO STARTED ALL OF THIS.
THEY TURNED LI INTO MISTER NEGATIVE.
AND SPIDERS. PETER, THERE ARE CREEPY SPIDERS EVERYWHERE.
DO YOU THINK HE'S TRYING TO REVERSE ENGINEER YOUR POWERS?
DEFINITELY WOULDN'T PUT IT PAST HIM.
OOF. IMAGINE THAT GUY SWINGING THROUGH MIDTOWN IN A GREEN THREE-PIECE SUIT.
DO YOU SEE ANYTHING ABOUT THE ANTI-SERUM?
MAYBE. THERE'S A BIG OSCORP PROPERTY MAP.
YES! HERE WE GO, GR-27. HE'S COOKING UP THE ANTI-SERUM ON THE UPPER WEST SIDE.
PERFECT.
LET ME GET YOU A CLEAR--

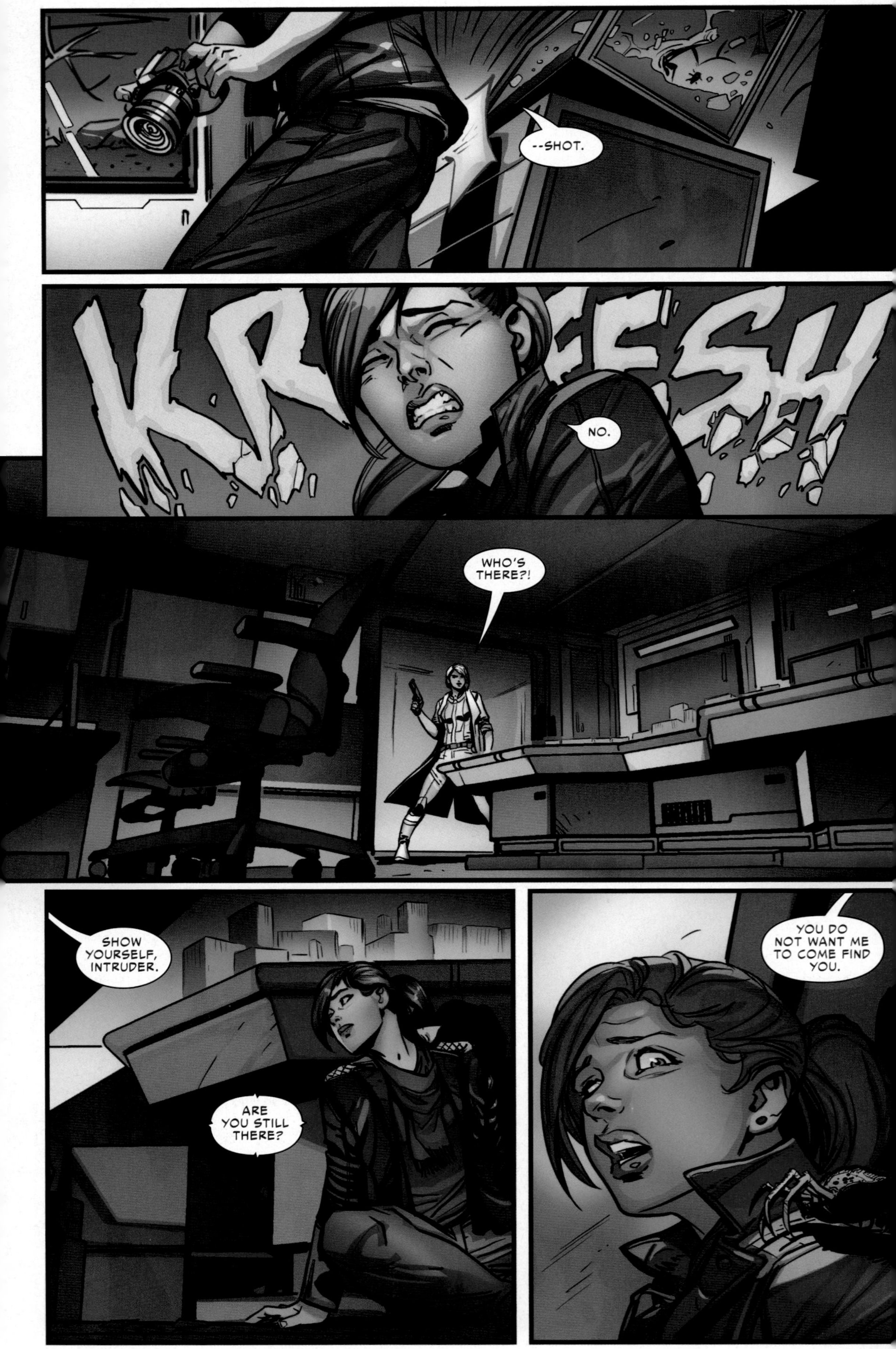
--SHOT.
KRSSH
NO.
WHO'S THERE?!
SHOW YOURSELF, INTRUDER.
ARE YOU STILL THERE?
YOU DO NOT WANT ME TO COME FIND YOU.

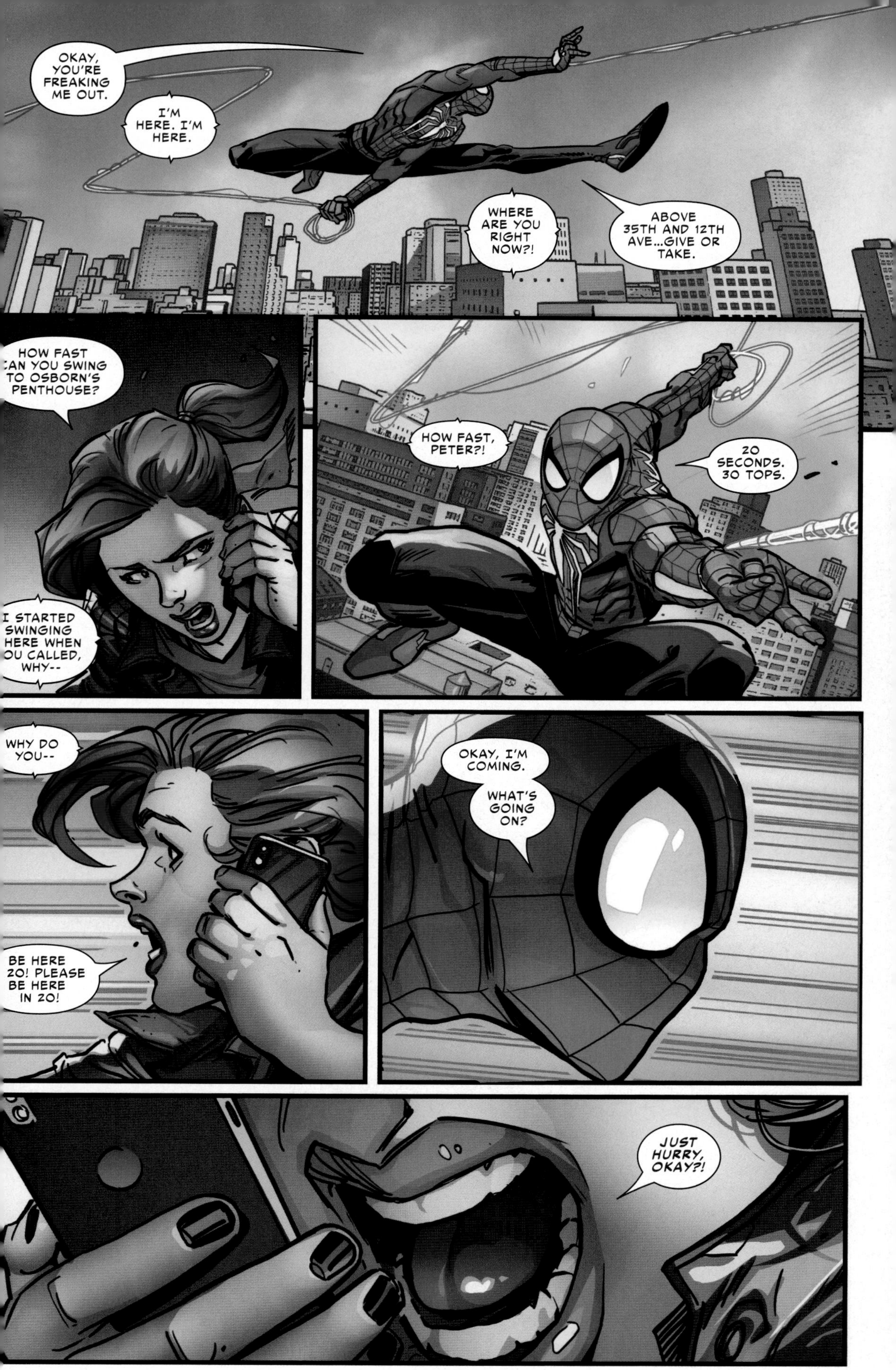
OKAY, YOU'RE FREAKING ME OUT.
I'M HERE. I'M HERE.
WHERE ARE YOU RIGHT NOW?!
ABOVE 35TH AND 12TH AVE...GIVE OR TAKE.
HOW FAST CAN YOU SWING TO OSBORN'S PENTHOUSE?
I STARTED SWINGING HERE WHEN OU CALLED, WHY--
HOW FAST, PETER?!
20 SECONDS. 30 TOPS.
WHY DO YOU--
BE HERE 20! PLEASE BE HERE IN 20!
OKAY, I'M COMING.
WHAT'S GOING ON?
JUST HURRY, OKAY?!

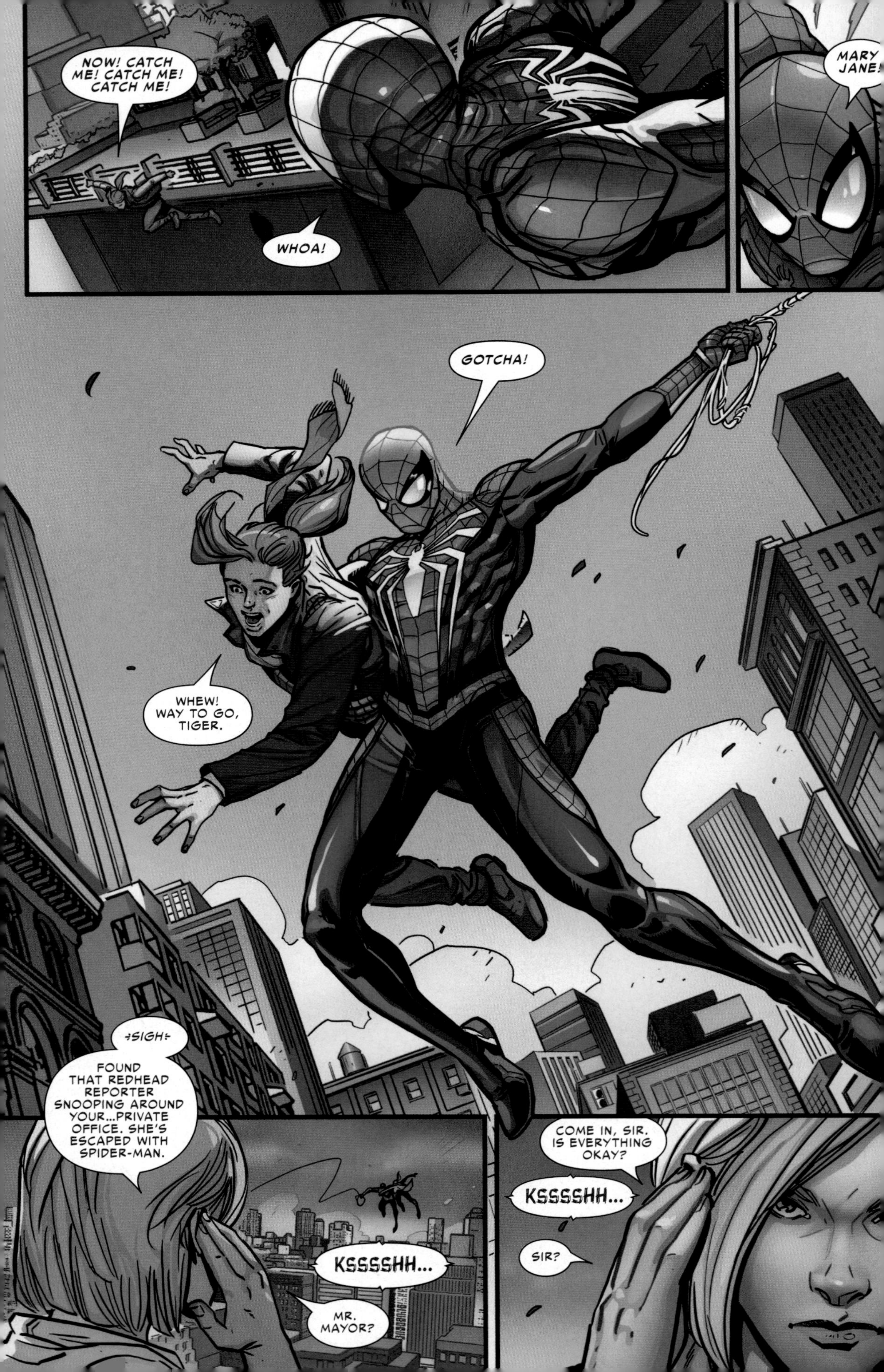
NOW! CATCH ME! CATCH ME! CATCH ME!
WHOA!
MARY JANE!
GOTCHA!
WHEW! WAY TO GO, TIGER.
-SIGH-
FOUND THAT REDHEAD REPORTER SNOOPING AROUND YOUR...PRIVATE OFFICE. SHE'S ESCAPED WITH SPIDER-MAN.
KSSSSHH...
MR. MAYOR?
COME IN, SIR. IS EVERYTHING OKAY?
KSSSSHH...
SIR?

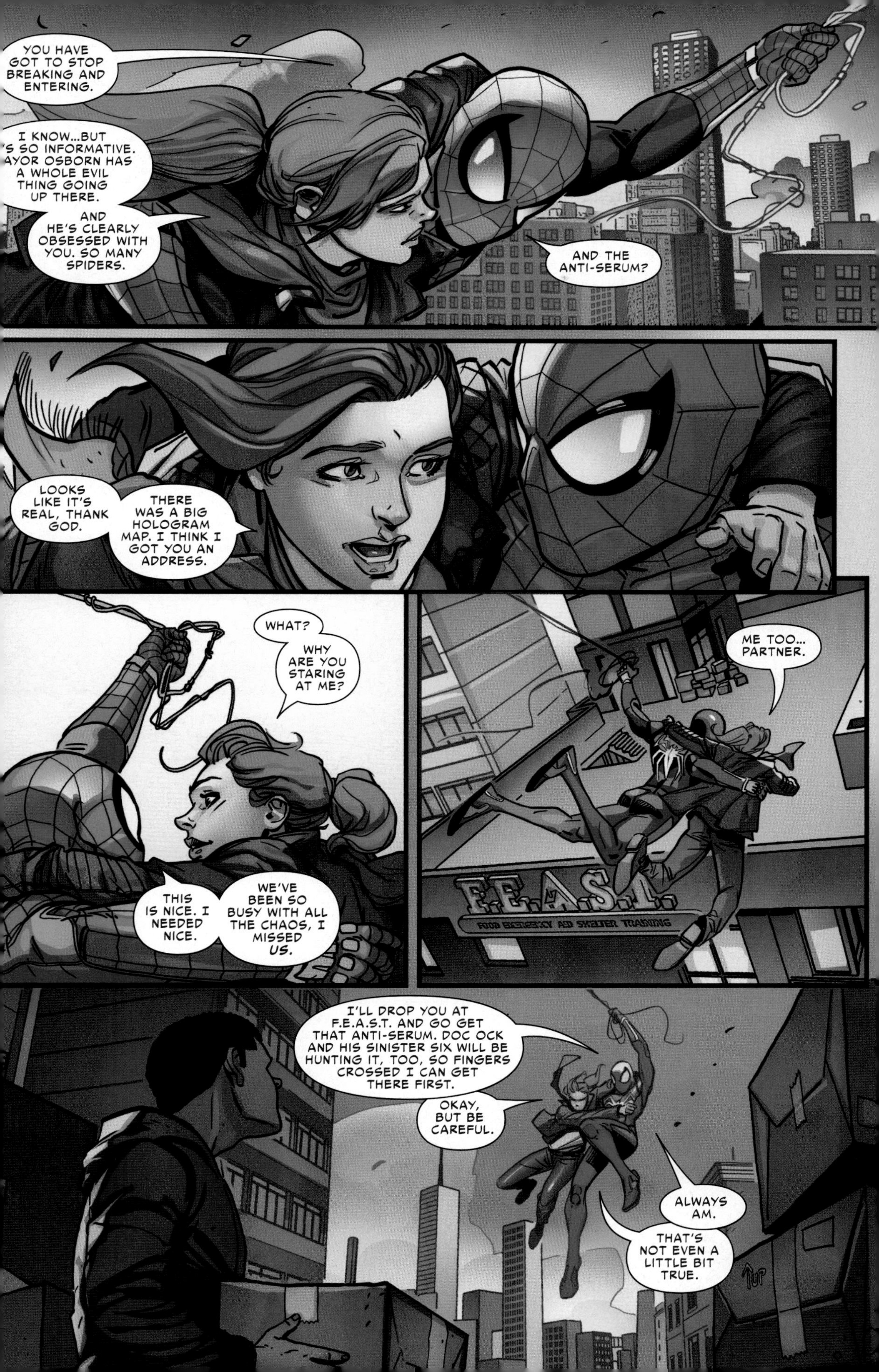
YOU HAVE GOT TO STOP BREAKING AND ENTERING.
I KNOW...BUT 'S SO INFORMATIVE. AYOR OSBORN HAS A WHOLE EVIL THING GOING UP THERE.
AND HE'S CLEARLY OBSESSED WITH YOU. SO MANY SPIDERS.
AND THE ANTI-SERUM?
LOOKS LIKE IT'S REAL, THANK GOD.
THERE WAS A BIG HOLOGRAM MAP. I THINK I GOT YOU AN ADDRESS.
WHAT?
WHY ARE YOU STARING AT ME?
THIS IS NICE. I NEEDED NICE.
WE'VE BEEN SO BUSY WITH ALL THE CHAOS, I MISSED *US*.
ME TOO... PARTNER.
F.E.A.S.T.
FOOD EMERGENCY AID SHELTER TRAINING
I'LL DROP YOU AT F.E.A.S.T. AND GO GET THAT ANTI-SERUM. DOC OCK AND HIS SINISTER SIX WILL BE HUNTING IT, TOO, SO FINGERS CROSSED I CAN GET THERE FIRST.
OKAY, BUT BE CAREFUL.
ALWAYS AM.
THAT'S NOT EVEN A LITTLE BIT TRUE.

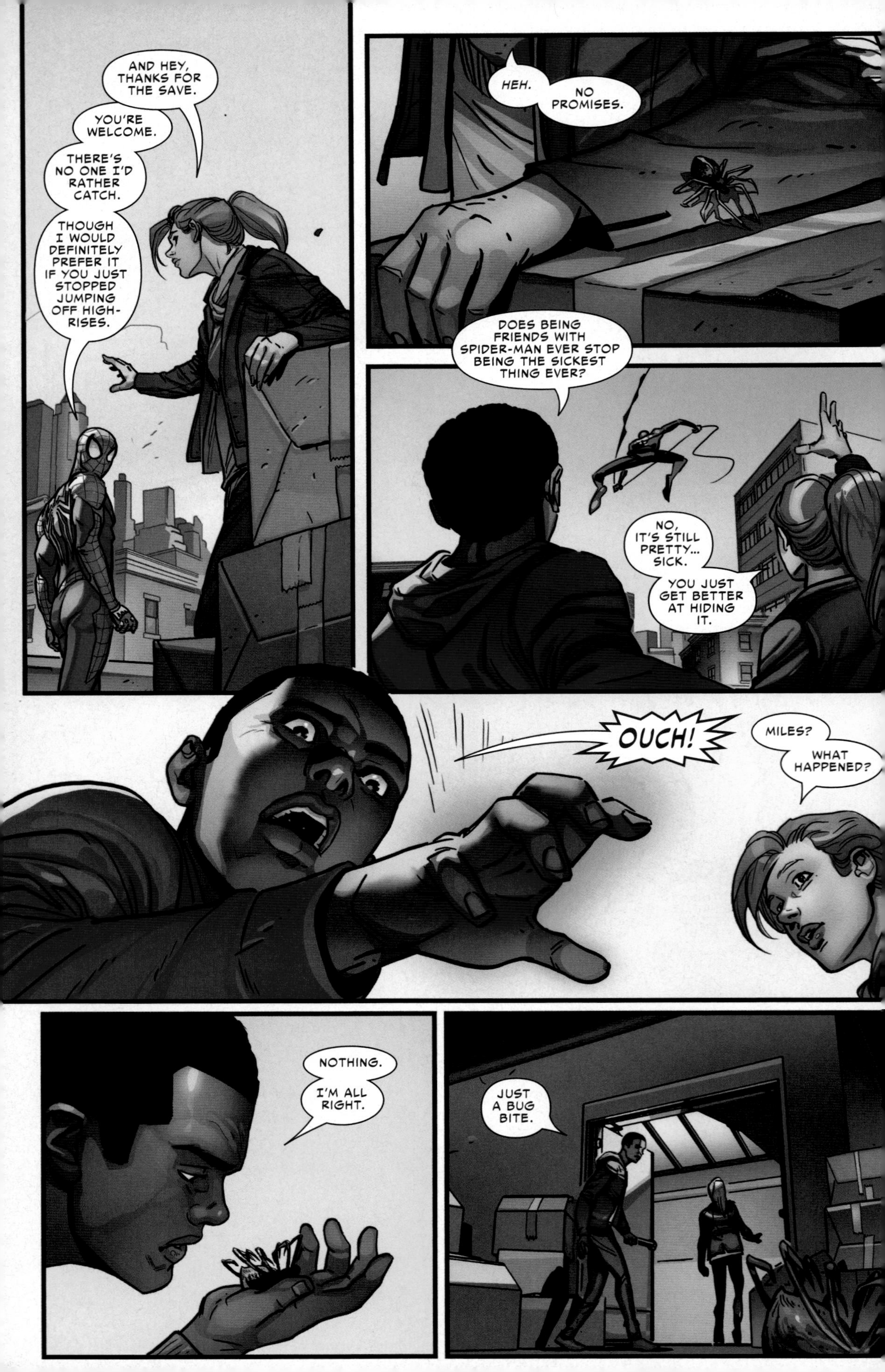
AND HEY, THANKS FOR THE SAVE.
YOU'RE WELCOME.
THERE'S NO ONE I'D RATHER CATCH.
THOUGH I WOULD DEFINITELY PREFER IT IF YOU JUST STOPPED JUMPING OFF HIGH-RISES.
HEH.
NO PROMISES.
DOES BEING FRIENDS WITH SPIDER-MAN EVER STOP BEING THE SICKEST THING EVER?
NO, IT'S STILL PRETTY... SICK.
YOU JUST GET BETTER AT HIDING IT.
OUCH!
MILES?
WHAT HAPPENED?
NOTHING.
I'M ALL RIGHT.
JUST A BUG BITE.

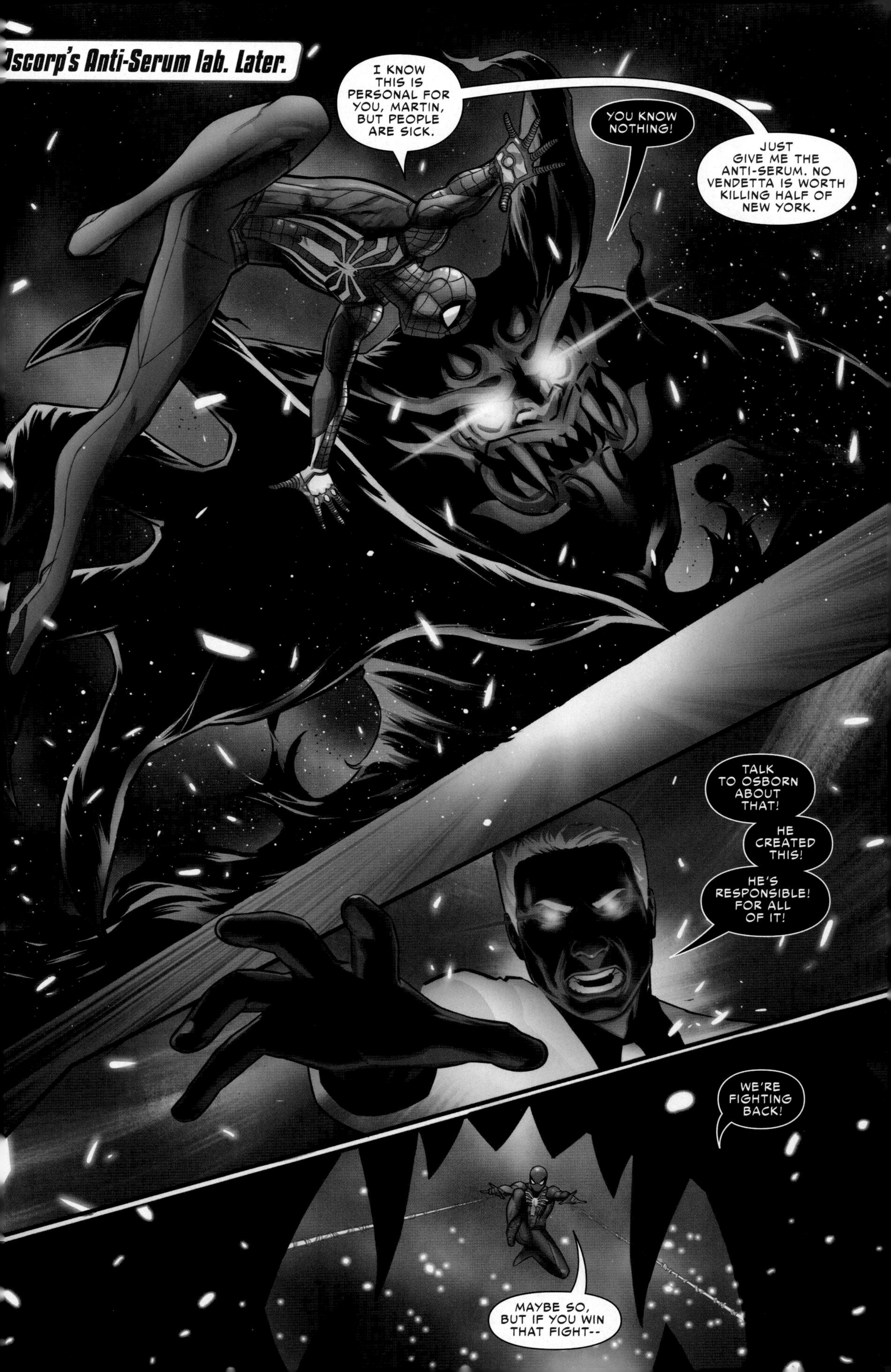

Oscorp's Anti-Serum lab. Later.
I KNOW THIS IS PERSONAL FOR YOU, MARTIN, BUT PEOPLE ARE SICK.
YOU KNOW NOTHING!
JUST GIVE ME THE ANTI-SERUM. NO VENDETTA IS WORTH KILLING HALF OF NEW YORK.
TALK TO OSBORN ABOUT THAT!
HE CREATED THIS!
HE'S RESPONSIBLE! FOR ALL OF IT!
WE'RE FIGHTING BACK!
MAYBE SO, BUT IF YOU WIN THAT FIGHT--

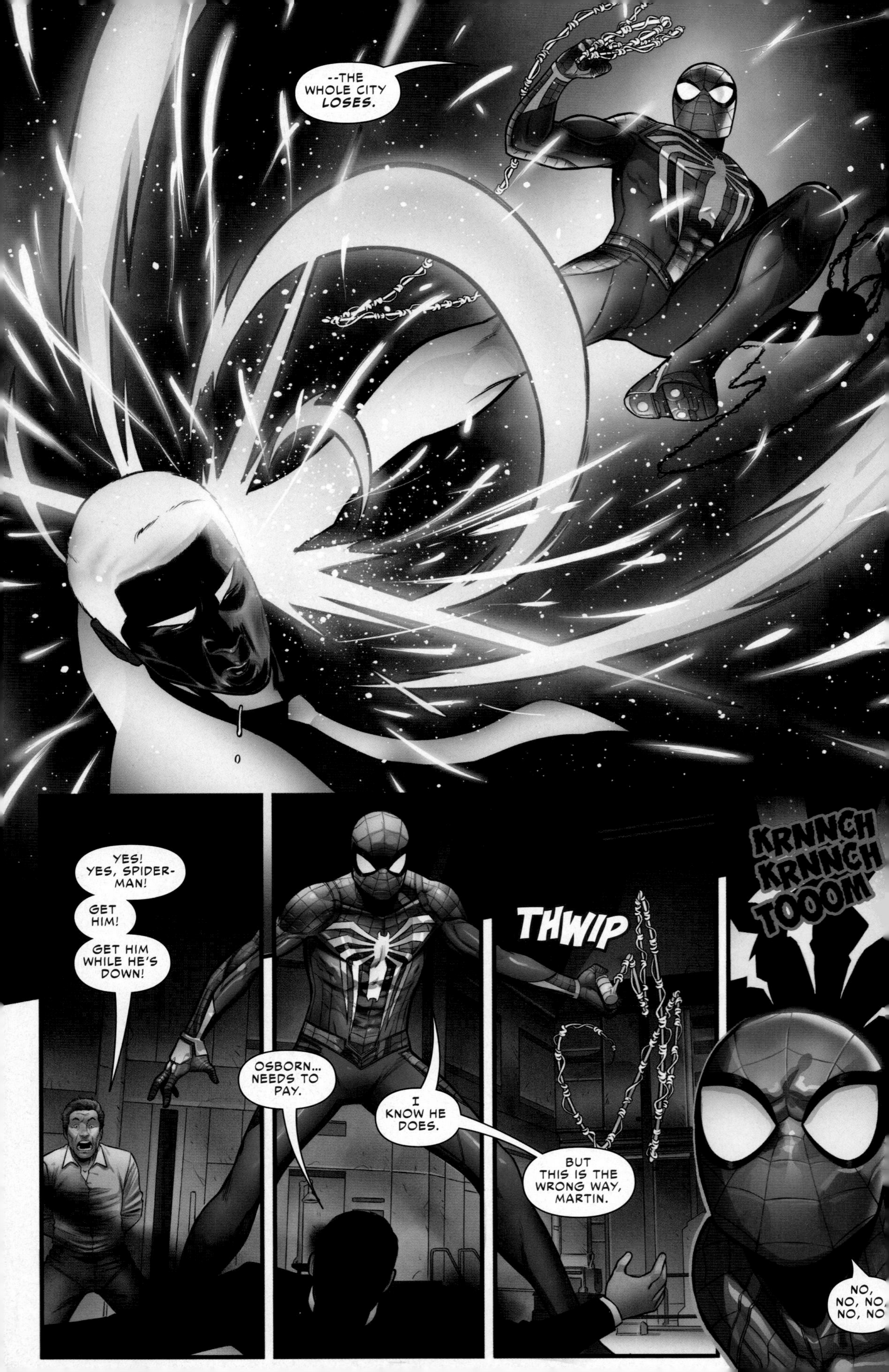
--THE WHOLE CITY *LOSES.*
YES! YES, SPIDER-MAN!
GET HIM!
GET HIM WHILE HE'S DOWN!
OSBORN... NEEDS TO PAY.
I KNOW HE DOES.
THWIP
BUT THIS IS THE WRONG WAY, MARTIN.
KRNNCH KRNNCH TOOOM
NO, NO, NO, NO, NO

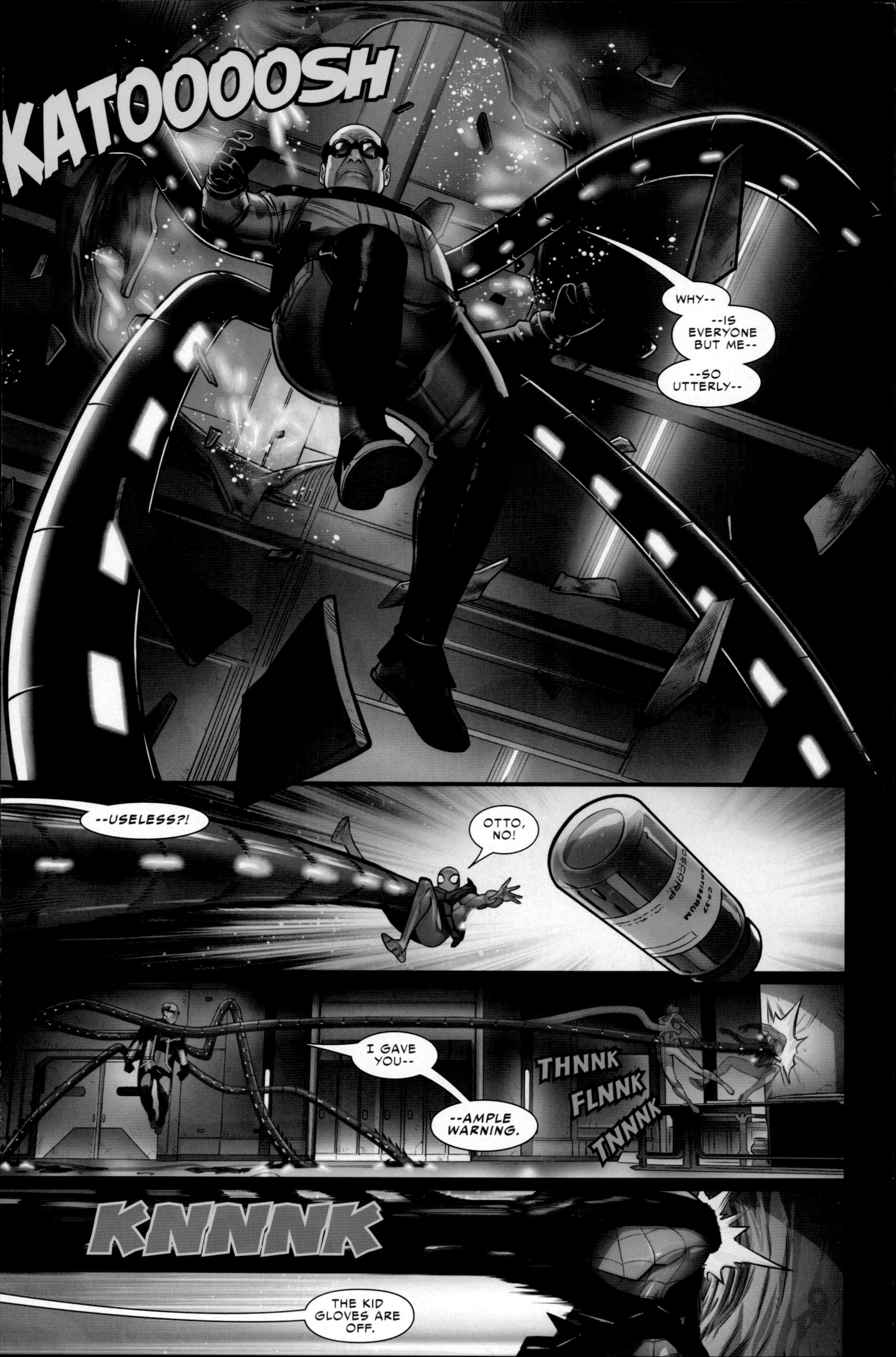
KATOOOOSH
WHY--
--IS EVERYONE BUT ME--
--SO UTTERLY--
--USELESS?!
OTTO, NO!
OSCORP
CR-27
ANTISERUM
I GAVE YOU--
--AMPLE WARNING.
THNNK
FLNNK
TNNNK
KNNNK
THE KID GLOVES ARE OFF.

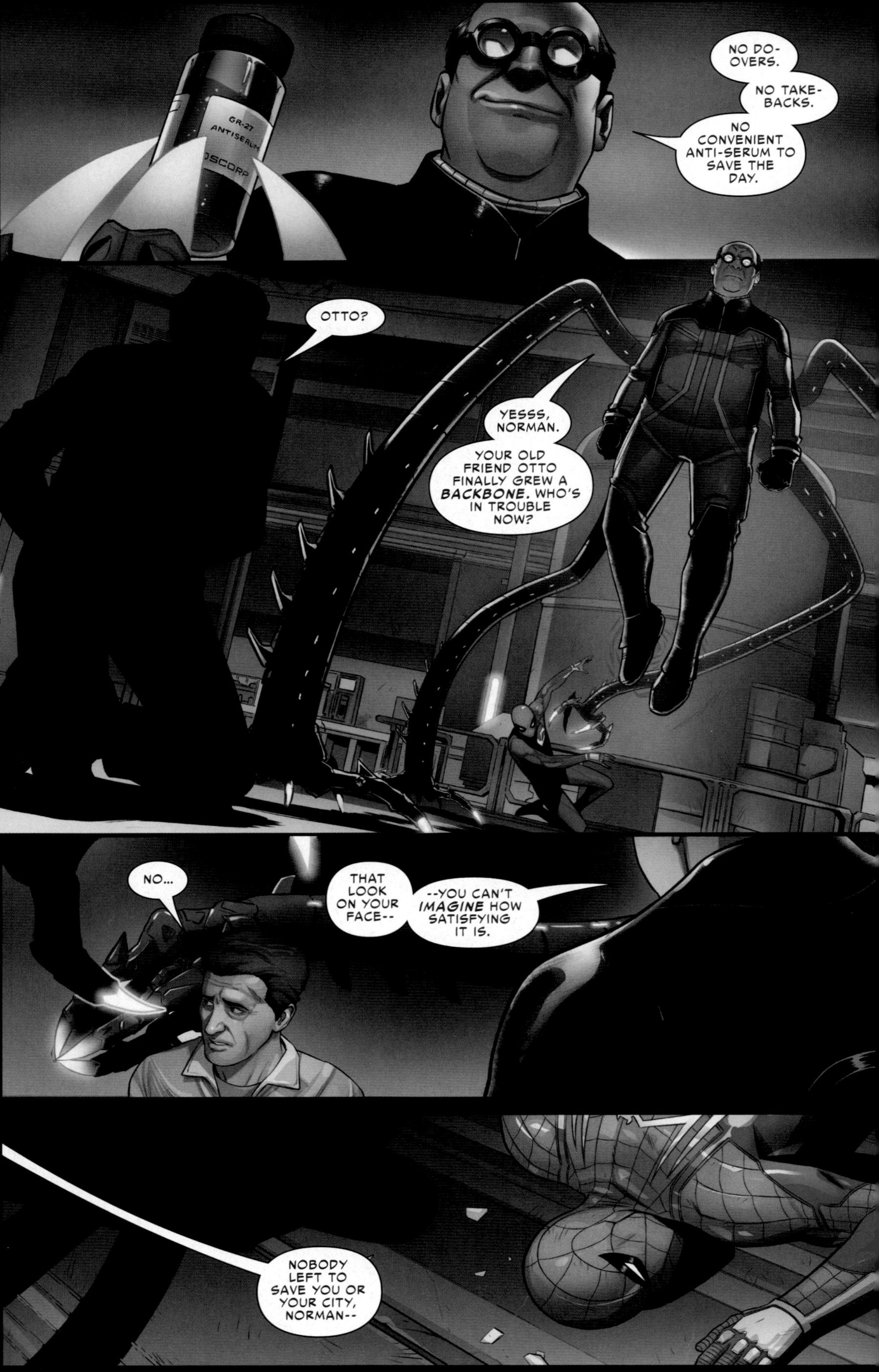
GR-27
ANTISERUM
OSCORP
NO DO-OVERS.
NO TAKE-BACKS.
NO CONVENIENT ANTI-SERUM TO SAVE THE DAY.
OTTO?
YESSS, NORMAN.
YOUR OLD FRIEND OTTO FINALLY GREW A **BACKBONE**. WHO'S IN TROUBLE NOW?
NO...
THAT LOOK ON YOUR FACE--
--YOU CAN'T *IMAGINE* HOW SATISFYING IT IS.
NOBODY LEFT TO SAVE YOU OR YOUR CITY, NORMAN--

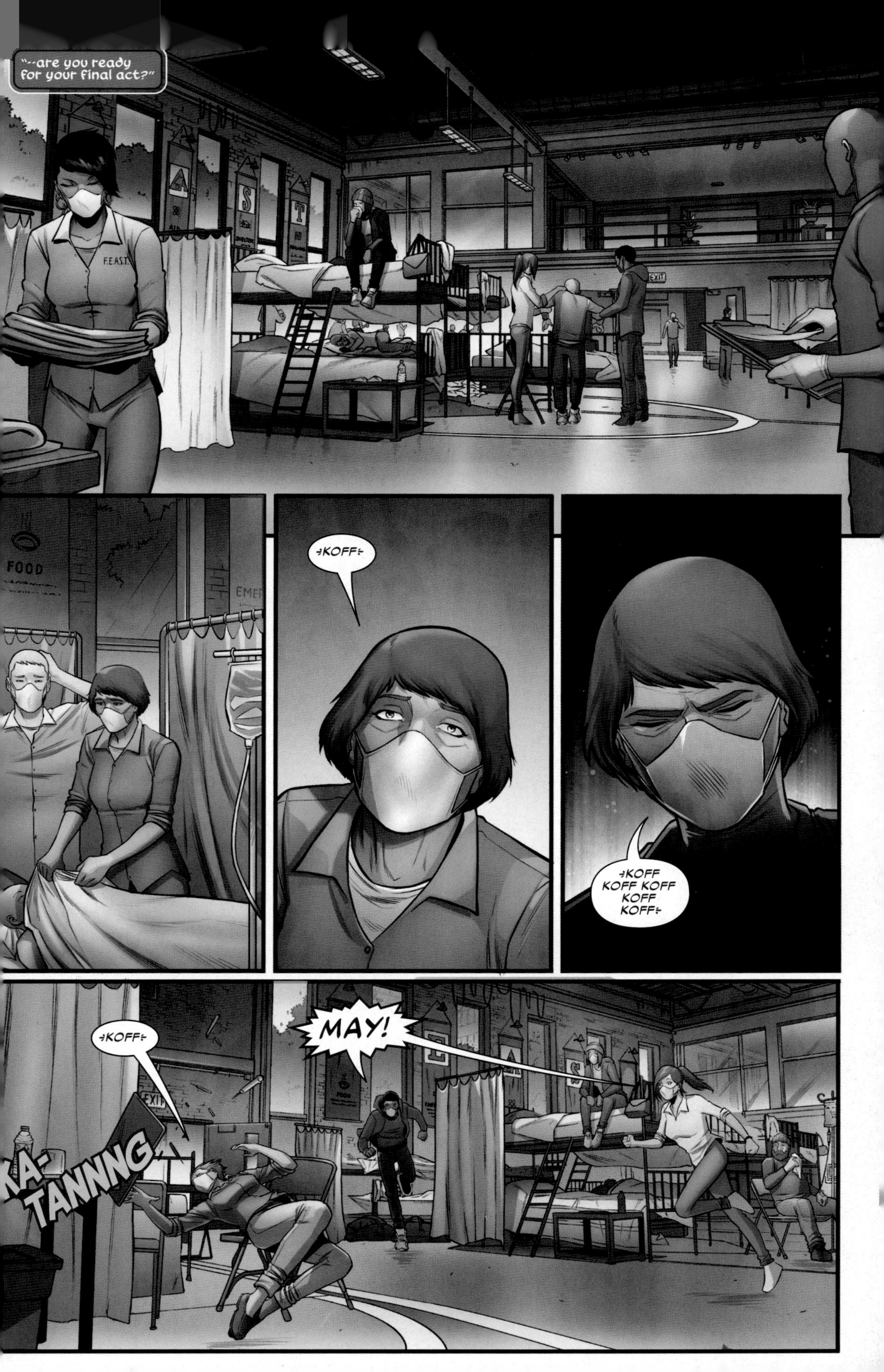
"--are you ready for your final act?"
F.E.A.S.T.
EXIT
FOOD
⇛KOFF⇚
⇛KOFF KOFF KOFF KOFF KOFF⇚
⇛KOFF⇚
MAY!
KA-TANNNG

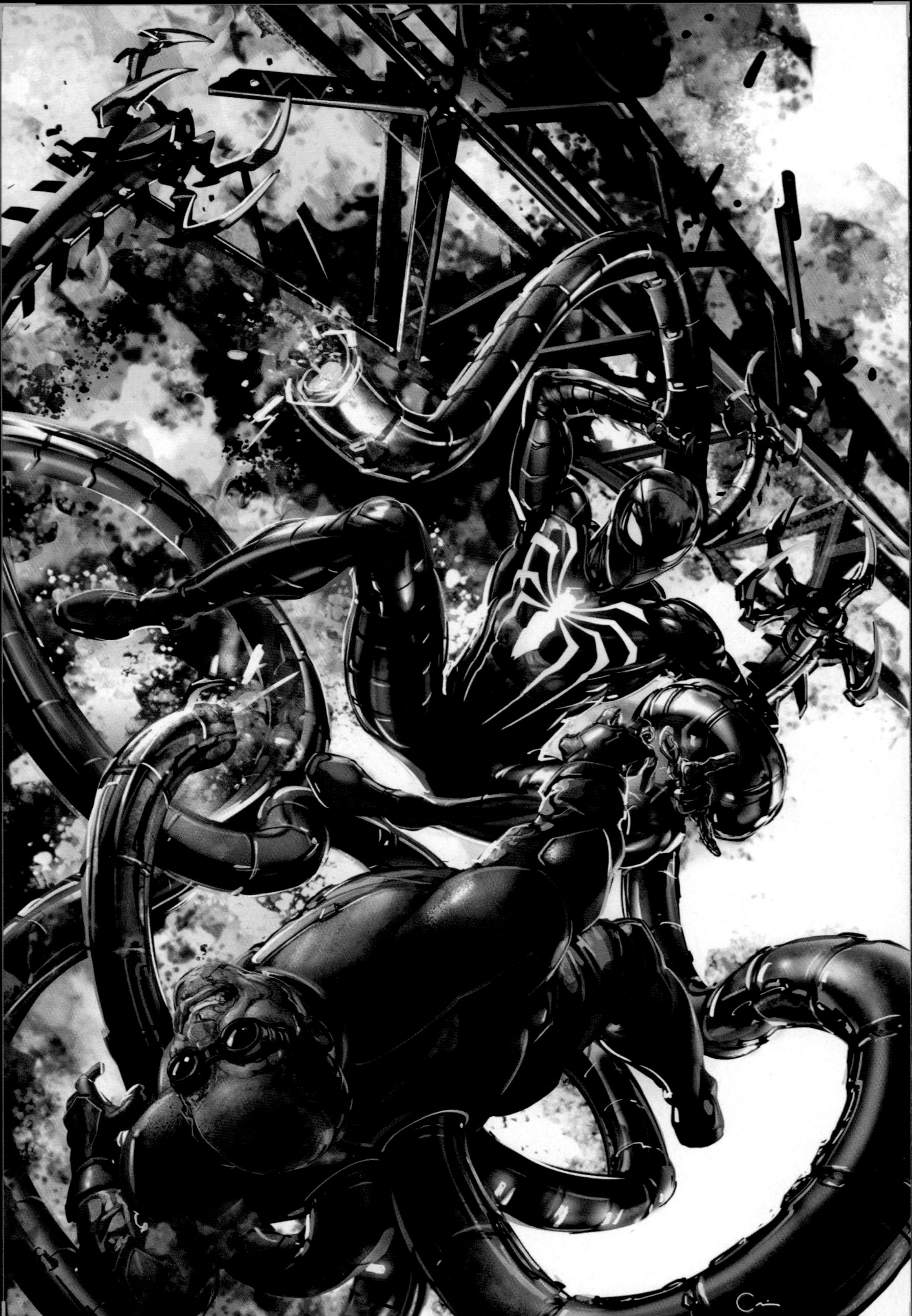

6

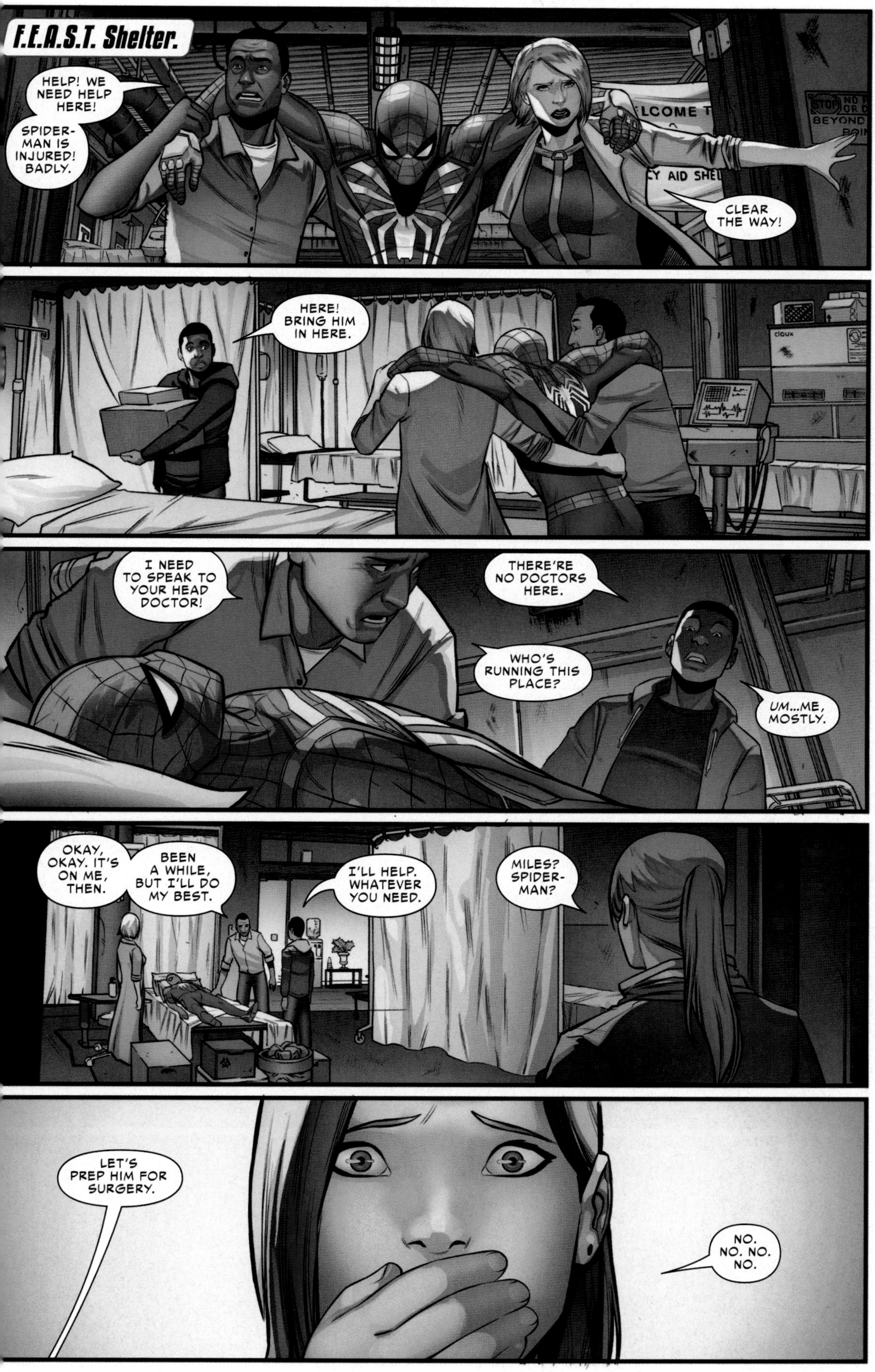

F.E.A.S.T. Shelter.
HELP! WE NEED HELP HERE!
SPIDER-MAN IS INJURED! BADLY.
CLEAR THE WAY!
HERE! BRING HIM IN HERE.
I NEED TO SPEAK TO YOUR HEAD DOCTOR!
THERE'RE NO DOCTORS HERE.
WHO'S RUNNING THIS PLACE?
UM...ME, MOSTLY.
OKAY, OKAY. IT'S ON ME, THEN.
BEEN A WHILE, BUT I'LL DO MY BEST.
I'LL HELP. WHATEVER YOU NEED.
MILES? SPIDER-MAN?
LET'S PREP HIM FOR SURGERY.
NO. NO. NO. NO.

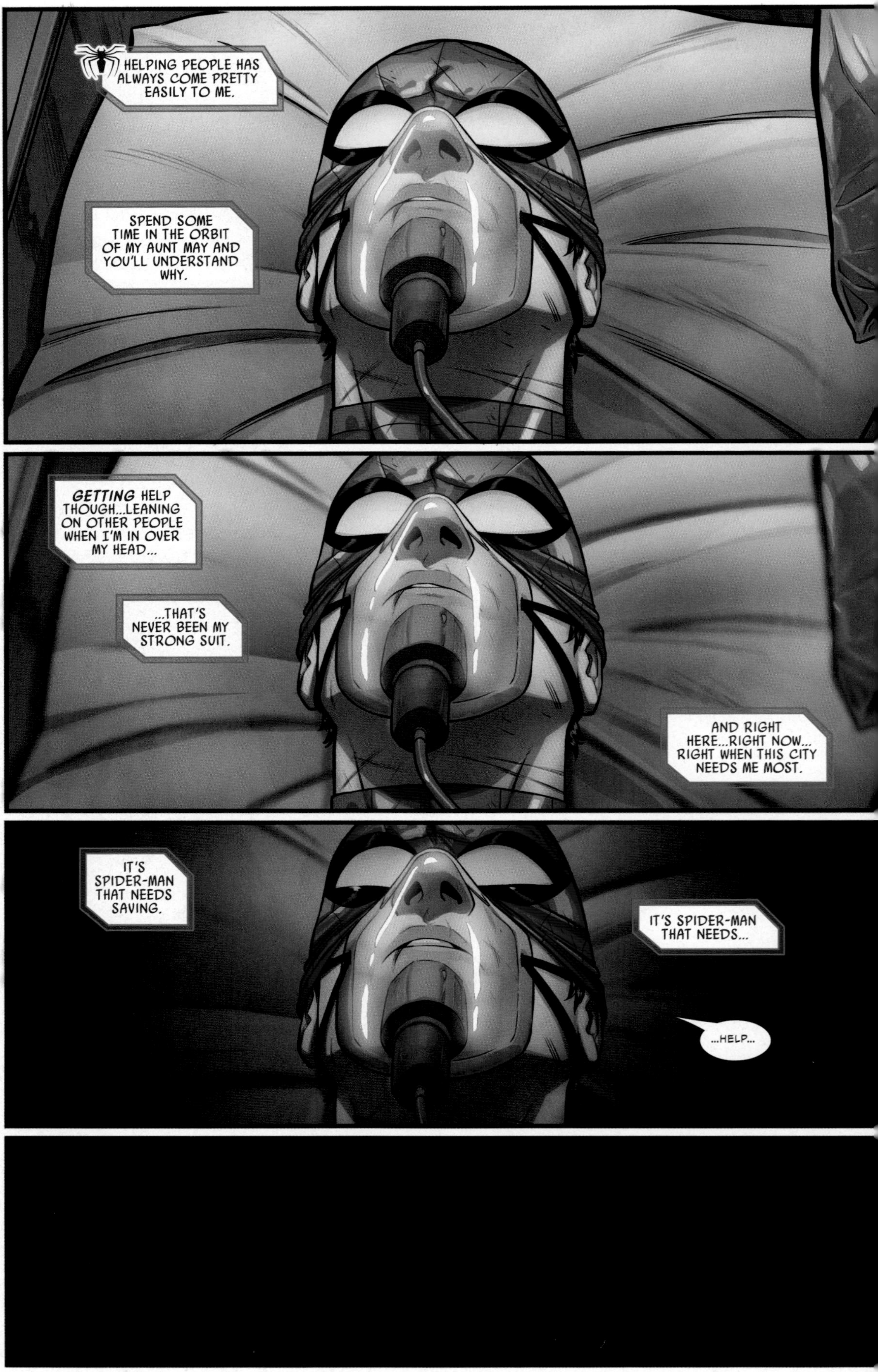
HELPING PEOPLE HAS ALWAYS COME PRETTY EASILY TO ME.
SPEND SOME TIME IN THE ORBIT OF MY AUNT MAY AND YOU'LL UNDERSTAND WHY.
GETTING HELP THOUGH...LEANING ON OTHER PEOPLE WHEN I'M IN OVER MY HEAD...
...THAT'S NEVER BEEN MY STRONG SUIT.
AND RIGHT HERE...RIGHT NOW... RIGHT WHEN THIS CITY NEEDS ME MOST.
IT'S SPIDER-MAN THAT NEEDS SAVING.
IT'S SPIDER-MAN THAT NEEDS...
...HELP...

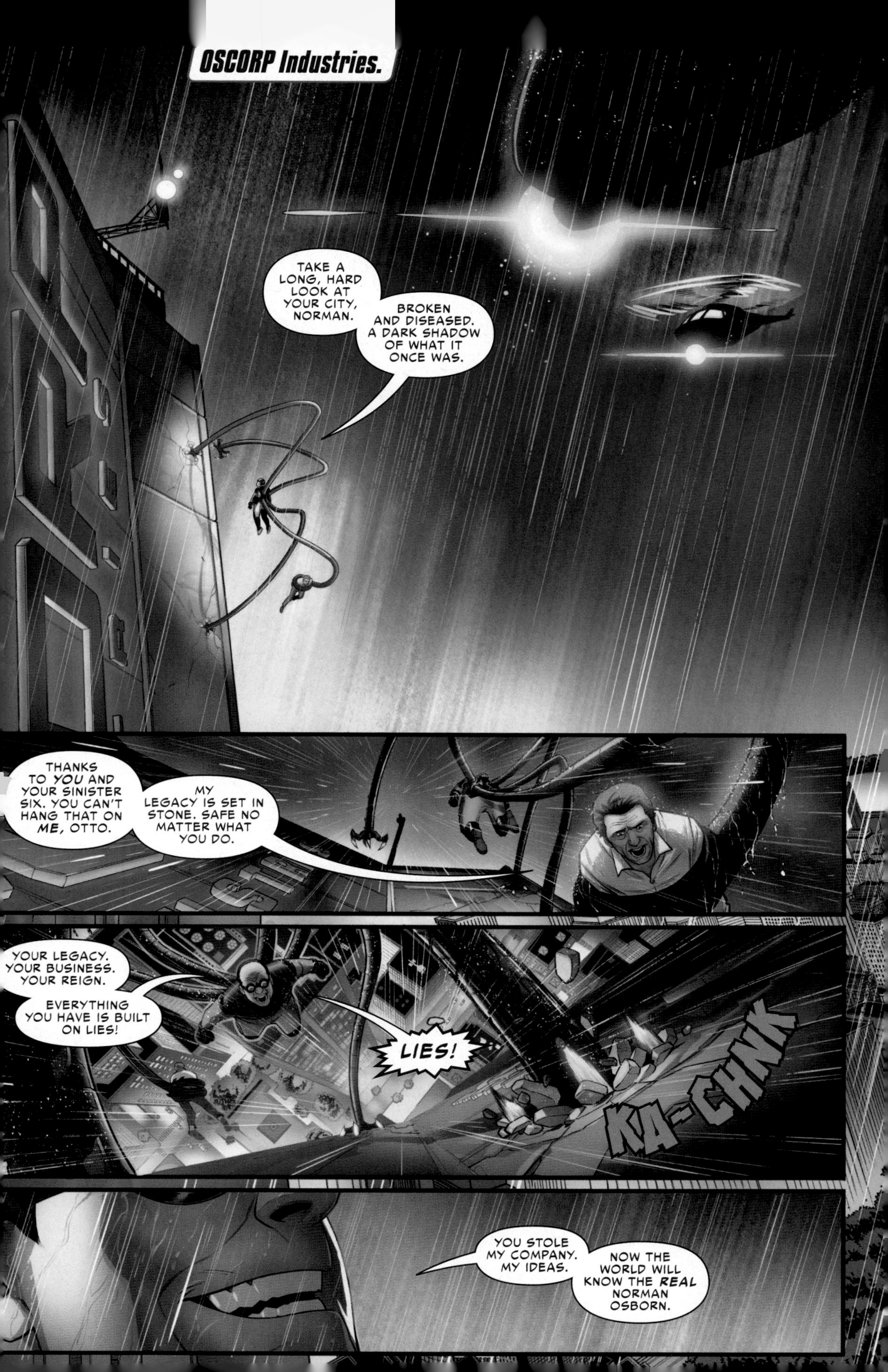
OSCORP Industries.
TAKE A LONG, HARD LOOK AT YOUR CITY, NORMAN.
BROKEN AND DISEASED. A DARK SHADOW OF WHAT IT ONCE WAS.
THANKS TO *YOU* AND YOUR SINISTER SIX. YOU CAN'T HANG THAT ON *ME*, OTTO.
MY LEGACY IS SET IN STONE. SAFE NO MATTER WHAT YOU DO.
YOUR LEGACY. YOUR BUSINESS. YOUR REIGN.
EVERYTHING YOU HAVE IS BUILT ON LIES!
LIES!
KA-CHNK
YOU STOLE MY COMPANY. MY IDEAS.
NOW THE WORLD WILL KNOW THE *REAL* NORMAN OSBORN.

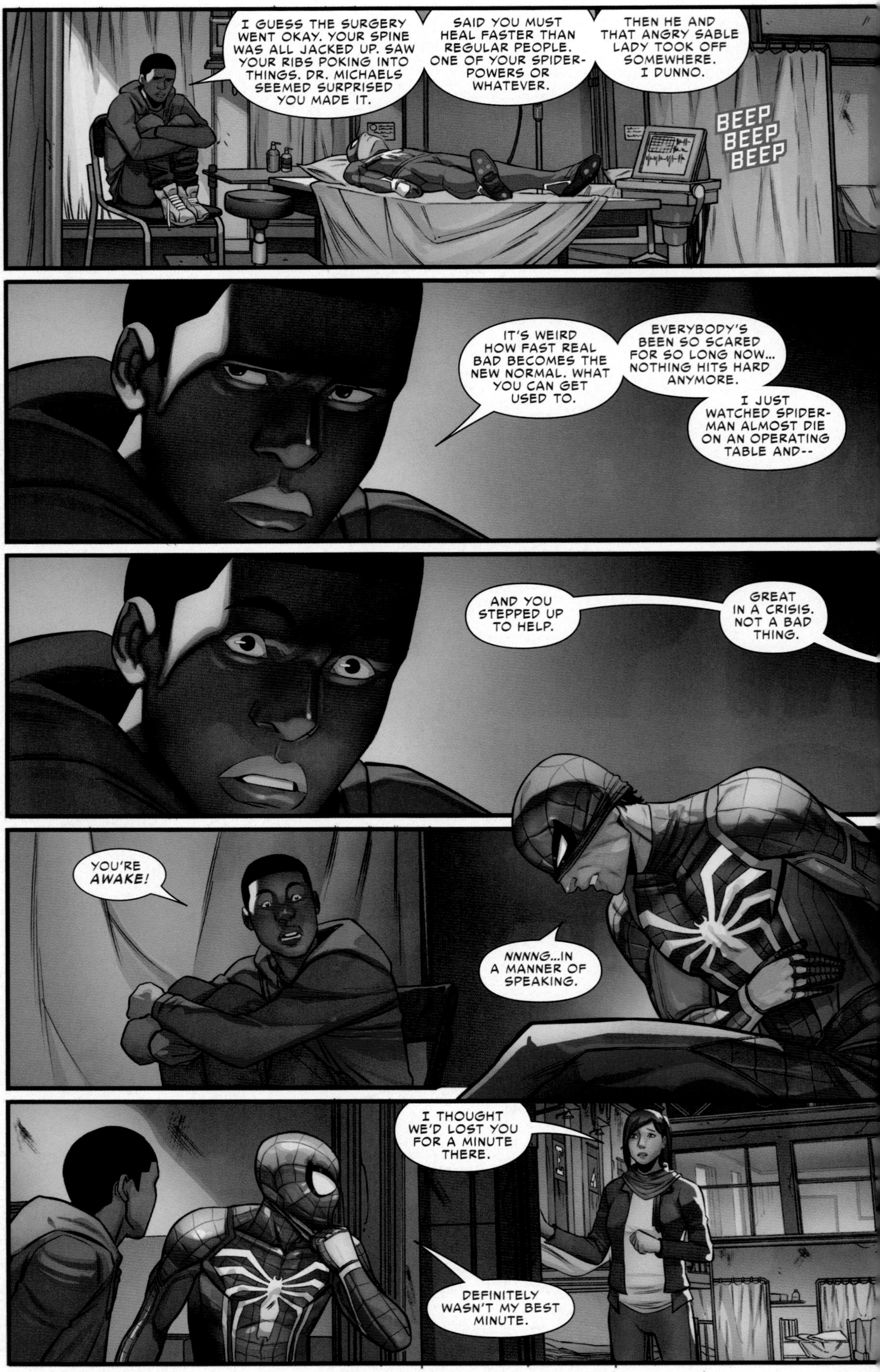
I GUESS THE SURGERY WENT OKAY. YOUR SPINE WAS ALL JACKED UP. SAW YOUR RIBS POKING INTO THINGS. DR. MICHAELS SEEMED SURPRISED YOU MADE IT.
SAID YOU MUST HEAL FASTER THAN REGULAR PEOPLE. ONE OF YOUR SPIDER-POWERS OR WHATEVER.
THEN HE AND THAT ANGRY SABLE LADY TOOK OFF SOMEWHERE. I DUNNO.
BEEP BEEP BEEP
IT'S WEIRD HOW FAST REAL BAD BECOMES THE NEW NORMAL. WHAT YOU CAN GET USED TO.
EVERYBODY'S BEEN SO SCARED FOR SO LONG NOW... NOTHING HITS HARD ANYMORE.
I JUST WATCHED SPIDER-MAN ALMOST DIE ON AN OPERATING TABLE AND--
AND YOU STEPPED UP TO HELP.
GREAT IN A CRISIS. NOT A BAD THING.
YOU'RE AWAKE!
NNNNG...IN A MANNER OF SPEAKING.
I THOUGHT WE'D LOST YOU FOR A MINUTE THERE.
DEFINITELY WASN'T MY BEST MINUTE.

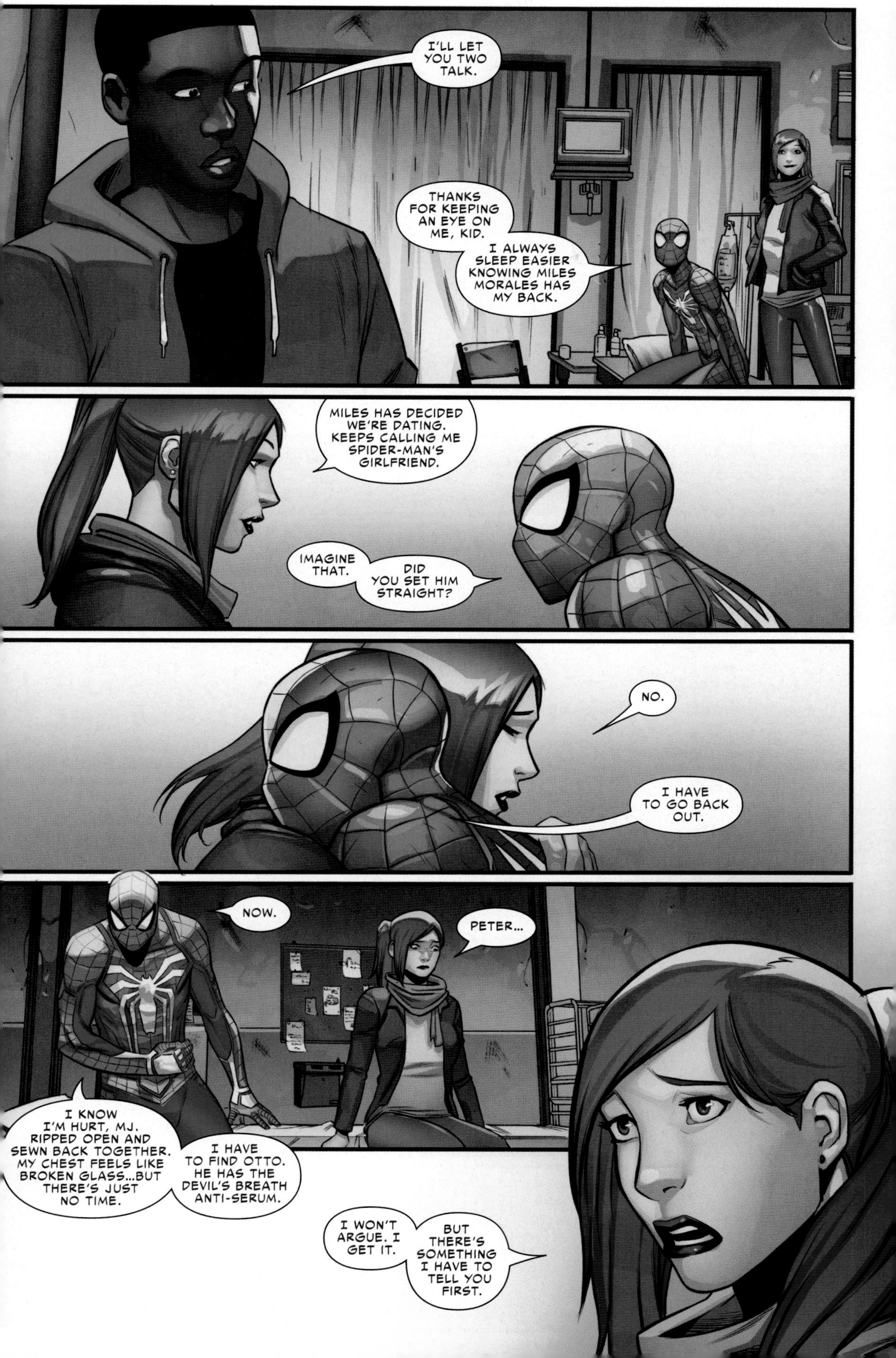
I'LL LET YOU TWO TALK.
THANKS FOR KEEPING AN EYE ON ME, KID.
I ALWAYS SLEEP EASIER KNOWING MILES MORALES HAS MY BACK.
MILES HAS DECIDED WE'RE DATING. KEEPS CALLING ME SPIDER-MAN'S GIRLFRIEND.
IMAGINE THAT.
DID YOU SET HIM STRAIGHT?
NO.
I HAVE TO GO BACK OUT.
NOW.
PETER...
I KNOW I'M HURT, MJ. RIPPED OPEN AND SEWN BACK TOGETHER. MY CHEST FEELS LIKE BROKEN GLASS...BUT THERE'S JUST NO TIME.
I HAVE TO FIND OTTO. HE HAS THE DEVIL'S BREATH ANTI-SERUM.
I WON'T ARGUE. I GET IT.
BUT THERE'S SOMETHING I HAVE TO TELL YOU FIRST.

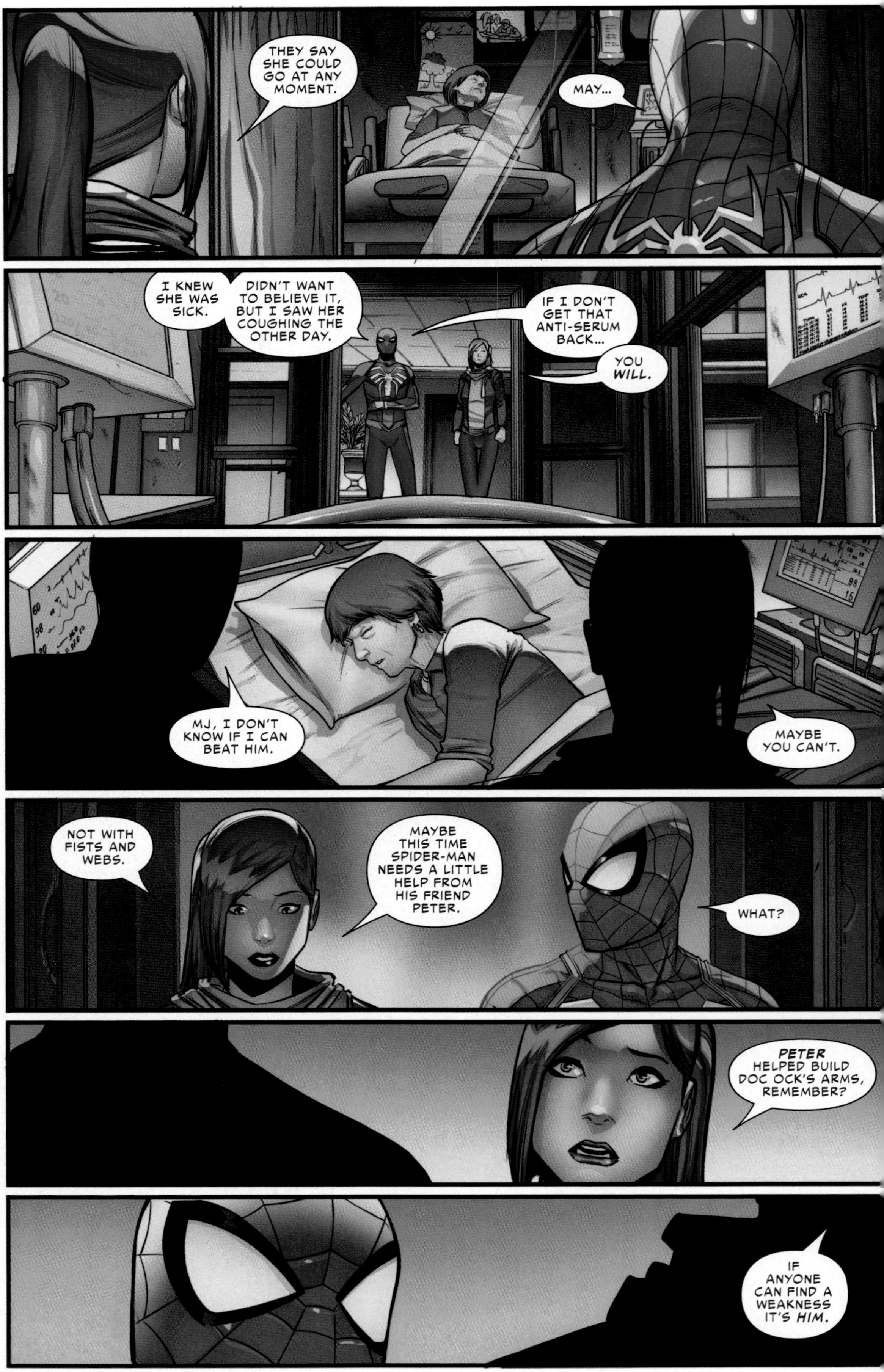
THEY SAY SHE COULD GO AT ANY MOMENT.
MAY...
I KNEW SHE WAS SICK.
DIDN'T WANT TO BELIEVE IT, BUT I SAW HER COUGHING THE OTHER DAY.
IF I DON'T GET THAT ANTI-SERUM BACK...
YOU *WILL.*
MJ, I DON'T KNOW IF I CAN BEAT HIM.
MAYBE YOU CAN'T.
NOT WITH FISTS AND WEBS.
MAYBE THIS TIME SPIDER-MAN NEEDS A LITTLE HELP FROM HIS FRIEND PETER.
WHAT?
PETER HELPED BUILD DOC OCK'S ARMS, REMEMBER?
IF ANYONE CAN FIND A WEAKNESS IT'S *HIM.*

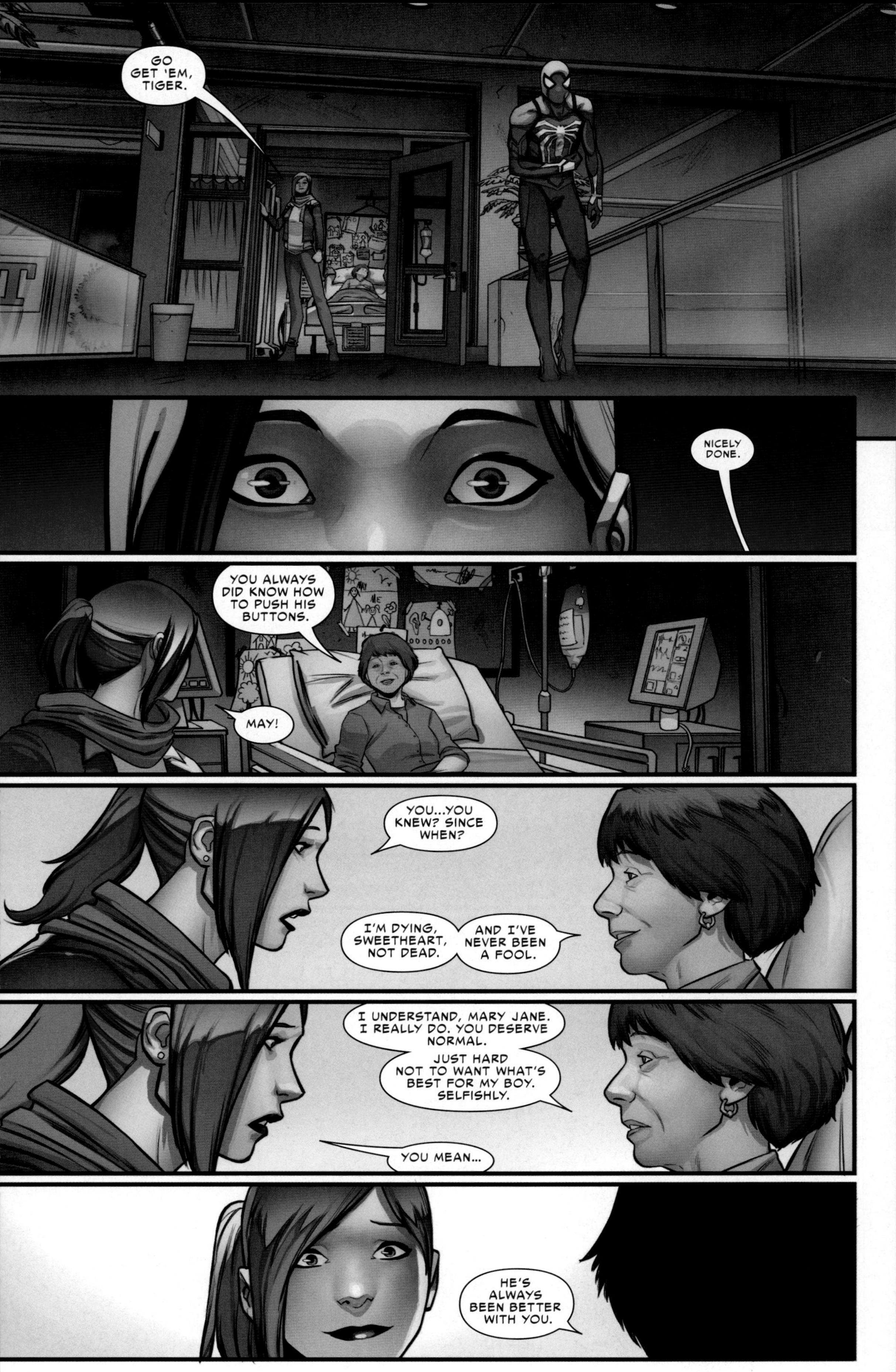
GO GET 'EM, TIGER.
NICELY DONE.
YOU ALWAYS DID KNOW HOW TO PUSH HIS BUTTONS.
MAY!
YOU...YOU KNEW? SINCE WHEN?
I'M DYING, SWEETHEART, NOT DEAD.
AND I'VE NEVER BEEN A FOOL.
I UNDERSTAND, MARY JANE. I REALLY DO. YOU DESERVE NORMAL.
JUST HARD NOT TO WANT WHAT'S BEST FOR MY BOY. SELFISHLY.
YOU MEAN...
HE'S ALWAYS BEEN BETTER WITH YOU.

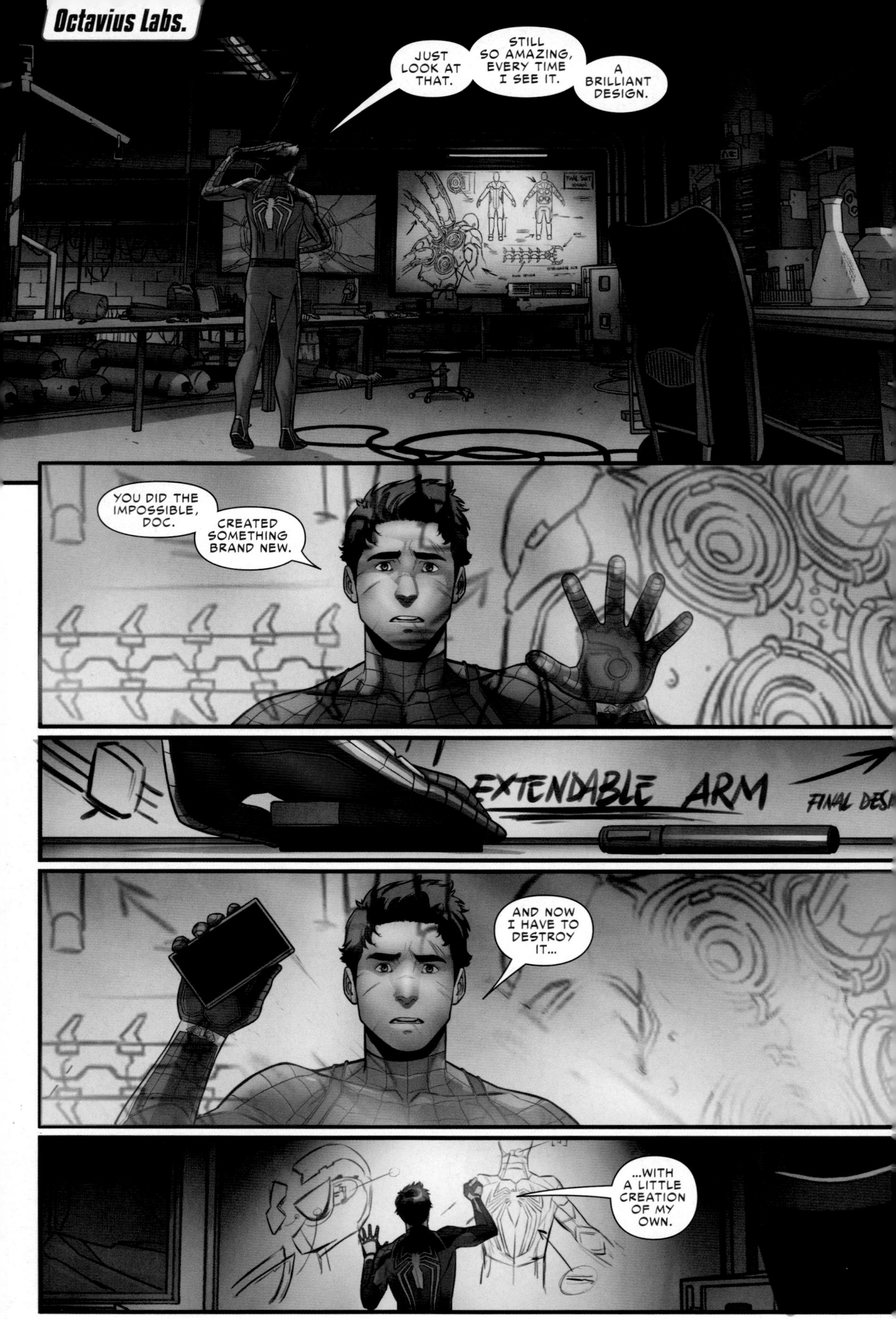
Octavius Labs.
JUST LOOK AT THAT.
STILL SO AMAZING, EVERY TIME I SEE IT.
A BRILLIANT DESIGN.
YOU DID THE IMPOSSIBLE, DOC.
CREATED SOMETHING BRAND NEW.
EXTENDABLE ARM
AND NOW I HAVE TO DESTROY IT...
...WITH A LITTLE CREATION OF MY OWN.

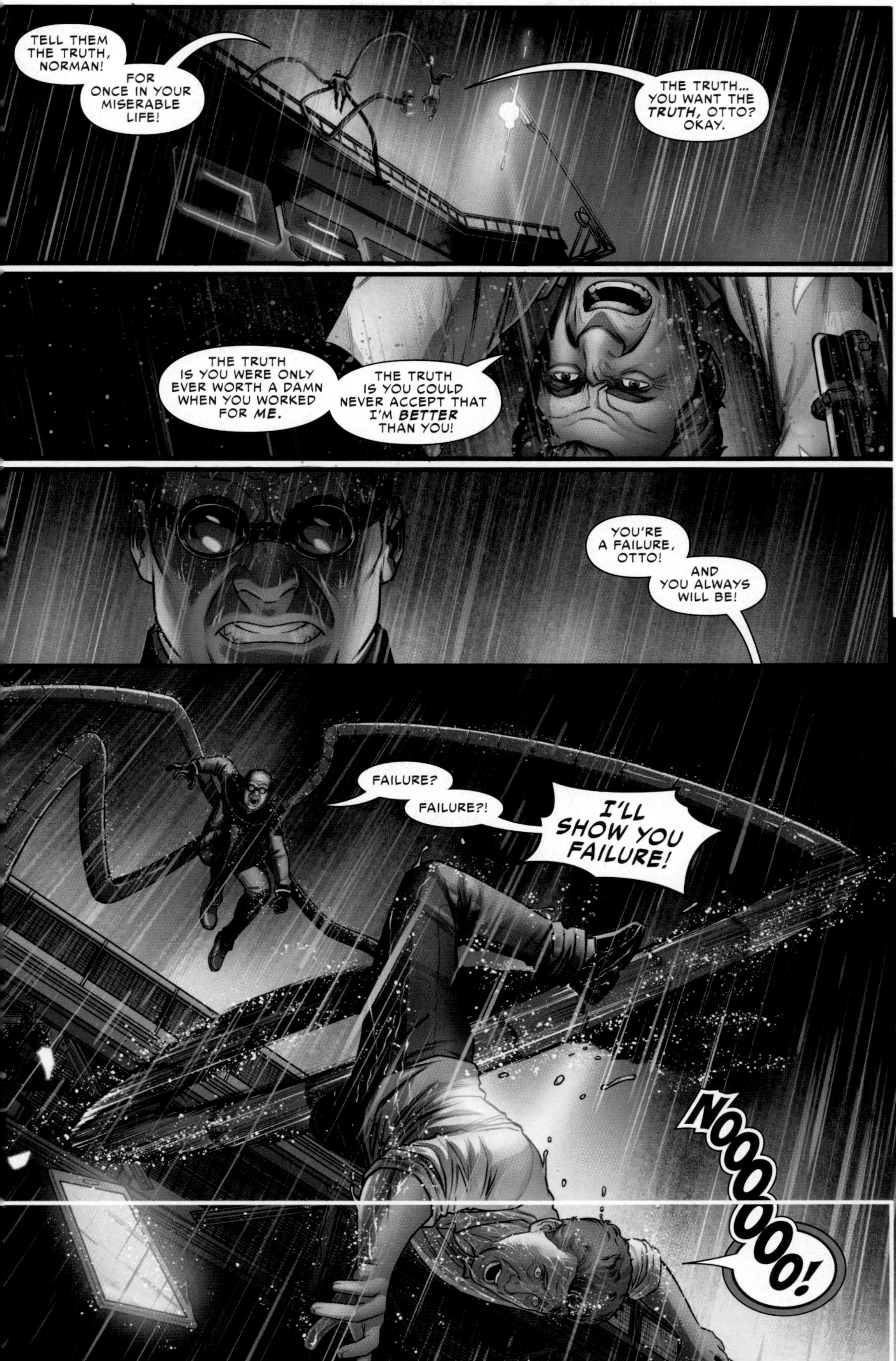
TELL THEM THE TRUTH, NORMAN!
FOR ONCE IN YOUR MISERABLE LIFE!
THE TRUTH... YOU WANT THE TRUTH, OTTO? OKAY.
THE TRUTH IS YOU COULD NEVER ACCEPT THAT I'M BETTER THAN YOU!
THE TRUTH IS YOU WERE ONLY EVER WORTH A DAMN WHEN YOU WORKED FOR ME.
YOU'RE A FAILURE, OTTO!
AND YOU ALWAYS WILL BE!
FAILURE?
FAILURE?!
I'LL SHOW YOU FAILURE!
NOOOOOO!

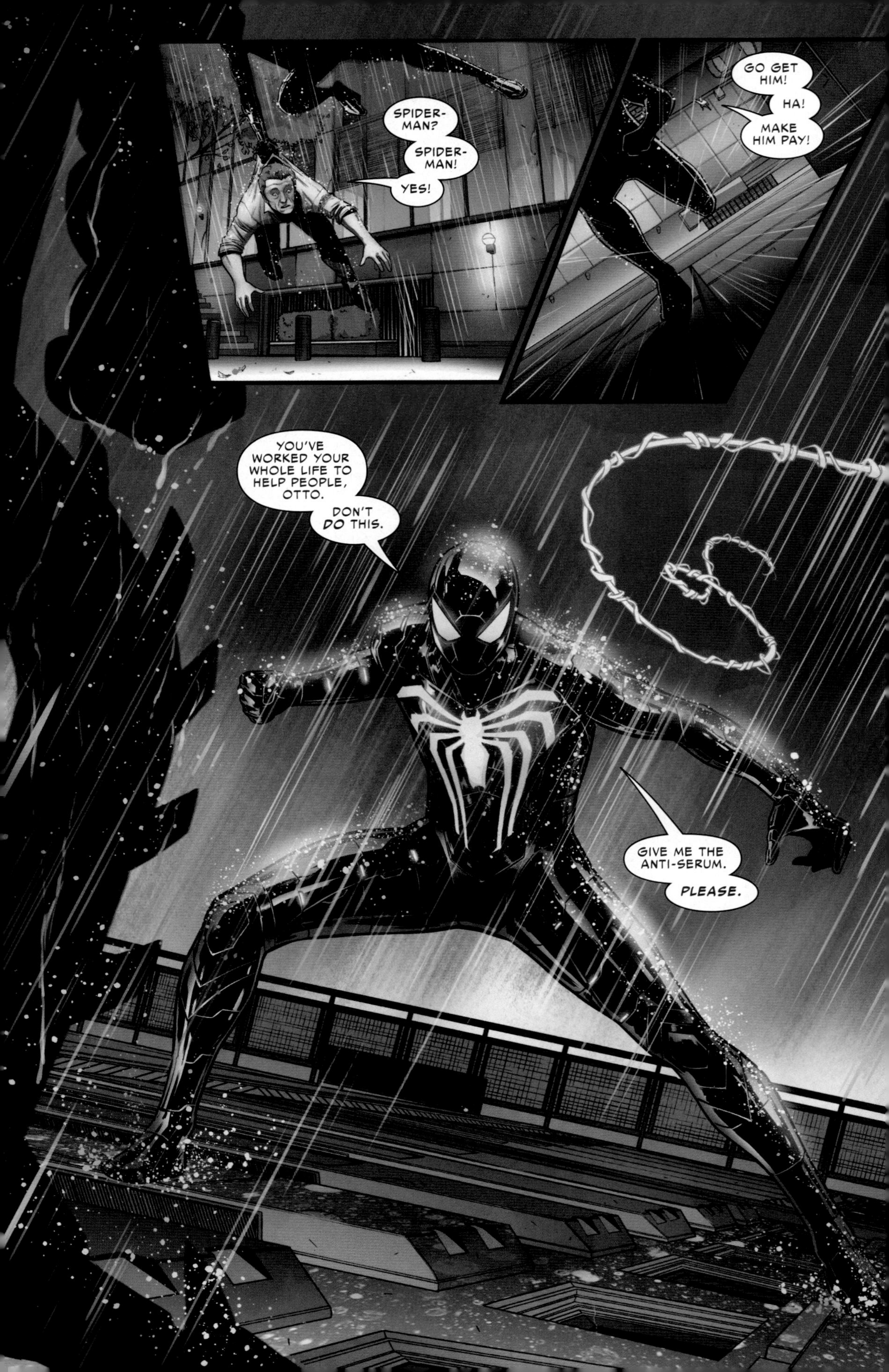
SPIDER-MAN?
SPIDER-MAN!
YES!
GO GET HIM!
HA!
MAKE HIM PAY!
YOU'VE WORKED YOUR WHOLE LIFE TO HELP PEOPLE, OTTO.
DON'T DO THIS.
GIVE ME THE ANTI-SERUM.
PLEASE.

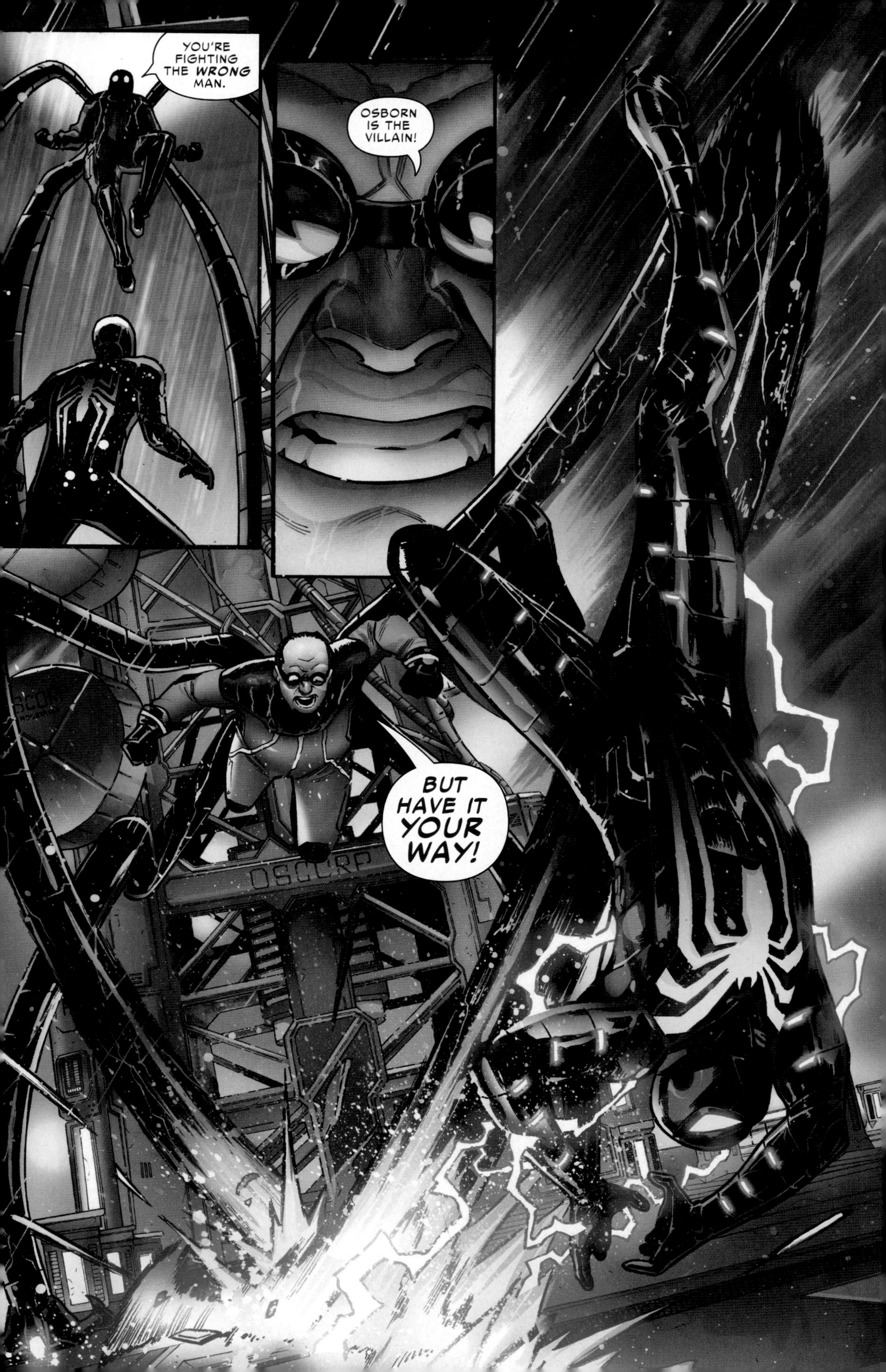
YOU'RE FIGHTING THE WRONG MAN.
OSBORN IS THE VILLAIN!
BUT HAVE IT YOUR WAY!

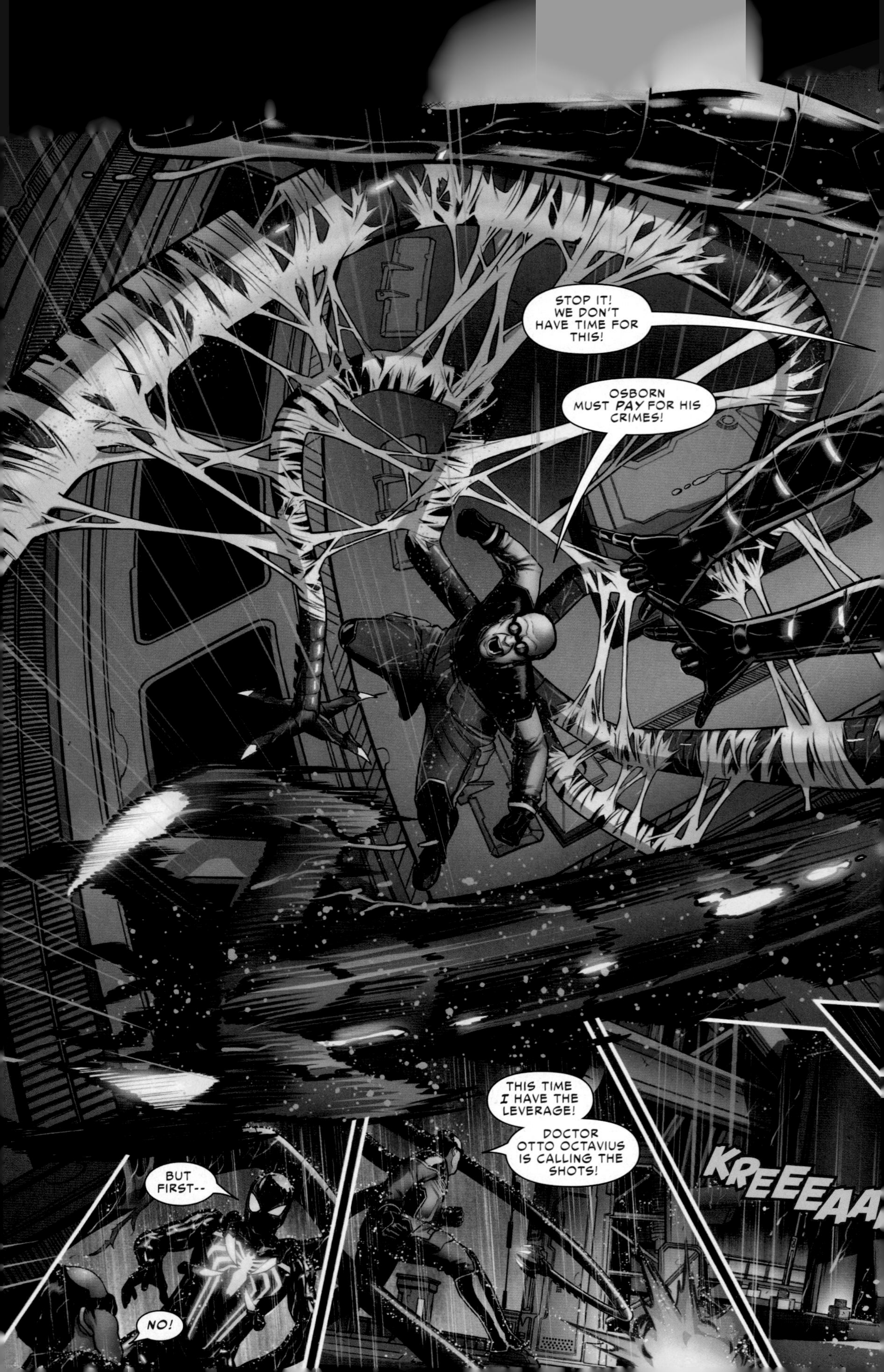
STOP IT! WE DON'T HAVE TIME FOR THIS!
OSBORN MUST PAY FOR HIS CRIMES!
THIS TIME I HAVE THE LEVERAGE!
DOCTOR OTTO OCTAVIUS IS CALLING THE SHOTS!
KREEEAA
BUT FIRST--
NO!

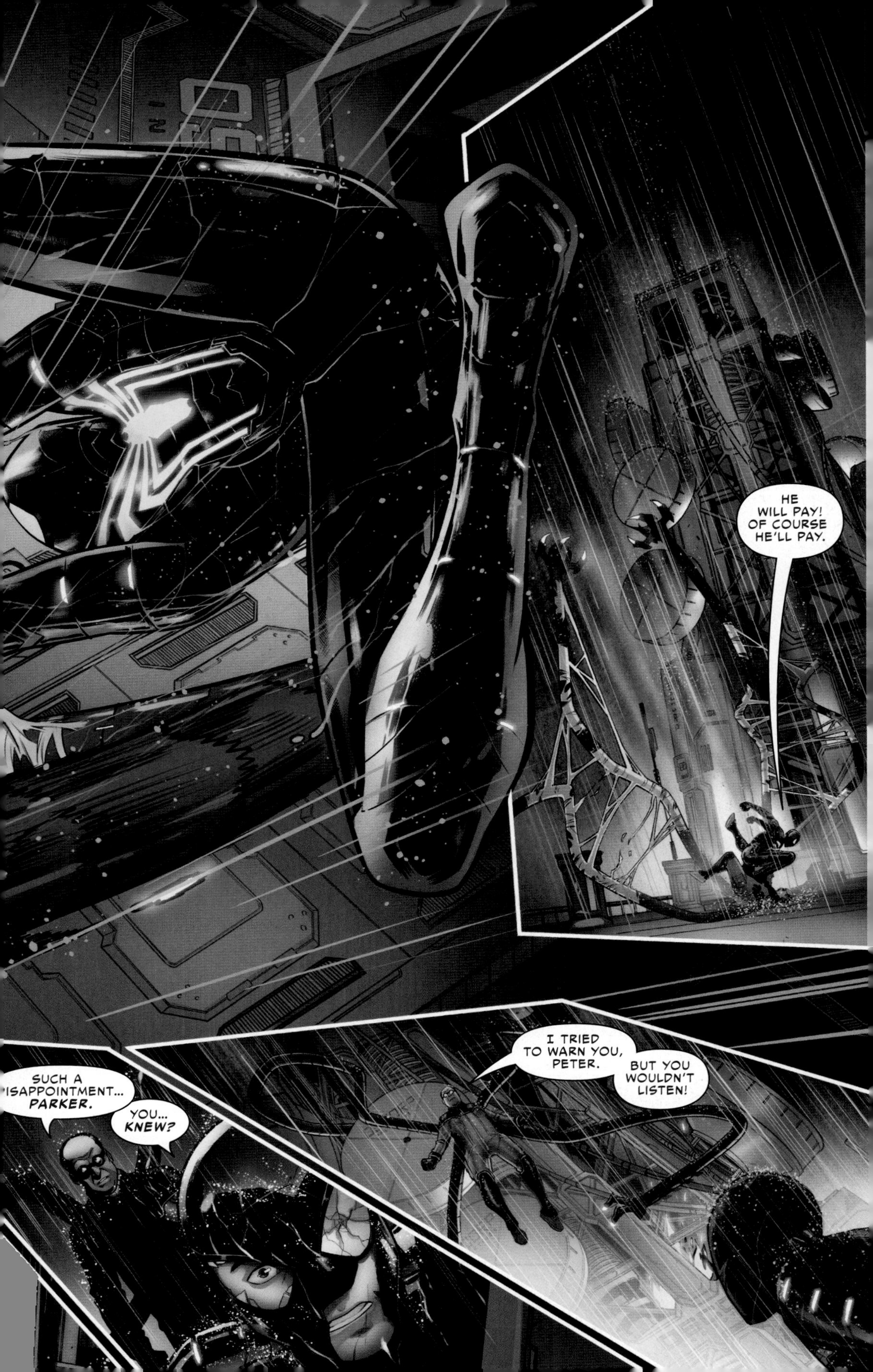
HE WILL PAY! OF COURSE HE'LL PAY.
SUCH A ISAPPOINTMENT... PARKER.
YOU... KNEW?
I TRIED TO WARN YOU, PETER.
BUT YOU WOULDN'T LISTEN!

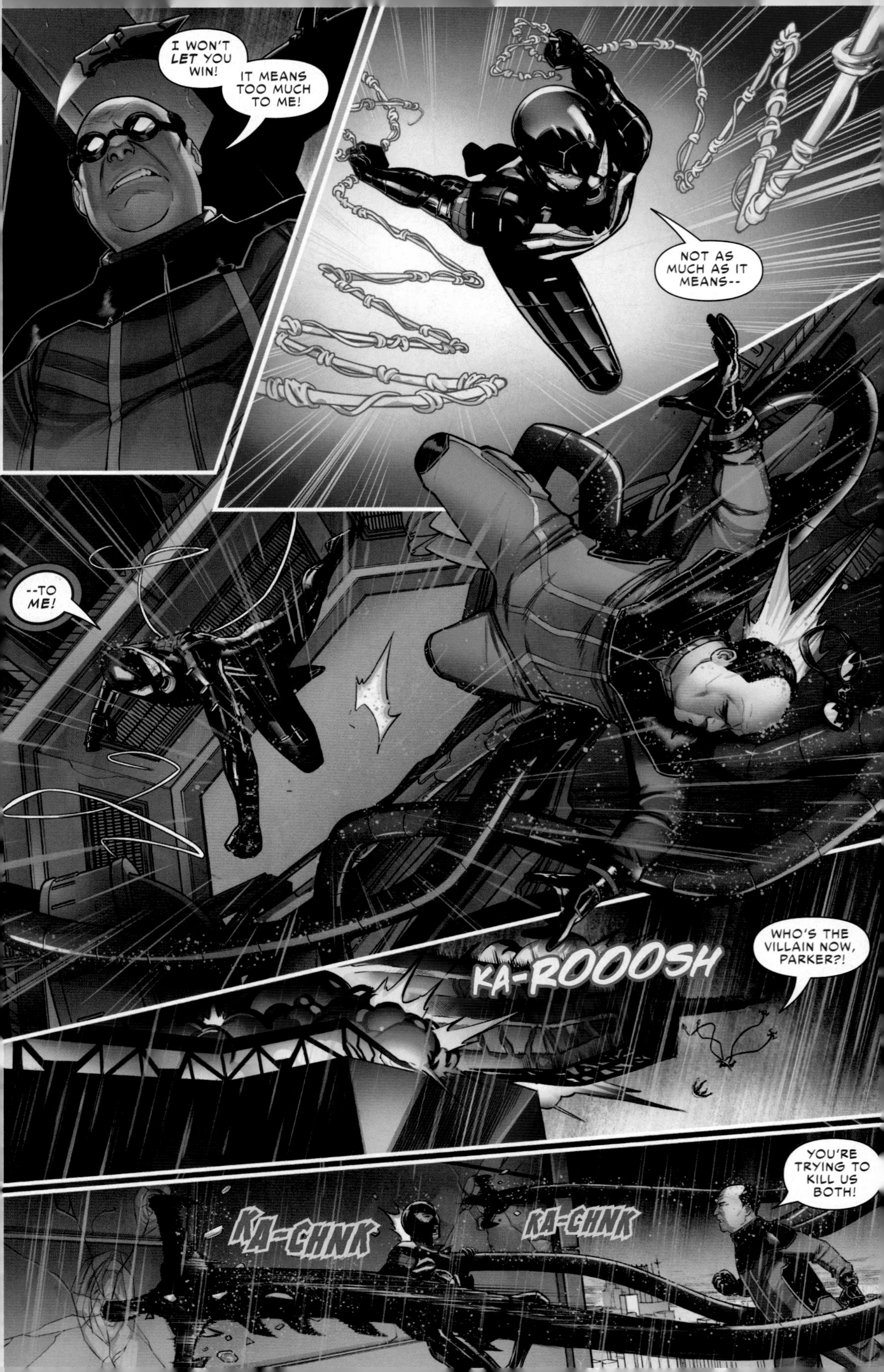
I WON'T *LET* YOU WIN!
IT MEANS TOO MUCH TO ME!
NOT AS MUCH AS IT MEANS--
--TO *ME*!
KA-ROOOOSH
WHO'S THE VILLAIN NOW, PARKER?!
YOU'RE TRYING TO KILL US BOTH!
KA-CHNK
KA-CHNK

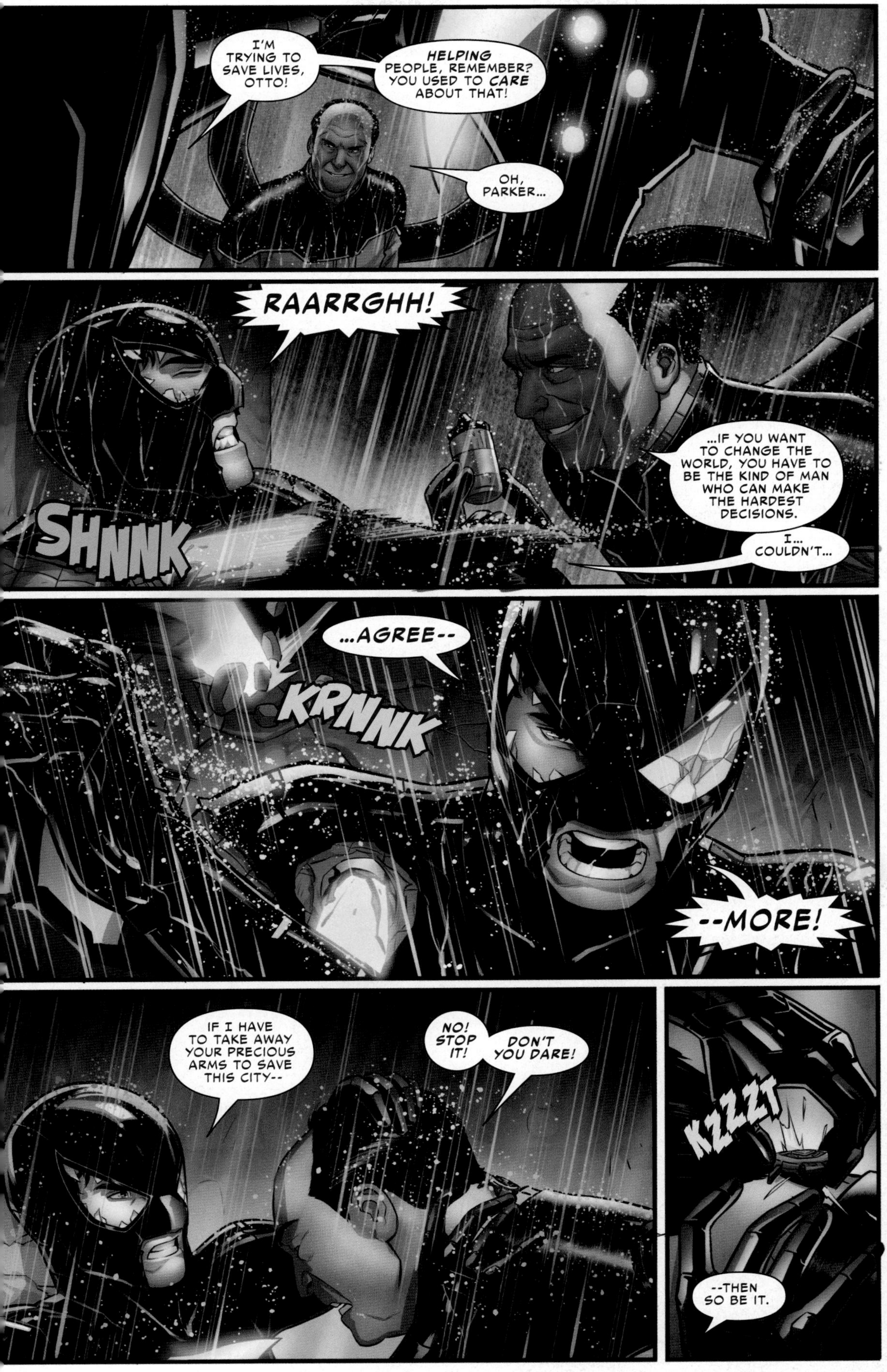

I'M TRYING TO SAVE LIVES, OTTO!
HELPING PEOPLE, REMEMBER? YOU USED TO CARE ABOUT THAT!
OH, PARKER...
RAARRGHH!
...IF YOU WANT TO CHANGE THE WORLD, YOU HAVE TO BE THE KIND OF MAN WHO CAN MAKE THE HARDEST DECISIONS.
SHNNK
I... COULDN'T...
...AGREE--
KRNNK
--MORE!
IF I HAVE TO TAKE AWAY YOUR PRECIOUS ARMS TO SAVE THIS CITY--
NO! STOP IT!
DON'T YOU DARE!
KZZZZT
--THEN SO BE IT.

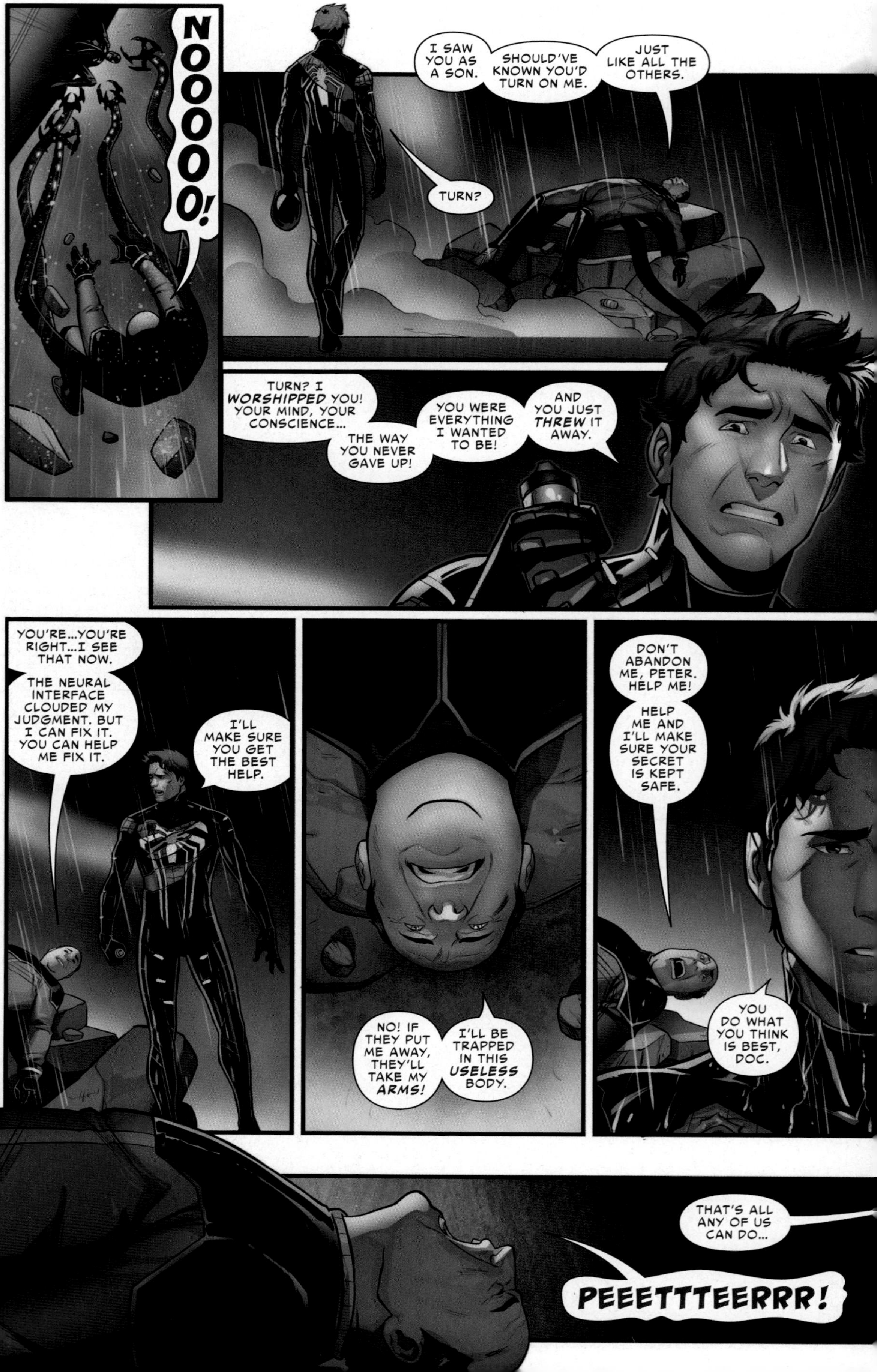
NOOOOOO!
I SAW YOU AS A SON.
SHOULD'VE KNOWN YOU'D TURN ON ME.
JUST LIKE ALL THE OTHERS.
TURN?
TURN? I WORSHIPPED YOU! YOUR MIND, YOUR CONSCIENCE...
THE WAY YOU NEVER GAVE UP!
YOU WERE EVERYTHING I WANTED TO BE!
AND YOU JUST THREW IT AWAY.
YOU'RE...YOU'RE RIGHT...I SEE THAT NOW.
THE NEURAL INTERFACE CLOUDED MY JUDGMENT. BUT I CAN FIX IT. YOU CAN HELP ME FIX IT.
I'LL MAKE SURE YOU GET THE BEST HELP.
NO! IF THEY PUT ME AWAY, THEY'LL TAKE MY ARMS!
I'LL BE TRAPPED IN THIS USELESS BODY.
DON'T ABANDON ME, PETER. HELP ME!
HELP ME AND I'LL MAKE SURE YOUR SECRET IS KEPT SAFE.
YOU DO WHAT YOU THINK IS BEST, DOC.
THAT'S ALL ANY OF US CAN DO...
PEEETTTEERRR!

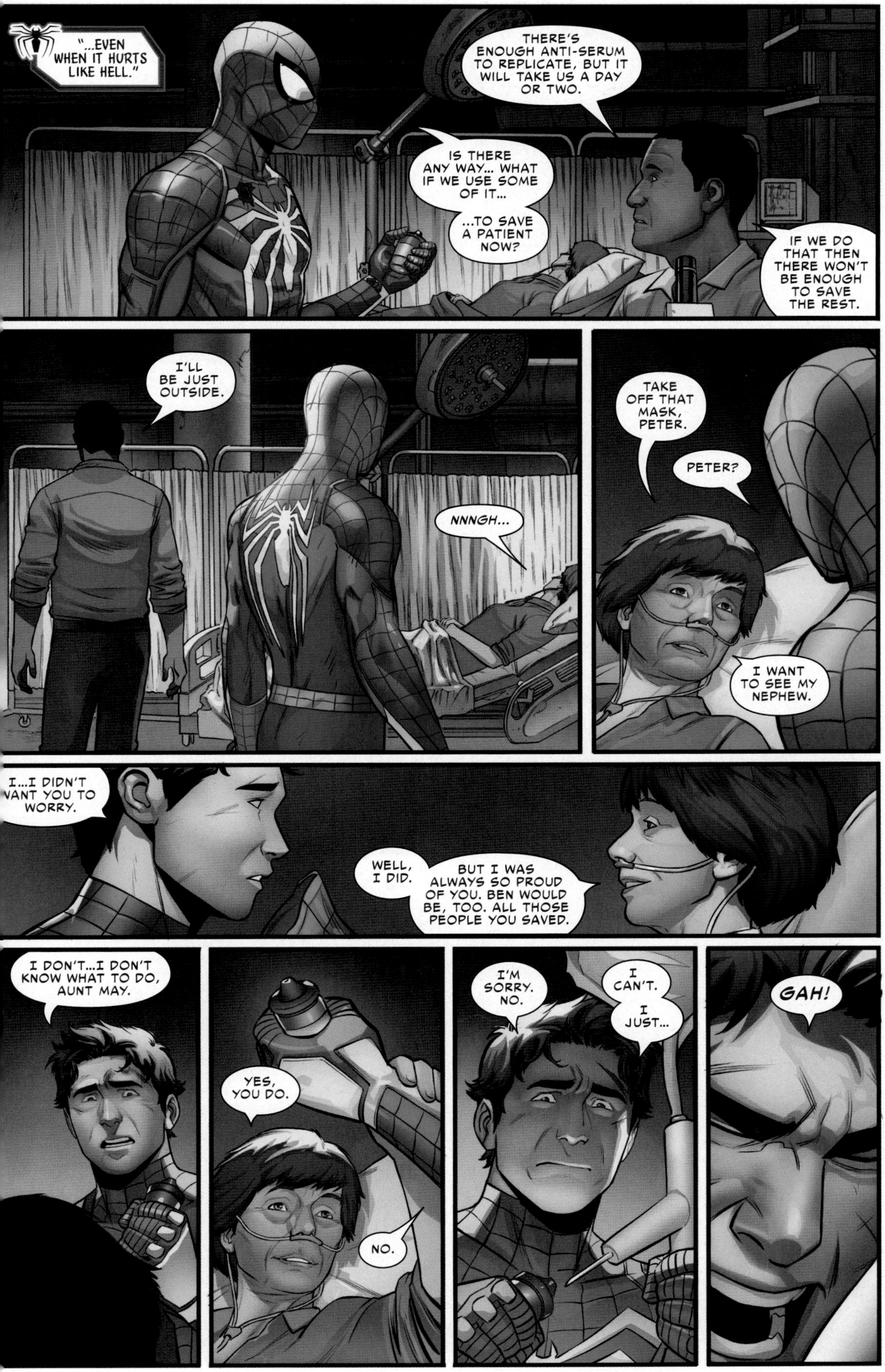
"...EVEN WHEN IT HURTS LIKE HELL."
THERE'S ENOUGH ANTI-SERUM TO REPLICATE, BUT IT WILL TAKE US A DAY OR TWO.
IS THERE ANY WAY... WHAT IF WE USE SOME OF IT...
...TO SAVE A PATIENT NOW?
IF WE DO THAT THEN THERE WON'T BE ENOUGH TO SAVE THE REST.
I'LL BE JUST OUTSIDE.
NNNGH...
TAKE OFF THAT MASK, PETER.
PETER?
I WANT TO SEE MY NEPHEW.
I...I DIDN'T WANT YOU TO WORRY.
WELL, I DID.
BUT I WAS ALWAYS SO PROUD OF YOU. BEN WOULD BE, TOO. ALL THOSE PEOPLE YOU SAVED.
I DON'T...I DON'T KNOW WHAT TO DO, AUNT MAY.
YES, YOU DO.
NO.
I'M SORRY. NO.
I CAN'T.
I JUST...
GAH!

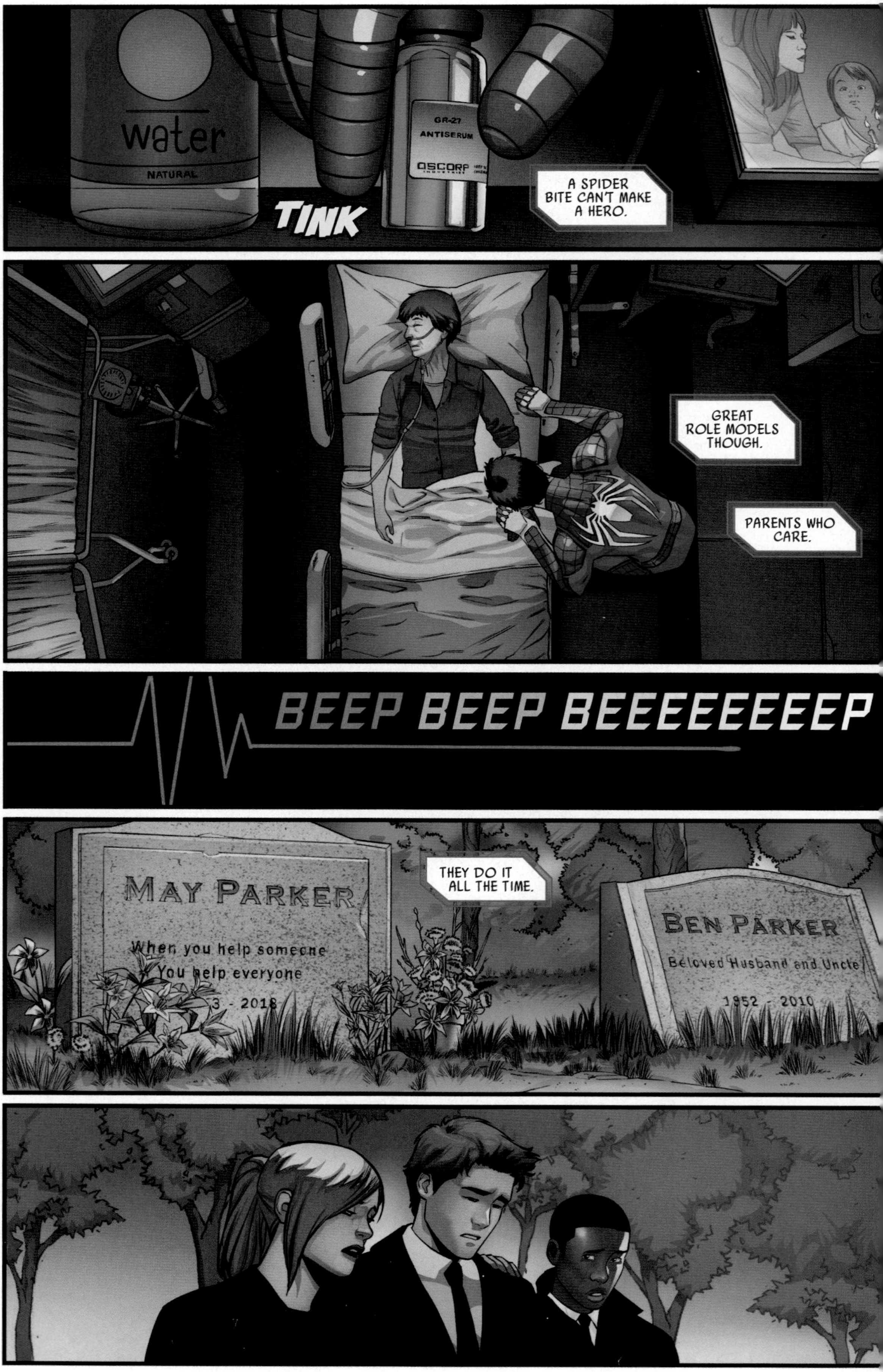
water
NATURAL
GR-27
ANTISERUM
OSCORP
TINK
A SPIDER BITE CAN'T MAKE A HERO.
GREAT ROLE MODELS THOUGH.
PARENTS WHO CARE.
BEEP BEEP BEEEEEEEEP
MAY PARKER
When you help someone
You help everyone
3 - 2018
THEY DO IT ALL THE TIME.
BEN PARKER
Beloved Husband and Uncle
1952 - 2010

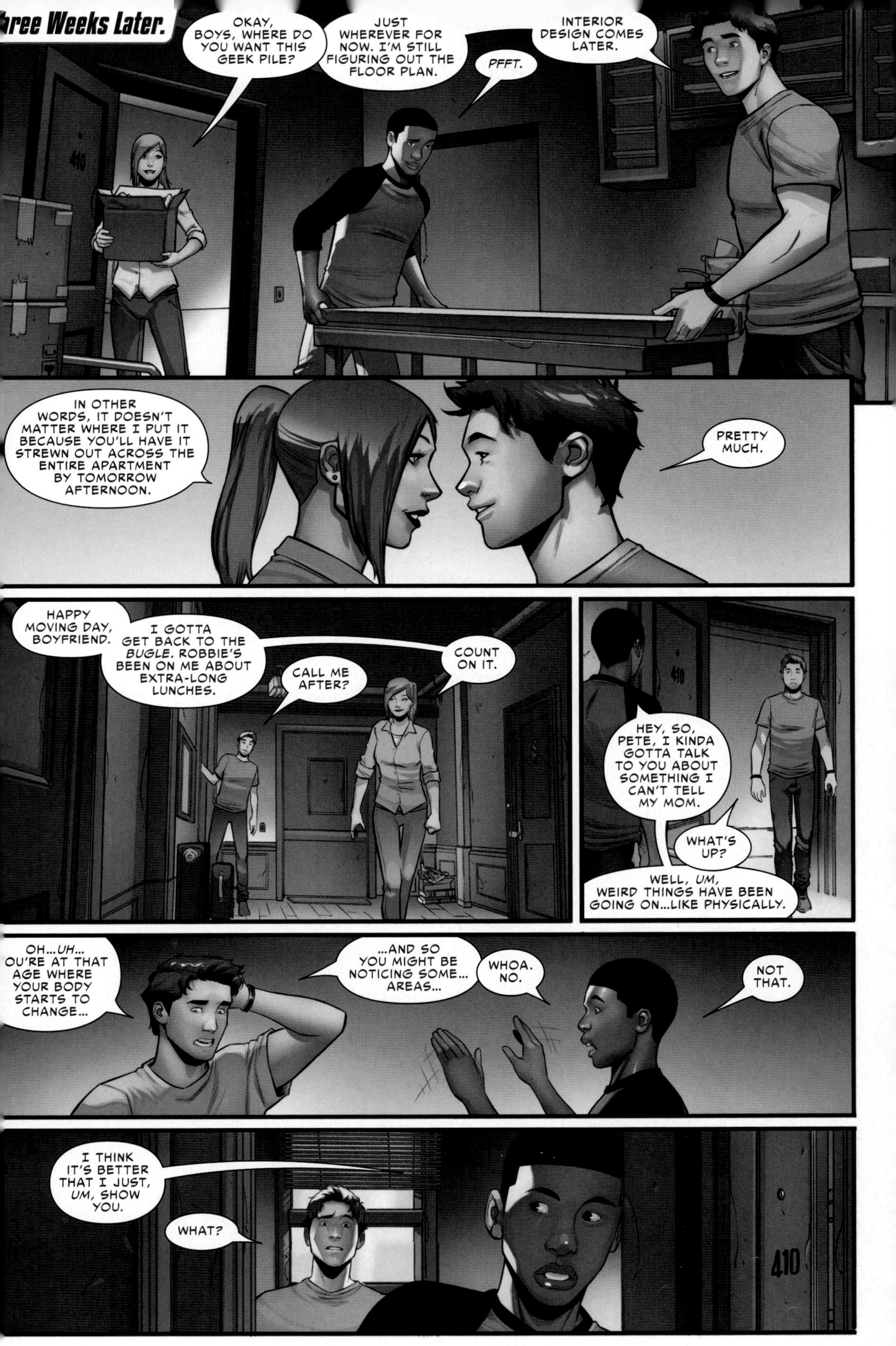

Three Weeks Later.
OKAY, BOYS, WHERE DO YOU WANT THIS GEEK PILE?
JUST WHEREVER FOR NOW. I'M STILL FIGURING OUT THE FLOOR PLAN.
PFFT.
INTERIOR DESIGN COMES LATER.
IN OTHER WORDS, IT DOESN'T MATTER WHERE I PUT IT BECAUSE YOU'LL HAVE IT STREWN OUT ACROSS THE ENTIRE APARTMENT BY TOMORROW AFTERNOON.
PRETTY MUCH.
HAPPY MOVING DAY, BOYFRIEND.
I GOTTA GET BACK TO THE BUGLE. ROBBIE'S BEEN ON ME ABOUT EXTRA-LONG LUNCHES.
CALL ME AFTER?
COUNT ON IT.
410
HEY, SO, PETE, I KINDA GOTTA TALK TO YOU ABOUT SOMETHING I CAN'T TELL MY MOM.
WHAT'S UP?
WELL, UM, WEIRD THINGS HAVE BEEN GOING ON...LIKE PHYSICALLY.
OH...UH... OU'RE AT THAT AGE WHERE YOUR BODY STARTS TO CHANGE...
...AND SO YOU MIGHT BE NOTICING SOME... AREAS...
WHOA. NO.
NOT THAT.
I THINK IT'S BETTER THAT I JUST, UM, SHOW YOU.
WHAT?
410

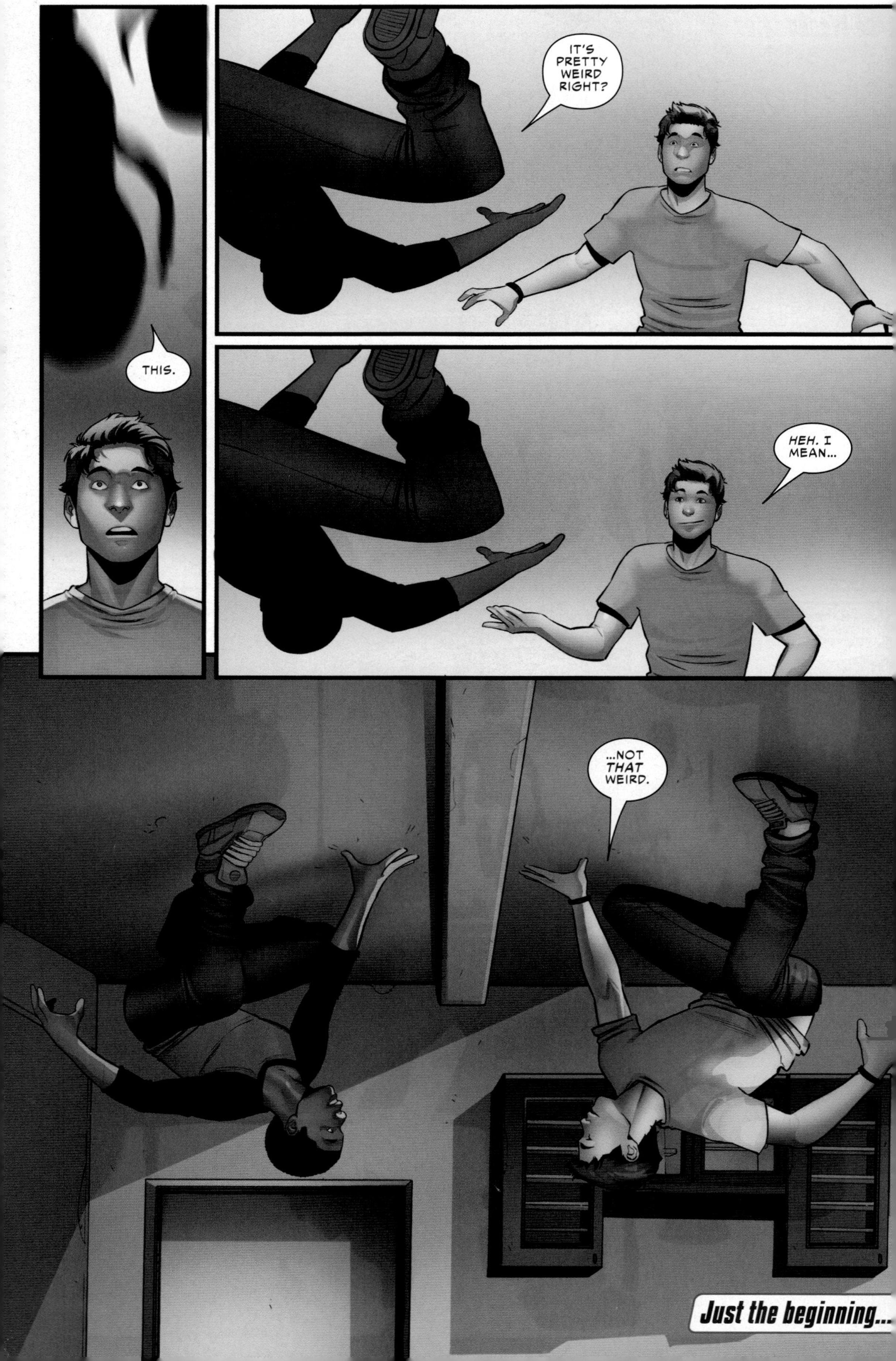
IT'S PRETTY WEIRD RIGHT?
THIS.
HEH. I MEAN...
...NOT THAT WEIRD.
Just the beginning...

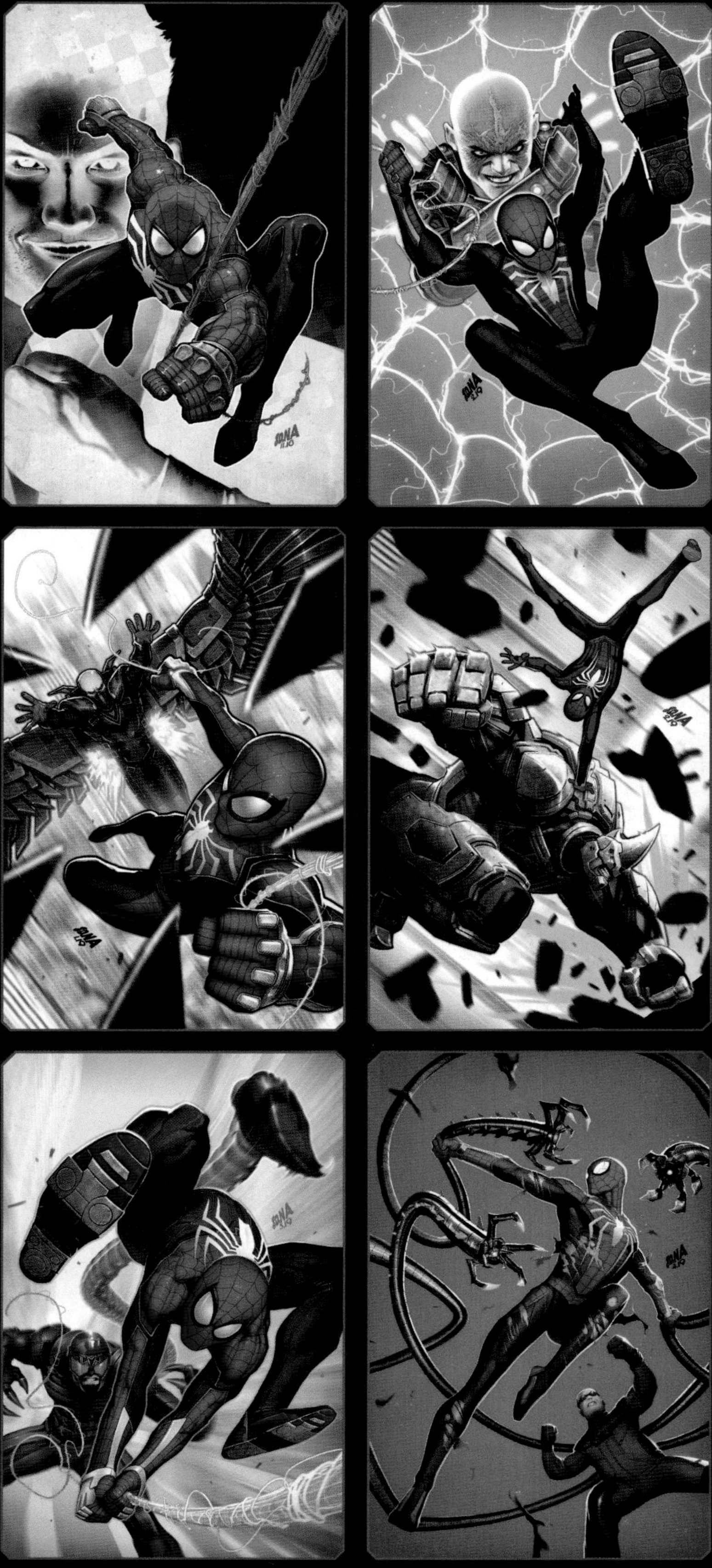

DAVID NAKAYAMA

#1-6 SINISTER SIX VARIANTS

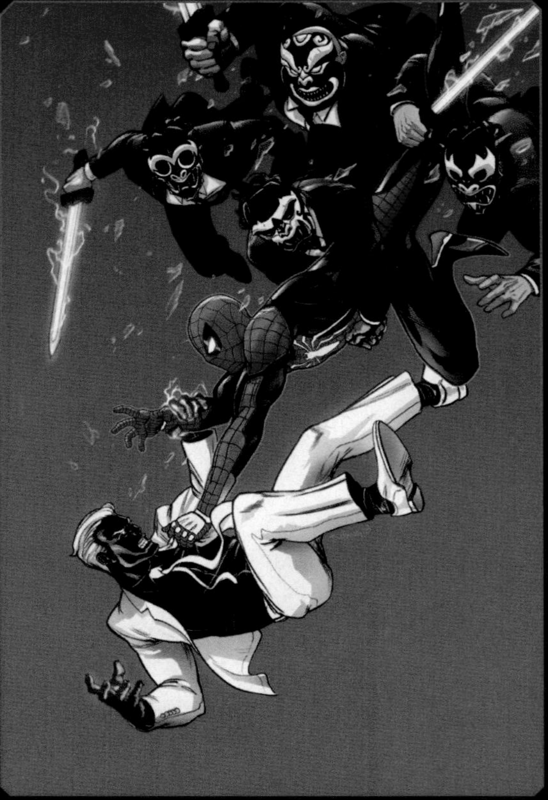

TIM TSANG

#1 VARIANT

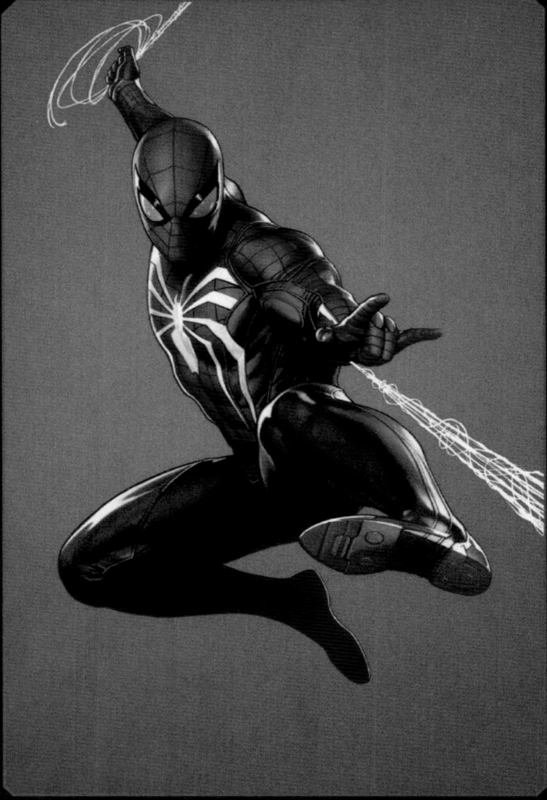

ADI GRANOV

#1 VARIANT

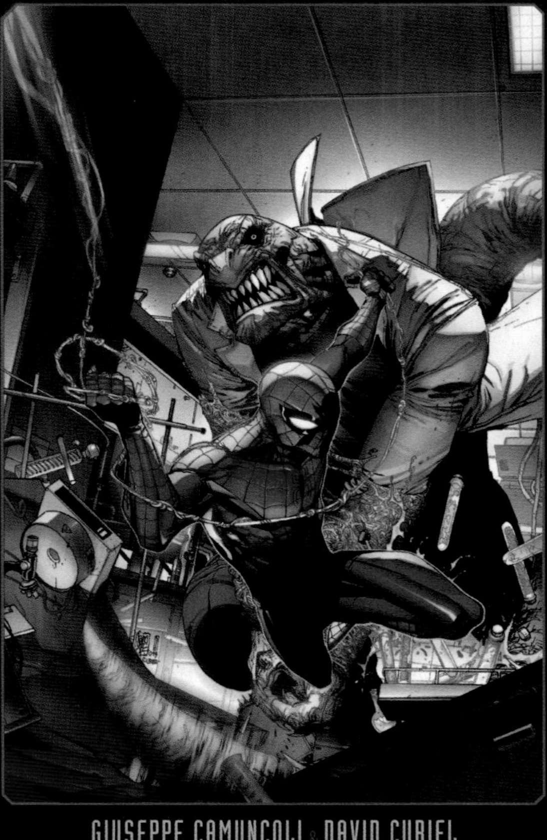

GIUSEPPE CAMUNCOLI & DAVID CURIEL

#1 SPIDER-MAN VILLAINS VARIANT

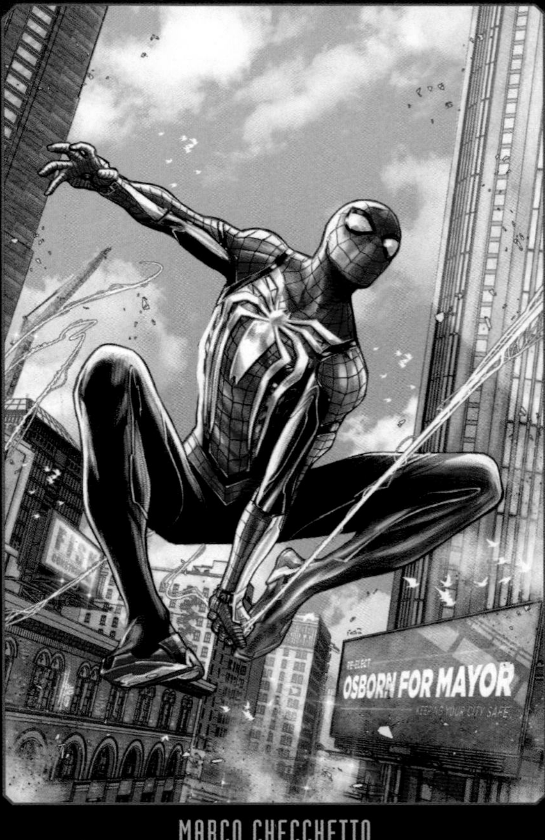
OSBORN FOR MAYOR

MARCO CHECCHETTO

#2 VARIANT

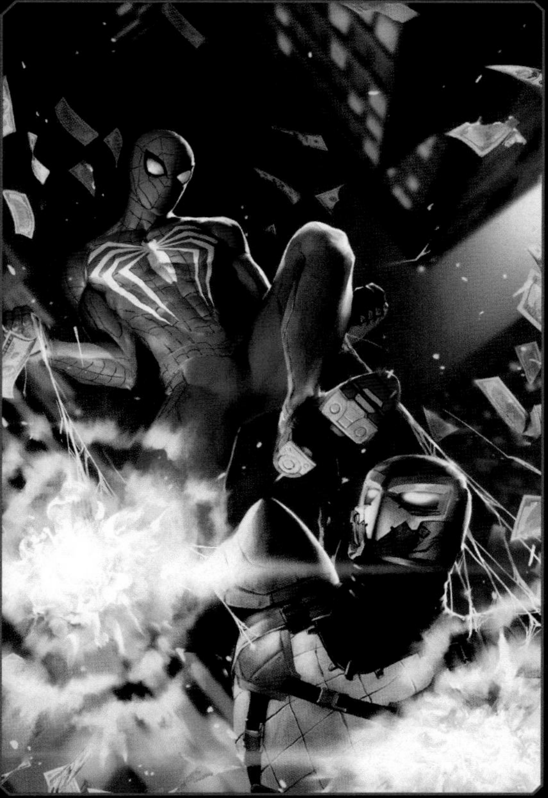

GANG HYUK LIM
#3 VARIANT

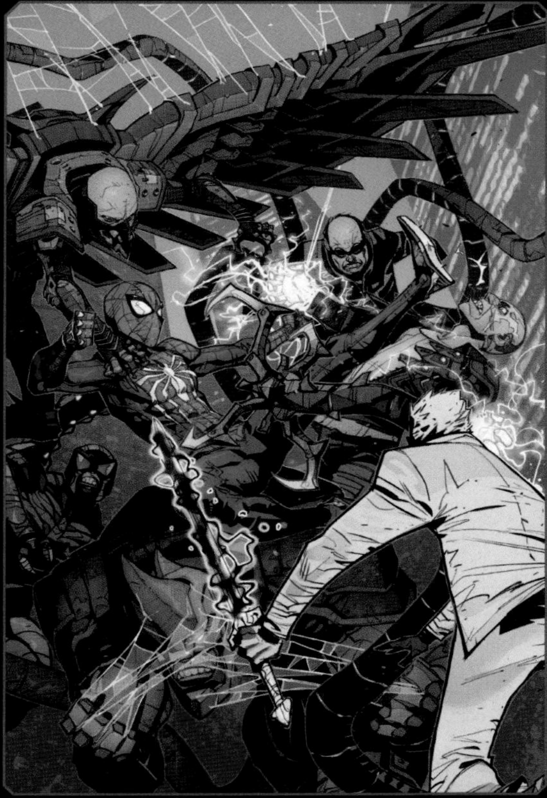

EDUARD PETROVICH
#4 VARIANT

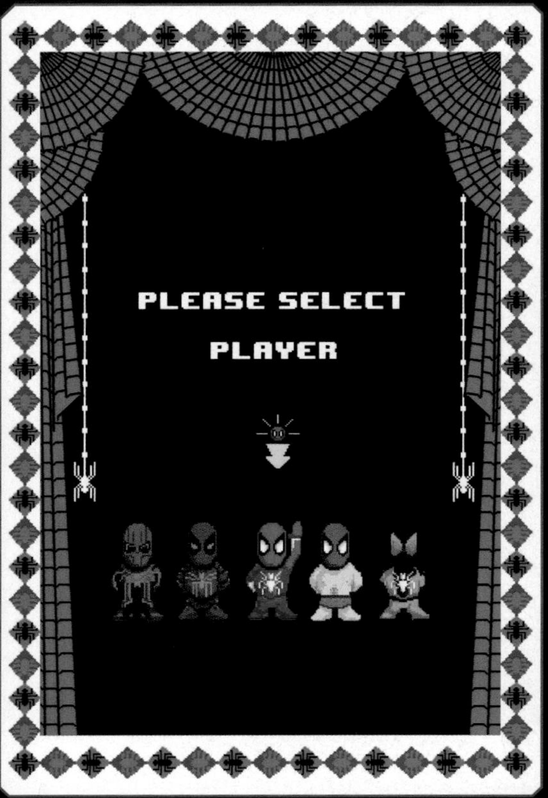
PLEASE SELECT
PLAYER

MATTHEW WAITE
#5 8-BIT VARIANT

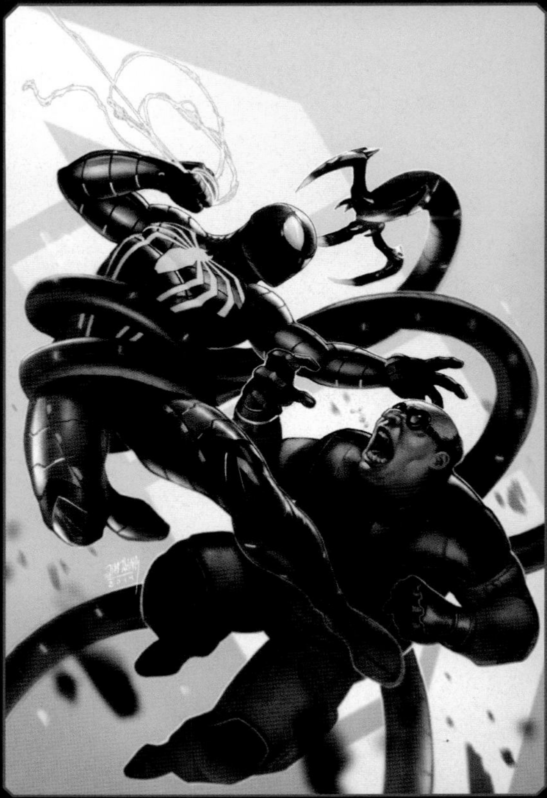

TIM TSANG
#6 VARIANT

WELCOME, WEB-HEADS!

And congratulations! You're here at the very beginning. The ground floor. The title screen, so to speak. The book that you hold in your hands, that you've no doubt already thrilled to every page, is not only the start of a brand-new SPIDER-MAN series but the first in a brand-new universe!

Welcome to the MARVEL GAMERVERSE, readers! Some of you may have already dipped a toe into this universe if you played last year's runaway hit *Marvel's Spider-Man* video game. Like the Marvel Cinematic Universe and others before it, what we're doing here is taking the classic Marvel characters you know and love and putting them into all-new, thrilling adventures aimed at long-term Marvel readers as well as those newer to the medium! The Insomniac Games team, and their amazing collaborators, Marvel Games, inspired by the classic Marvel comic books, built this storyline for the game that is now the groundwork for these comics. Talk about full circle!

If you've already played the game and think you know the whole story—think again. We're going to be delving into unexplored scenes from the original story, fleshing out secondary characters and plotlines and, as we get further into the series, telling completely new tales set in this exciting world.

In fact, get ready for a showdown in our very next issue between Spider-Man and a classic villain redesigned especially for this comic series that'll be sure to have the fandom buzzing!

In the meantime, with MARVEL'S SPIDER-MAN: CITY AT WAR having roots in the video game proper, we wanted to give you all a sneak peek behind the scenes of the game's development each issue, so all you die-hard gamers will get a deeper look into the initial development of this world after each installment of the story! Turn the page for a glimpse into the development of the game's Peter Parker!

See you next month!
—**Mark Basso**

PETER PARKER

While Spider-Man is in his prime as a crimefighting super hero, Peter Parker would rather devote his energy to changing the world through science and the amazing technology he's developing with Otto Octavius. As a 23-year-old recent college graduate struggling to maintain his job, pay his bills and find time to protect his personal relationships, Peter is trying to figure life out while also protecting the fates of millions of innocent New Yorkers threatened by rising evil.

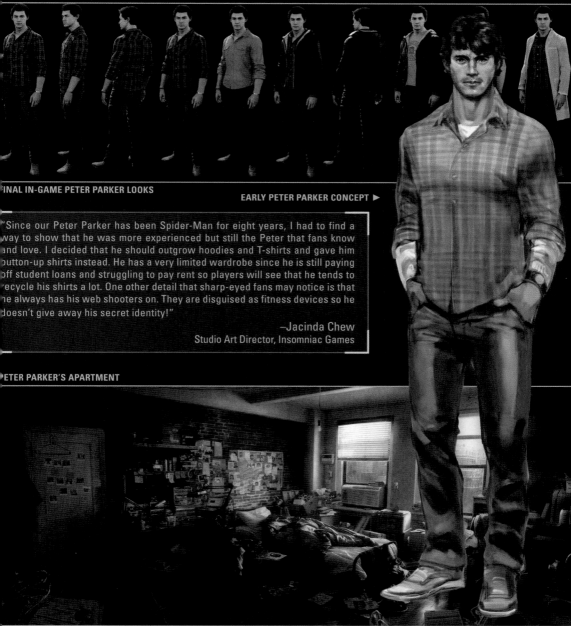

FINAL IN-GAME PETER PARKER LOOKS

EARLY PETER PARKER CONCEPT ▶

"Since our Peter Parker has been Spider-Man for eight years, I had to find a way to show that he was more experienced but still the Peter that fans know and love. I decided that he should outgrow hoodies and T-shirts and gave him button-up shirts instead. He has a very limited wardrobe since he is still paying off student loans and struggling to pay rent so players will see that he tends to recycle his shirts a lot. One other detail that sharp-eyed fans may notice is that he always has his web shooters on. They are disguised as fitness devices so he doesn't give away his secret identity!"

–Jacinda Chew
Studio Art Director, Insomniac Games

PETER PARKER'S APARTMENT

Welcome back, gang. A heavy end to this issue, but it's the toughest challenges that forge the greatest heroes. And speaking of forging heroes, we wanted to take this opportunity to share another peek behind the scenes—and reveal the creation of a character!

When we started development of this series, we knew we wanted to be faithful to the storyline of the *Marvel's Spider-Man* game while also expanding on it in new and meaningful ways that you can only see in this comic. And what's more impactful than redesigning a classic Spider-Man villain for this universe? We put our heads together with the Marvel Games folks and…well, I just happen to have Marvel Games VP and Creative Director Bill Rosemann here to expound upon our undertaking! Take it away, Bill!

Hello, Web-Heads! If you haven't already guessed, everyone at Marvel Games and Insomniac Games are card-carrying, Underoos-wearing True Believers. How far back does our fandom go? Yours Truly just stumbled upon photos of the spectacular Spider-Man cake that my mom made for my 8th birthday. So it's been a special thrill and honor to be given the opportunity to collaborate on Marvel's Spider-Man and pour our love for decades of the wall-crawler's comic books into the game…and to now see everything come full circle as our game's story leaps to life in comic book form!

The issue you hold in your hands also presented an amazing opportunity to add to the game's mythology by adding a super villain not yet seen on the screen. Given the web-slinger's renowned rogues' gallery, we had many infamous faces to choose from, but as a tribute to game co-writer Christos Gage, there was only one choice. In the game's J. Jonah Jameson podcasts, Christos wrote a few hilarious mentions of "a Nazi made of bees," which, as all astute fans know, was a nod to the sinister Swarm! A former evil scientist whose body is comprised of sentient bees? How could we not try to create the game's never-before-seen version? And as with all the villains in the game, how could we tackle the challenge of reimagining him so that he felt authentic both to his original design and to our modern aesthetic?

That challenge went straight to series artist Michele Bandini! Michele immersed himself in the high-tech takes on Spider-Man's villains in the game and immediately set to work on a souped-up, scientific-focused interpretation of Swarm to fit this world. Pairing the classic cape (and, well, bees) of the original look, Michele worked out a more mechanical version of our buzzing baddie, including some unique abilities as detailed in his design sheet below:

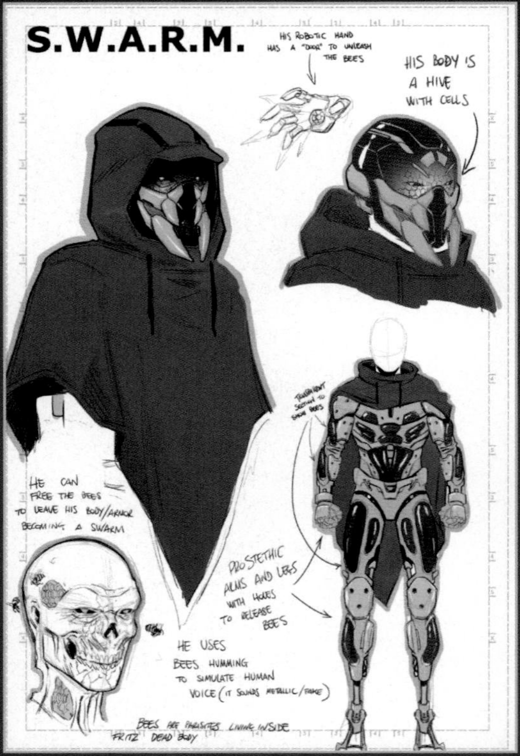
S.W.A.R.M.
HIS ROBOTIC HAND HAS A "DOOR" TO UNLEASH THE BEES
HIS BODY IS A HIVE WITH CELLS
HE CAN FREE THE BEES TO LEAVE HIS BODY/ARMOR BECOMING A SWARM
PROSTETHIC ARMS AND LEGS WITH HOLES TO RELEASE BEES
HE USES BEES HUMMING TO SIMULATE HUMAN VOICE (IT SOUNDS METALLIC/FAKE)
BEES ARE PARASITES LIVING INSIDE FRITZ DEAD BODY

Hope you all dug the result! Let us know your thoughts on Swarm, and the SPIDER-MAN: CITY AT WAR comic, by writing to us at **GAMERVERSE@marvel.com** and marking your message **"OKAY TO PRINT."** In the meantime, check out the next page for more on Miles Morales, and be sure to join us next month as Mary Jane's investigation uncovers a startling discovery…

–Mark Basso

MILES MORALES

Miles Morales is a bright, tech-savvy teen—and major Spider-Man fanboy. After Miles suffers a devastating loss, Peter Parker recognizes key similarities between his own life and the teen's and steps up to mentor him—further empowering Miles to grow. With a little added "encouragement" from Spider-Man, Miles is poised to become a hero just like his idol.

FINAL IN-GAME MILES MORALES LOOKS

"There was a careful balancing act between making Miles look properly nerd chic and streetwear-style teenager hip enough to be believable as a Spider-Man fanboy, technology expert, scientific savant, and legitimate Brooklyn High School student. He provides the player a relatable glimpse into the collision of the super hero and the modern human worlds."

—Eric Monacelli
Director of Game Production, Marvel Games

MILES MORALES ROUGHS

"In the Ultimate comics, Miles and Peter are normally around the same age, but I wanted to make sure we set their looks apart due to their age difference in our game. Miles can have more fun with his wardrobe and wears funny T-shirts and cool shoes. He doesn't have to worry about shedding his clothes all over New York City to fight crime."

—Jacinda Chew
Studio Art Director,
Insomniac Games

WELCOME BACK, WEB-HEADS!

Since Mary Jane is at the center of the action in this issue, we thought now would be a good time to put the spotlight on everyone's favorite redhead. The version of MJ that appears in the *Marvel's Spider-Man* game is both familiar and different at the same time to longtime comic book readers. Mary Jane has had many jobs over the years—model, soap opera actress and Stark employee, to name just a few—but *Daily Bugle* reporter is a new venture for the iconic character.

Here's Marvel Games VP and Creative Director Bill Rosemann to shed further light on MJ's evolution!

In another amazing example of Insomniac Games' mission to "respect the DNA of the franchise, but don't be afraid to mix things up," the team very smartly proposed to make Mary Jane a crusading reporter for the *Daily Bugle*, which, while never having been done in the comics or movies, feels like an authentic and deserved update to her character. Given how the beloved newspaper has been woven throughout Spidey's history, this fresh twist gives MJ agency, her own separate heroic arc and a logical reason why she would insert herself into the heart of our escalating drama, forming an evolving partnership with both Peter and Spider-Man.

Check out the next page for a further look at reporter-on-the-rise Mary Jane! And send your thoughts on this and anything else related to the SPIDER-MAN: CITY AT WAR comic by writing to us at GAMERVERSE@marvel.com and marking your message "OKAY TO PRINT." Be sure to join us next month to discover MJ's fate…

—**Martin Biro**

MARY JANE WATSON

Incisive and independent, MJ is an emerging investigative journalist for the *Daily Bugle*. Burrowing her way into Wilson Fisk's network, MJ soon digs deep into the mystery of the dangerous masked gang known as the Inner Demons. She's also embroiled in a delicate relationship with Peter Parker as they navigate repairing a damaged romantic connection with a more businesslike partnership that may require more mutual trust than ever before.

FINAL IN-GAME MARY JANE WATSON LOOKS

"Insomniac Games worked with us on a fresh take for Mary Jane Watson that stands uniquely on its own. MJ's self-assured, brave and confident while being stylish and charismatic. We wanted to give her many opportunities throughout the game to be the hero. Her look and tone needed to reflect her character development as the game progresses, and the team pulled it off with charm and wit."

–Eric Monacelli
Director of Game Production, Marvel Games

"MJ originally had an office job in our storyline, and she had a corporate look to match. Her design changed when she became a reporter and a playable character. She has her signature red hair, but it's in a ponytail so it doesn't get in the way of her movements. She is practical but has a stylish tomboy look to all of her clothes."

–Jacinda Chew
Studio Art Director, Insomniac Games

MARY JANE WATSON'S APARTMENT ▼

OTTO OCTAVIUS

While focusing on perfecting groundbreaking neural technology that allows patients to control prosthetics through thought, Otto Octavius has become the mentor Peter has been searching for since the death of his beloved Uncle Ben. But when Peter discovers that Otto has been twisted into the scheming Doctor Octopus, responsible for the crime spree and viral outbreak ravaging New York City, he will have to fight at his absolute peak as Spider-Man to save all he holds dear.

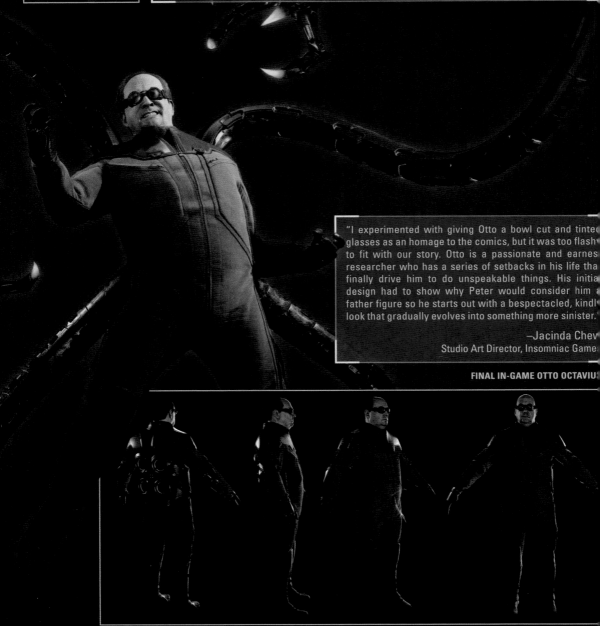

"I experimented with giving Otto a bowl cut and tinted glasses as an homage to the comics, but it was too flashy to fit with our story. Otto is a passionate and earnest researcher who has a series of setbacks in his life that finally drive him to do unspeakable things. His initial design had to show why Peter would consider him a father figure so he starts out with a bespectacled, kindly look that gradually evolves into something more sinister."

—Jacinda Chew
Studio Art Director, Insomniac Games

FINAL IN-GAME OTTO OCTAVIUS

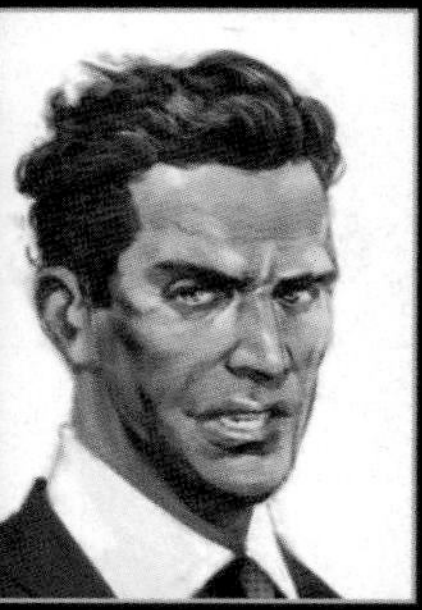

NORMAN OSBORN

Norman Osborn is an extremely successful businessman who built his fortune on experimental technology, making powerful enemies as his own stature and that of his business, OsCorp, grows. Osborn parlayed his financial success into a term as mayor of Marvel's New York and is seeking re-election. Mayor Osborn imposes iron-fisted order throughout Manhattan as the city descends into disarray following Kingpin's capture and the rise of Mister Negative and his Inner Demons.

▼ **NORMAN OSBORN CONCEPT ART** ►

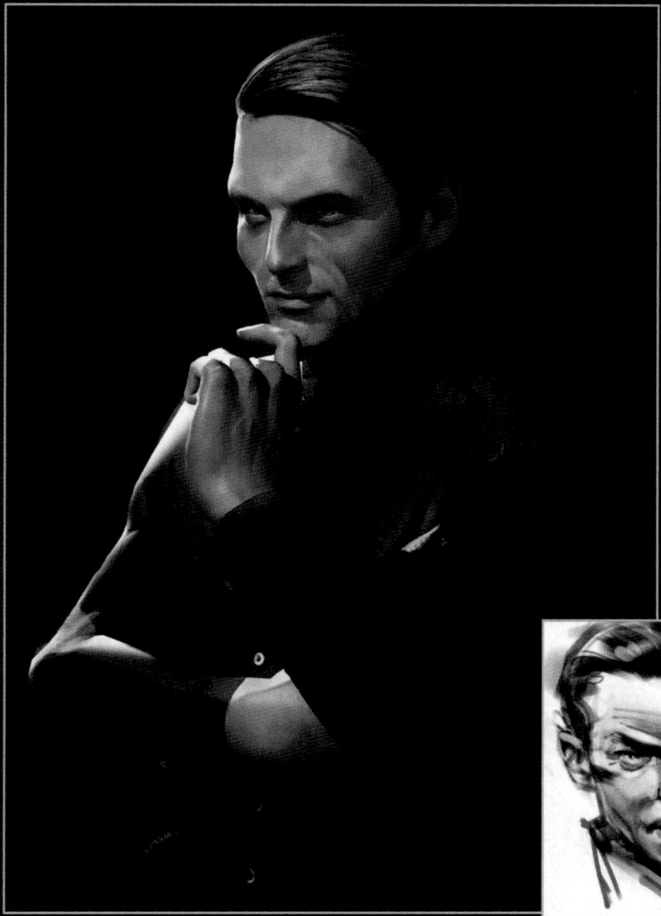

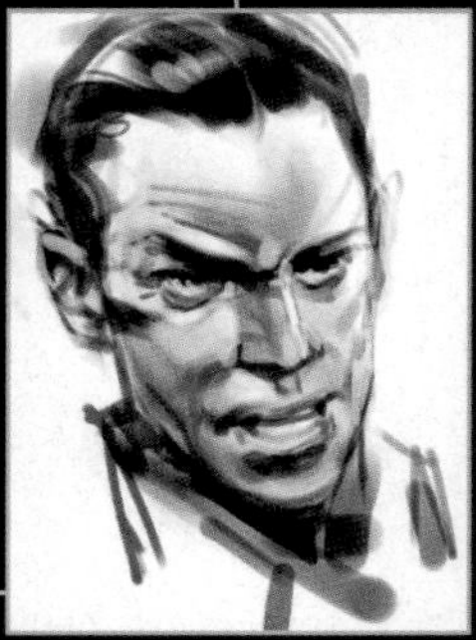

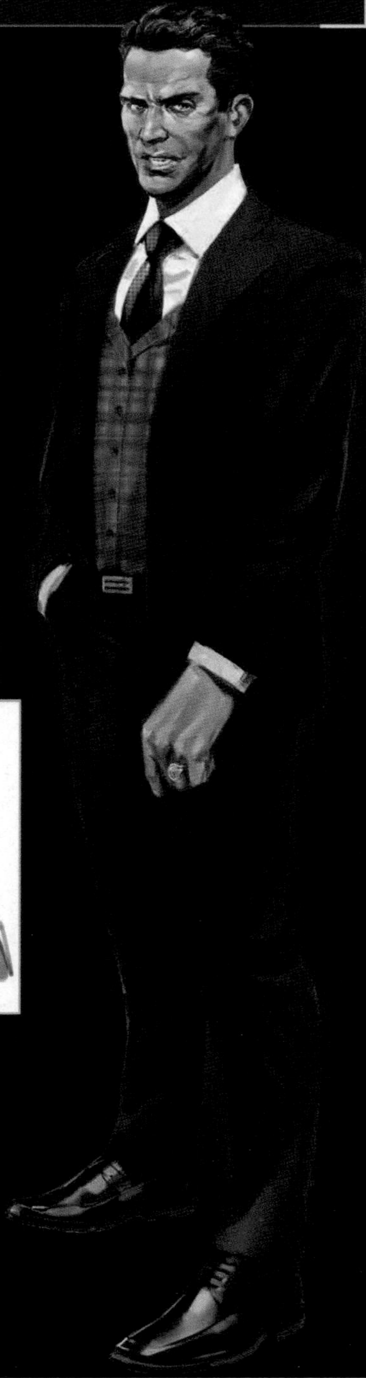

"Norman was one of my favorite characters to design. His smug arrogance was something I wanted to ooze out of every pore. He has an enviable head of red hair and his suits have a '60s feeling to reflect that era of masculinity. His penthouse is in mid-century modern style, designed to intimidate and impress with tall ceilings and cold modern lines."

–Jacinda Chew
Studio Art Director, Insomniac Games

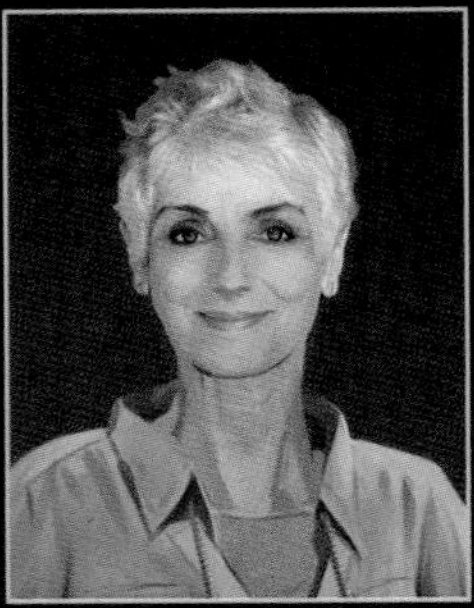

AUNT MAY

Peter Parker's beloved Aunt May runs Martin Li's F.E.A.S.T. shelter in Marvel's New York. As a living reminder of Peter's original failure to use his powers responsibly, May acts as a motherly figure for Peter and helps him navigate his chaotic and complicated life.

▼ AUNT MAY CONCEPT ART ►

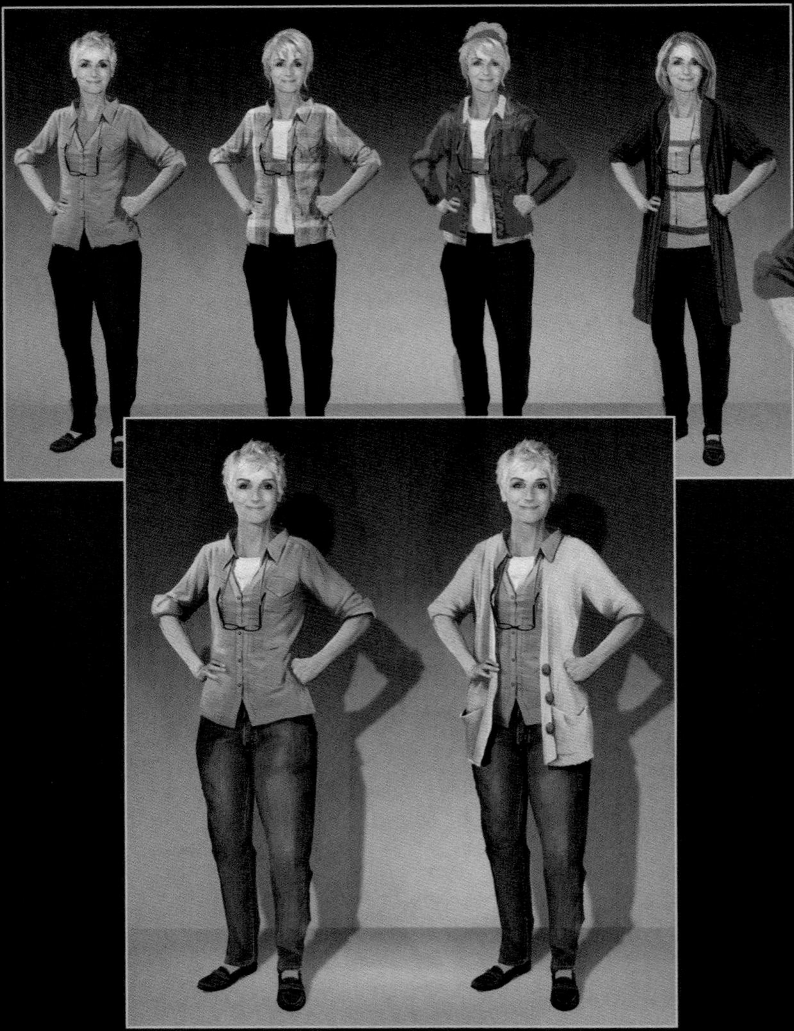

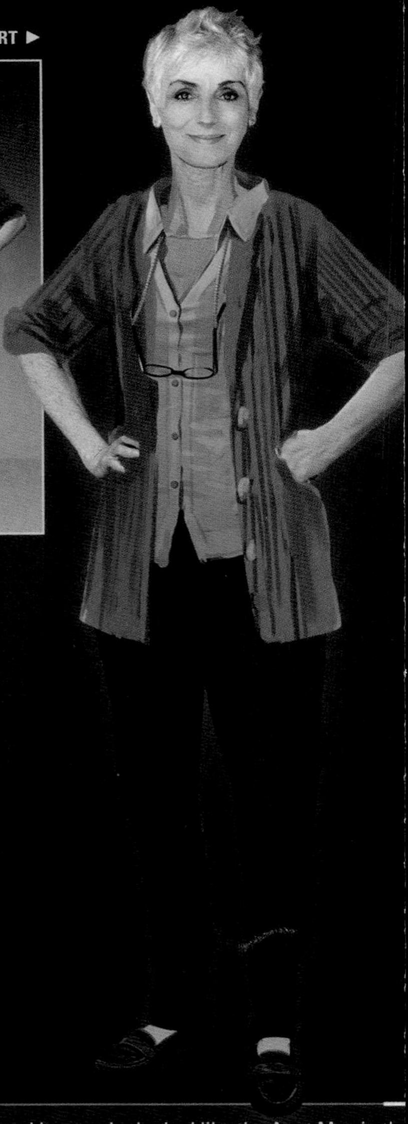

"It was really important that Aunt May felt vibrant and maternal. I originally designed her so she looked like the Aunt May in the early comics so she was much older and frail, but the design ultimately didn't align with the story. She runs a homeless shelte for Martin Li and is always busy helping others rather than taking care of herself. She has to feel like she would never slow down. I traded her white hair for red hair and added more color to her skin and clothing to reflect this."

–Jacinda Chew
Studio Art Director, Insomniac Games

EXCLUSIVE preview!

MARVEL
SPIDER-MAN
SCRIPT BOOK

ON SALE JANUARY 2020!

Marvel is proud to present a unique look behind the scenes of a video game phenomenon! *Marvel's Spider-Man* for PlayStation 4, developed by Insomniac Games, raised the bar for super hero adventures with its stunning graphics, fully realized world and plot filled with intrigue, action and emotion. Now the script for the title's "golden path" story is published for the first time—offering fans unprecedented insight into a crucial part of video game development.

PLUS: Learn about the video game scripting process in an in-depth interview with the teams from Marvel Games and Insomniac Games, whose tireless efforts helped bring *Marvel's Spider-Man* to life!

BEGIN CINEMATIC CAMERA:

ON YURI'S HELICOPTER as she surveys the scene below:

> **YURI WATANABE**
> (through her radio)
> Okay, looks like things are somewhat under control...

CUT TO: KRABOOM! A huge explosion from behind her--at the RAFT supermax prison!

SPIDER-MAN leaps into the frame and hangs onto the side of a lamppost.

BACK TO Yuri and Spider-Man as they react to the explosion--

> **SPIDER-MAN**
> I thought you said the Raft was secure?!

> **YURI WATANABE**
> (through radio)
> It was. Let's go.

Spider-Man LEAPS up to the WOUNDED CHOPPER to take a ride over to the Raft.

They see ELECTRICAL ARCS blast through the sky:

> **YURI WATANABE (CONT'D)**
> (through radio)
> Maybe it's not as bad as it looks.

> **SPIDER-MAN**
> Love the optimism.

Then:
> **SPIDER-MAN (CONT'D)**
> But in my experience...

> **SPIDER-MAN (CONT'D)**
> ...when it looks bad...

The camera pans and we see ELECTRO charging up to attack them.

> **SPIDER-MAN (CONT'D)**
> ...it's usually worse.

CUT TO: Spider-Man, as he realizes they're in trouble-- .
> **SPIDER-MAN (CONT'D)**
> <eyes go wide> Look out!

But it's too late. A massive bolt of electricity shoots out of the shadows and hits the helicopter-- FZZZKOW!

The already-shaky helicopter spins out of control. As it spins, Yuri is thrown around inside the cockpit:

> **SPIDER-MAN (CONT'D)**
> Yuri!

He grabs onto her, but the force of the spinning chopper is too much:

> **YURI WATANABE**
> I'm slipping!

Then she falls:

Spider-Man acts quickly and shoots out a web to catch her--THWIP!

He yanks her back up toward him--

> **SPIDER-MAN**
> Gotcha.

Then he grabs the yoke:

> **SPIDER-MAN (CONT'D)**
> Hold on--!

He steers the helicopter back to a semblance of control, but it CRASHES into the cellblock anyway. SMASH TO BLACK:

FADE IN FROM BLACK:

We are now INSIDE the Raft. The crashed helicopter is on the floor, and there's a hole in the ceiling.

Spider-Man descends, clutching Yuri, in front of the crashed helicopter.

> **SPIDER-MAN (CONT'D)**
> You okay?

> **YURI WATANABE**
> Yeah.

Just as they get their feet--FROOOOSH! Electro flies by.

CLOSE ON Electro as he gets to the end of the hallway ahead and then turns back to Spider-Man and Yuri:

> **ELECTRO**
> Welcome to the party.

Then he CHARGES UP and electricity CRACKLES all around him, sparking off the metal structures...

> **ELECTRO (CONT'D)**
> Just in time for the fireworks...

As he turns away--SKZZZZZZ! The sparks from the electrical trail ZAP the circuits.

ALL OF THE DOORS in the cellblock crank open-- CRAKOW!

As the inmates come out, some of them might say something:

> **RYKERS PRISONER #3**
> Looks like we made parole, boys!

ON SPIDER-MAN as he sees this:

> **SPIDER-MAN**
> Electro? Why is he letting everyone out?

IN GAMEPLAY Yuri starts running off a side hallway, leaving Spider-Man behind.

> **YURI WATANABE**
> I'll head for the main control center and see how bad the situation is.

Spider-Man follows the trail of destruction into the RAFT.

> **SPIDER-MAN**
> Got it--I'll go join the party.

BEGIN GAMEPLAY:

> **SPIDER-MAN (CONT'D)**
> Everyone just quietly go back into your cell and lock the door behind you! Okay? Please?

When the first room is cleared, Spider-Man will pull open some doors, and then we will CUT TO:

BEGIN CINEMATIC CAMERA:

Suddenly RHINO hurls a pillar at Spider-Man-- CRASH!

Spider-Man falls back in a heap, then looks up:

> **SPIDER-MAN (CONT'D)**
> (pained)
> Hi, Rhino.

Rhino STOMPS and readies to charge

> **RHINO**
> Hope you like surprises, spider.

Rhino and Electro escape deeper into the RAFT.

END CINEMATIC CAMERA.

Rhino charges on, escaping, causing rubble to collapse behind him to prevent pursuit. Spider-Man struggles to his feet.

> **SPIDER-MAN**
> (recovering, to himself)
> Surprise? What is he talking about?

Spider-Man will now parkour over some objects and shoot through an opening in a doorway.

Then he gets a call from Yuri--BEEP!

> **YURI WATANABE**
> (through radio)
> Spider-Man, I made it to the control room. What's your status?

> **YURI WATANABE (CONT'D)**
> (through radio)
> Hey, what's your status?

> **SPIDER-MAN**
> Me? Just trapped in a prison with every criminal I've put away in the last eight years. No biggie.

Yuri's next line will be interrupted by Scorpion when he grabs Spider-Man in the next scene:

> **YURI WATANABE**
> (though radio; NOTE: Line will be interrupted by Scorpion grabbing Spider-Man)
> Electro must be working for someone--he's not the type to help others unless there's something in it for him. If I can get the camera system back online, I can look back at who helped him get out of his cell in the first place. But the system's fried, along with everything else in this place. Just stay on Electro--he's the biggest threat.

As soon as the player presses the button to begin the web-tunnel, we CUT TO:

BEGIN CINEMATIC CAMERA:

ANGLE ON a SCORPION TAIL that descends from behind him. As his tail DRIPS POISON we hear Yuri talk to Spider-Man (continuation of previous line), then--

SHHKLACK! Mac Gargan, A.K.A. SCORPION, strikes out with his tail and wraps up Spider-Man.

As Scorpion brings Spider-Man close:

> **SCORPION**
> (laughing/sneering)
> This is too good to be true...

> **SPIDER-MAN**
> (while getting choked)
> Scorpion--can you hold on a minute? I was in the middle of a phone call and it was business--

KRABOOM! An explosion wipes the screen with fire as Spider-Man dives to safety.

Spider-Man lies on the ground, gathering his wits. He stands and recovers, then notices that--

SCORPION IS GONE.

> **SPIDER-MAN (CONT'D)**
> Right. Okay, then.

END CINEMATIC CAMERA.

RESUME GAMEPLAY:

When Yuri calls back:

> **YURI WATANABE**
> (through phone)
> Lost you for a second there--you okay?

> **SPIDER-MAN**
> (as we're fighting)
> Not really. Electro, Rhino and now Scorpion are all on the loose. What's going on in the rest of the prison?

> **YURI WATANABE**
> (through radio)
> Camera system's almost up. I'll give you a sitrep soon.

> **SPIDER-MAN**
> (as we're fighting)
> Okay, I'll keep tracking Electro...

Then, when the room is clear, BLAM! A door flies open and we see Electro waiting on the other side: When Electro leads the player up the FIRST SHAFT:

> **ELECTRO**
> (yelling down from above)
> Up here!

Spider-Man runs up the shaft and vaults over the top lip and then TRANSITIONS TO--

Now we begin the exterior chase segment with Electro. The chase moves all around the Raft and underneath.

At one point, Spider-Man catches up with Electro and we see a WEB-ZIP PROMPT appear. When the player web-zips, CUT TO:

BEGIN CINEMATIC CAMERA:

Spider-Man flies toward Electro:

> **SPIDER-MAN**
> Gotcha.

But just as he reaches Electro, ADRIAN TOOMES, A.K.A. THE VULTURE, swoops in and grabs Spider-Man.

Vulture carries Spider-Man straight up into the sky. As he does:

> **VULTURE**
> Long time, no see.

> **SPIDER-MAN**
> Vulture?!

Then Spider-Man WEBS HIM IN THE FACE:

> **VULTURE**
> We're going to have so much f--

> **SPIDER-MAN**
> Sorry, no time to talk.

Vulture releases Spider-Man, then FLIES AWAY into the dark night sky.

Spider-Man falls back down toward the RAFT, and we smoothly transition into gameplay:

END CINEMATIC CAMERA.

BEGIN GAMEPLAY:

The chase continues.

As soon as Spider-Man starts swinging, he gets a call from Yuri:

> **YURI WATANABE**
> (through radio)
> Okay, I got the security cameras back online.

> **SPIDER-MAN**
> (while swinging)
> How does it look?

> **YURI WATANABE**
> (through radio)
> Well...it looks like the entire population of the Raft has escaped.

> **YURI WATANABE (CONT'D)**
> (through radio)
> Including Martin Li. That makes FIVE of your worst enemies that are now on the loose.

> **SPIDER-MAN**
> (laughing)
> Ha. For a second there I thought you were serious.

> **YURI WATANABE**
> (through radio)
> I *am* serious.

CLICK!

> **SPIDER-MAN**
> (laughing-to-serious)
> Ha! Uh, Yuri? Okay, seriously, I REALLY need you to be joking right now. Yuri?!

As they reach the end of the chase, Electro takes a sharp left back into the RAFT, and Spider-Man follows.

Spider-Man chases Electro up the tower, running up the wall, avoiding hazards and Electro's attacks.

> **ELECTRO**
> Keep chasing--party's almost over. Last chance to stop him...

Spider-Man sees Electro heading upward. Electro keeps him at bay with some blasts.

When Spider-Man reaches the roof, CUT TO:

BEGIN CINEMATIC CAMERA:

EXT. TOP OF TOWER - NIGHT

Spider-Man emerges at the top of the tower into a WIDE-OPEN SPACE. Dillon is at the far end of the space.

Cameras and music set us up for an epic encounter. Feels like we're about to do a wicked boss fight! Cool!

> **ELECTRO**
> How do you like my new suit?

> **SPIDER-MAN**
> Dashing. Where'd you get it?

> **ELECTRO**
> It's an exclusive club.

VULTURE flies by--wearing a super-cool new suit. As the camera tracks him, we reveal RHINO in all his bigbadassnes.

Spider-Man is starting to feel a little out of his depth:

Then, from behind Spider-Man, SCORPION scampers up the wall and joins the fight.

And then a helicopter flies by and MISTER NEGATIVE jumps down off the skid and into the arena.

Spider-Man is now SURROUNDED by villains. This feels like it's going to be one tough fight.

Rhino leans in, about to charge at Spider-Man, but Li interrupts:

> **MISTER NEGATIVE**
> Remember, he said not to kill him.

Spider-Man looks at Li. He's actually relieved but still on edge:

> **SPIDER-MAN**
> Good idea. In fact, we don't have to do this at all if you don't want to--

> **RHINO**
> We definitely want to.

Then--BIG FIGHT SEQUENCE! But there's just too many of them.

The super villains overwhelm Spider-Man and he's left on the ground, busted up.

Then--DOC OCK RISES into the frame, having just scaled the outside wall.

Spider-Man's eye-lenses go wide in shock.

> **SPIDER-MAN**
> (shocked, to himself)
> Doctor Octavius?

Otto pulls Spider-Man close so that we can see Spider-Man's mask in the reflection of Otto's trademark goggles:

> **OTTO**
> (quietly, sinister)
> First and final warning. Stay out of our way.

Otto then THROWS Spider-Man off the rooftop. After a moment, we hear/see a distant SPLASH!

ON OTTO as he turns to the Sinister Six...

> **OTTO (CONT'D)**
> Each of you has a job to do. Your debts will be repaid when we're done.

Beat.

> **OTTO (CONT'D)**
> Go!

The villains disperse, each heading off the rooftop in their own way.

PULL BACK TO REVEAL Otto watching, looking across the river at the city. OTTO'S THEME MUSIC swells as he rises on his four arms, watching his "friends" descend upon New York.

FADE TO BLACK: